Revolutionary and Early American Wars

The
MILITARY HISTORY
of the
UNITED STATES

Christopher Chant

Revolutionary and Early American Wars

WEBSTER'S HOME LIBRARY™
NEW YORK

Published 1997 by
Webster's Home Library™
Webster's Unified, Inc.
99 White Plains Rd.
Tarrytown, NY 10591

All rights reserved. No part of this book may be reproduced or utilized in any form or by any means electronic or mechanical including photocopying, recording, or by any information storage and retrieval system, without permission from the copyright holders.

©Marshall Cavendish Corporation 1992

The publishers wish to thank the following organizations who have supplied photographs:

The National Archive, Washington, United States Navy, United States Marines, United States Army, United States Air Force, Department of Defense, Library of Congress, and The Smithsonian Institution.

The publishers gratefully thank the following organizations for the use of archive material for the following witness accounts:

U.S. Army Military History Institute, Carlisle Barracks, PA.

Page 24: From the Revolutionary War Miscellaneous Collection —Letter, August 13, 1775, Robert Magaw, Thompson's Rifle Regiment. Also from *The British Invasion from the North. The Campaigns of Generals Carlton and Burgoyne from Canada 1776-1777, with the journal of Liet. William Digby of the 53rd or Shropshire regiment of foot,* by James Phinney Baxter (Albany, 1887).

Page 46-47: *Traditions and Reminiscence Chiefly of the American Revolution in the South* by Joseph Johnson, M.D. (Charleston, 1853).

Page 76-77: *Memoir of John Stark* by Thomas Mullen (Concord, 1877).

Page 114-116: The Sol Feinstone Collection of the American Revolution.

Page 150: A collection of items from *History of Pittsfield Massachusetts* by Joseph E. Smith, (Boston 1869); and *The Life of Major John Paterson* by Thomas Egleston, (New York, 1898).

Page 173: *History of the Late War in the Western Country* by Robert Breckenridge McAfee, (Lexington, 1816).

Page 241: *The War in Florida by a Staff Officer* by Woodburne Potter, (Baltimore, 1836).

Page 242: *Notices of Florida: The Campaign* by M.M. Cohen (New York, 1836).

Page 249: From *Order of the Indian Wars Collection,* U.S. Army Military History Institute, Carlisle Barracks, PA.

Page 250: *Letters From the Frontiers* by Major General George A. McCall, (Philadelphia, 1868).

Printed and bound in Malaysia

The arms of the United States reflect the nation's varied origins.

Publisher's Note

The Military History of the United States provides an objective work of reference on the wars, both great and small, fought by American forces. The first volume of the collection, Revolutionary and Early American Wars, focuses on events leading to the separation of the thirteen colonies from Great Britain up to the famous stand-off led by Colonel William Barrett Travis and 154 Texan defenders at the Alamo. Combining both historical fact as well as military strategy, this work helps readers comprehend the important decisions made at the time— decisions which led to military victories as well as humbling defeats.

Revolutionary and Early American Wars incorporates first-hand accounts in the form of letters and diary entries written by the battle participants, witnesses, as well as the victims of each campaign. These entries allow the reader to go back in time and participate in the historical events, to see through the writer's eyes and to feel the same emotions—the fear and the anticipation—they experienced over two hundred years ago.

Readers will learn about the wars waged against the Native American tribes as the young nation of America expanded westward. They will review the events that led to the War of 1812 and examine the skirmishes fought by the newly formed navy against pirates in the Caribbean and North Africa. They will identify the progression of technology from the evolution of firearms from the musket to the cannon to the uniforms worn in the various periods displayed in fullcolor throughout the text.

Though many works about individual American wars and campaigns have been published, this collection is specifically designed for use as an overview, highlighting the developments of the American military within the context of the United States' steady emergence as a world power. As such, The Military History of the United States not only examines major military campaigns, but also examines the evolution of the American military establishment and military thinking.

The narrative text covers the major wars and minor conflicts involving American forces since 1776. The organization is broadly chronological. Along with the incisive narrative, the work contains hundreds of illustrations including engravings and paintings, along with maps and colorful drawings of uniforms and important weapons.

Following the text there is a comprehensive glossary of technical terms as well as an extensive English language bibliography of currently available publications. A special feature of the bibliography is the supplementary annotation that provides the reader with a brief sketch of the content and scope of the books. This work also contains an A-Z Index for quick reference, as well as cross-reference panels throughout the text alluding to other major personalities and events.

It is hoped that a working knowledge of the components of The Military History of the United States will enable the reader to make the fullest use of the collection, enhancing its value as a research tool and educational reference source. Perhaps by looking at the past, the decisions that were made and their outcomes, readers can attempt to understand our roots and the events that brought us to our current status as world power. For only with a firm understanding of the rich history inherited from the nation's founders can, in some way, the foggy road of our future be made just a little more clear.

American calvary at the Battle of Guildford Court House on March 15, 1781.

Contents

Origins of the War	12
The First Continental Congress	15
The Battles of Lexington and Concord	16
The Siege of Boston	19
The Battle of Bunker Hill	23
Revitalized British Effort	31
The Creation of an American Army	33
Washington to Supreme Military Command	34
The Importance of Militia Units	38
The Invasion of Quebec	40
Lake Champlain, the Key	43
American Advantages From the Loss of Boston	45
The Declaration of Independence	49
Washington's Greatest Achievement	52
Lack of British Strategy	53
The British Invade New York	56
The Battle of White Plains	59
Washington Retreats From New York	61
The Battle of Trenton	63
Another British Delay	65
Support From the French	67
The Battle of the Brandywine	70
Burgoyne's Invasion of New York	72
The Battle of Fort Stanwix	76
Burgoyne's Fatal Gamble	79
The Second Battle of Saratoga	80
The Ordeal at Valley Forge	85
Von Steuben Revives the Continental Army	87
The Battle of Monmouth Court House	88
France Enters the War	89
Development of American Sea Power	90
Static Warfare in New York	93
The British Invasion of Georgia	96
The Americans Lose Charleston	100
The Battle of Camden	104
American Fortunes at Their Lowest Ebb	105
The Treason of Benedict Arnold	107
The Battle of King's Mountain	108
The Battle of Cowpens	110
The Battle of Guildford Court House	116
American Victory in Sight	119
Cornwallis Bottles Himself Up at Yorktown	123
The Second Battle of the Delaware Capes	127

Contents

British Surrender at Yorktown	131	The Assault at Penobscot	189
Formal Independence for the United States	134	The Creation of the Marine Band	191
		The War of 1812	192
The "Generalship" Factor	138	The Battle of Horseshoe Bend	197
Demobilization for the Continental Army	141	The Treaty of Ghent	199
		Early American Firearms	204
British Occupation of American Territory	146	The First Seminole War	206
		The Beginnings of the U.S. Navy	220
Shays' Rebellion	149	The Black Hawk War	235
The 1787 Constitutional Conversion	151	The Battle of Bad Axe River	237
American Sources of Weapon Procurement	153	The Second Seminole War	237
		Differences Between the First and Second Seminole Wars	240
The Whiskey Rebellion	154		
The Maumee War	156	The Battle of Lake Okeechobee	247
The Battle of Fallen Timbers	162	Army Exploration Teams in the West	247
The Shawnee War	163	The Texas Revolution	252
The Battle of the Tippecanoe	166	The Undermanned Alamo	258
The Louisiana Purchase	176	The Fall of the Alamo	260
Exploration in the West	178	The "Goliad Massacre"	261
The Creek War	179	The Battle of San Jacinto	262
The Beginnings of the U.S. Marine Corps	180		
The Battle of Lake Champlain	185	Glossary	264
The Battle of Princeton	186	Bibliography	268
The Taking of Fort Nassau	187	Index	269

The surrender of General Burgoyne at Saratoga on October 16, 1777.

THE MILITARY HISTORY OF THE UNITED STATES

Origins of the War

The United States of America was created by the Revolutionary War out of 13 British colonies on the eastern seaboard of North America. The upheaval that followed the colonies' attempt to separate themselves from Great Britain was considerable, and during it modern history's first democratic republic came into being when the Declaration of Independence was signed on July 4, 1776. The Revolutionary War had already started in 1775, and its outcome was to force the British to recognize the existence of the new nation and give up its claims to the region.

Ironically, the American Revolution was caused by the final British triumph over the French for effective control of what is now the United States and Canada. As an outgrowth of the Seven Years' War, fought in Europe between 1756 and 1763, the French and Indian War started in 1754, ended in 1760, and was a decisive British victory that removed the French threat to the inhabitants of Great Britain's American colonies. The Treaty of Paris that formally ended the war in February 1763 also ceded the French possessions in Canada and in America east of the Mississippi River to the British, who created the far smaller British colony of Quebec along the St. Lawrence River.

Historical forces were already at work, pushing the colonies toward a separation from British rule. These forces gathered momentum at the end of the French and Indian War when the British, who were determined to strengthen their control in North America, announced that a per-

Paul Revere's engraving of the Boston Massacre was a clever and effective piece of propaganda for the American cause. In the real event on March 5, 1770, the British opened fire on a riotous mob of toughs, many of them armed with clubs and other weapons, who were pelting them with rocks and pieces of ice. Copied from a more detailed engraving by Henry Pelham, Revere's version of the event shows the British firing on a peaceful assembly of unarmed and defenseless Boston citizens.

12

REVOLUTIONARY AND EARLY AMERICAN WARS

The strength of American feeling against the British is revealed by an episode that took place in Boston on January 27, 1774, as a protest against the customs dues imposed by the British. Angry Americans stormed into the house of John Malcolm, a British revenue officer. Malcolm wounded several Americans with his sword, but was seized, lowered from a window, and then tarred and feathered.

manent force of 10,000 British troops was to be stationed on the American frontiers. The colonists were shocked by the additional news that the colonies themselves would have to pay a large part of the cost for a force they felt was not needed since the defeat of France and which was probably to be used for the suppression of American liberties. This was just one of several British tax moves that greatly angered Americans, who had for some time already called for "no taxation without representation" in the British parliament.

From 1763, colonial leaders urged the creation of American popular assemblies to levy taxes on Americans for American purposes, but the British constantly refused to allow the creation of such bodies.

The provisions of the Stamp Act and the Sugar Act had already caused great resentment among the colonists. Between 1770 and 1774, there was growing violence and unrest, especially in the northern colonies. The British had felt themselves forced into repressive action in the so-called "Battle of Golden Hill" in New York during January 1770 and the "Boston Massacre" during March 1770. More serious trouble broke out on the western frontier of North Carolina during 1771, when a group of frontier settlers (self-styled "Regulators" mainly of Irish and Scottish descent) rose against the local aristocracy and called for intervention from London on their behalf. The governor sent in the colonial militia, which firmly defeated the Regulators in the Alamance Creek fight of May 16, 1771.

13

THE MILITARY HISTORY OF THE UNITED STATES

Among many British laws unpopular in the American colonies, the Stamp Act was perhaps the one that provoked the strongest feelings. In August 1775, American militants in Boston burned copies of the act's proclamation that had arrived from Great Britain.

The "Boston Tea Party"

The last straw for the British was the "Boston Tea Party" of December 16, 1773, when a group of Bostonians badly disguised as Indians, threw a consignment of British tea into the city's harbor to indicate their disgust with British taxation of the colonies. In the following year, the passage of the Quebec Act by the British parliament also alarmed the Americans. This new act expanded Quebec to the Ohio and Mississippi rivers, which was seen in the American colonies as a direct threat to the economic interests of Virginia and Pennsylvania.

Time was rapidly running out for the British to set matters right in their North American colonies. Colonial leaders had been trying since 1763 to persuade the British government to see the justice of

Boston
For further references see pages
12, 13, 15, 16, 17, 23, 25, 33, 40, 44, *44, 49.*

14

the colonists' points of view, and to convince the rulers that colonial hopes were both practical and not anti-British On two counts, the British made the wrong moves: on the one hand they failed to appreciate the revised and workable type of imperial union proposed by the colonists, and on the other, they also failed to act strongly enough to impose effective British rule on the colonies.

After the "Boston Tea Party," Parliament, with the full support of King George III, pushed through legislation that became known in the colonies as the "Intolerable Acts." These closed the port of Boston, infringed several of the colonists' rights and, to add insult to injury, imposed military rule on Massachusetts, which was now controlled directly by Major General Sir Thomas Gage. Gage was heavy-handed in his control of the colony, and this played into the hands of the American leaders, who had already raised colonial fears of increasingly repressive British rule. It is probable, therefore, that the declaration of martial rule in Massachusetts was the spark that ignited the tinder of the American Revolution.

The First Continental Congress Meets

On September 5, 1774, the First Continental Congress met in Philadelphia for a session that lasted until October 26 of the same year. The Congress drafted petitions to the king and Parliament in an effort to win repeal of the "Intolerable Acts." It also created a series of intercolonial agreements to prevent the import of British goods and the export of American ones to Great Britain, hoping in this way to exert financial pressure on the British. To make sure that these agreements were enforced, committees were formed in nearly every county, town, and city, and these committees soon became the real organs of government in the colonies. On this base, an organization of assemblies, congresses, conventions supervised by a few committees of safety

Another measure that infuriated the colonists was the British tax on the import of tea. On December 16, 1773, a group of protesters disguised as Indians boarded a British ship that had just arrived in Boston harbor and threw its cargo of tea into the sea. The British reacted by reducing the amount of self-government Massachusetts was allowed.

developed, although in greater secrecy. The British thus lost political control of the colonies at the grass-roots level. At the same time, this fledgling American government assumed control of the various militia forces, and thus paved the way for the creation of an American army.

The focus of activity in the short term was Massachusetts, and within Massachusetts the city of Boston. Here the Provincial Congress ordered that in each town one-third of the militia should be organized into "minuteman" units able to respond to a crisis at a moment's notice. To provide these forces with the required supplies, the Provincial Congress ordered the collection of ammunition and other stores at a depot in Concord, about 20 miles northwest of Boston.

Paul Revere's Ride

On April 18, 1775, Gage ordered a detachment of 700 British troops to march from Boston and seize the Concord depot. The plans were made in the greatest secrecy and the force marched off during the night, but the colonists had been expecting such a move. In a celebrated "midnight ride," Paul Revere, John Dawes, and Dr. Samuel Prescott rode ahead of the British force to warn the American patriots of the British move. Thus, when the British force marched into Lexington, slightly more than halfway from Boston to Concord, at dawn on April 19 they found that 70 American minutemen under Captain John Parker had taken up position on the village green. A

Above left: Depicted in its opening session in Philadelphia on September 5, 1774, the First Continental Congress marked the first genuinely "national" move by the American colonies. The congress urged the British to repeal the "Intolerable Acts," but also launched a series of agreements to limit British goods being imported into the 13 colonies.
Above: News of the Declaration of Independence is announced to the people of Boston.

REVOLUTIONARY AND EARLY AMERICAN WARS

gun was fired - and to this day it is not known whether it was an American or a British finger which pulled the trigger that fired this "shot heard 'round the world" - and the British regulars fired a volley into the minutemen before charging with their bayonets. The minutemen broke and dispersed, leaving eight of their men dead and another 10 wounded on Lexington Green.

The Revolutionary War had started. Major John Pitcairn pushed on with his British soldiers to Concord and found that the Americans had evacuated most of the supplies, burned the rest and set off back to Boston. By this time, the efforts of the "midnight riders" had raised the countryside into a hornet's nest of American minutemen and militia. The British force marched back toward Boston as fast as they could, but from behind what seemed to be every rock, tree, and house, American fire poured out at them. By the time the force reached Charlestown, just north of Boston, with the aid of a relief column sent out to meet it, the British had lost 73 killed, 174 wounded, and 26 missing out of a total of 1,800 men. On the other side of the fence, almost literally, the Americans had suffered another 77 casualties to add to their 18 at Lexington.

In purely military terms, the Americans had not done as well as they might have hoped. During the course of the day they fired 75,000 rounds at the British and caused relatively few casualties. But more important by far was the boost in morale given to the revolution by the steadfast resistance of these New England citizens who had shown that no longer were Americans prepared to stand for British

Right: The most celebrated of the "midnight riders," Paul Revere raced through the Massachusetts countryside on the night of April 18-19, 1775, to warn patriots that the British were advancing on Concord.

17

THE MILITARY HISTORY OF THE UNITED STATES

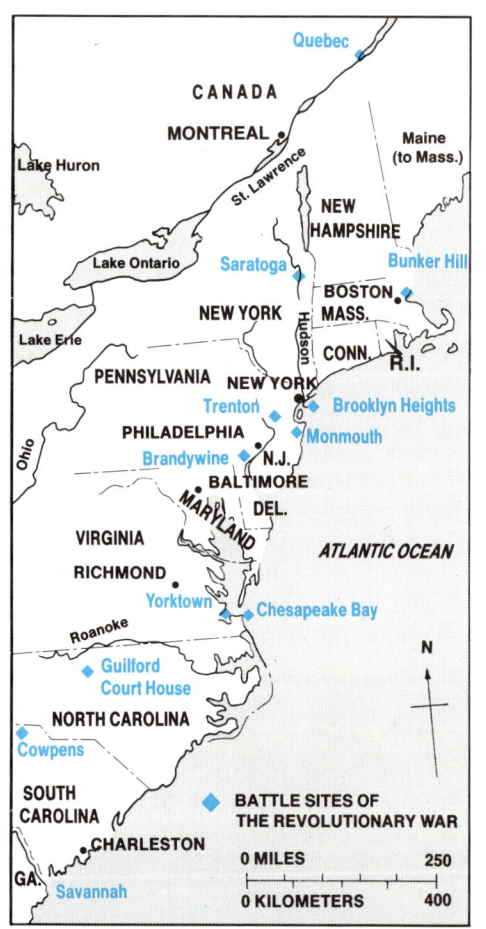

Left: Contemporary illustrations liked to emphasize that the "minutemen" were ordinary farmers. Called by a "midnight rider," this minuteman sets off for battle, leaving behind his anguished mother, wife, and child.
Above left: The American colonies and the main battle sites of the Revolutionary War.
Above: The Battle of Lexington, where the American Revolution truly started.

REVOLUTIONARY AND EARLY AMERICAN WARS

Below: The Battle of Concord before the British withdrawal to Boston.

domination through armed strength. Messengers rode throughout the 13 colonies as fast as exhausted horses could carry them, and within a short time, every colonist between New Hampshire and Georgia "knew" that the British had started a savage and unprovoked attack which had been repulsed by Massachusetts farmers, whose only thought had been to save their families and homes. It was a propaganda masterstroke, though probably not planned as such. Other colonial militia forces were called to arms, and offers of aid poured in to the Provincial Congress.

The Siege of Boston

In Boston, the Provincial Congress had decided to raise a force of 13,600 volunteers to besiege the British garrison of the city, and overall command of this Massachusetts force was entrusted to Major General Artemas Ward. Offers of aid from other colonies were gratefully accepted, and soon detachments were arriving from Connecticut, New Hampshire and Rhode Island so that the small British garrison was trapped by 15,000 Americans.

19

Benedict Arnold was a key figure in the Revolutionary War. This capable military commander served the American cause well during the first stage of the war, but was then paid to "turn his coat" and support the British in the second.

The uprising was also spreading to other parts of the colonies. The two most notable episodes were the capture of Ticonderoga and Crown Point, British forts on Lakes George and Champlain that formed the best route by which British forces could march from Quebec into the Hudson River valley in order to move on New York and the New England colonies. Ticonderoga was taken by Connecticut militia under Colonel Benedict Arnold on May 10, 1775, while Crown Point was taken two days later by Vermont militia, the "Green Mountain Boys" under Colonel Ethan Allen, who had refused to accept a command under Arnold.

The capture of these two places helped to prevent the move of British reinforcements from Quebec and also provided the revolutionary forces with much useful equipment, including some artillery. On the other side of the coin, however, Allen's

Major General, British Army (1775-1781)

From 1767, British generals had two coats: one was a gold-laced type for state occasions, while the other was a plainer "frock" in scarlet with blue facings and some gold embroidery. This major general is seen with his coat buttoned across his chest in the manner considered fashionable at the time for generals in the field. The coats of lieutenant generals had their button holes set in triplets while those for major generals were set in pairs. There was no uniformity of epaulets, which were often not worn.

refusal to serve under Arnold is an early example of the problem that would often be faced by revolutionary leaders in uniting colonial forces under a single command.

Two days after the capture of Fort Ticonderoga, the Americans achieved success in the first "naval" action of the war. In Machias Bay, Maine (then a part of Massachusetts), a group of lumbermen under Jeremiah O'Brien captured the British armed cutter *Margaretta*.

On the day that Fort Ticonderoga fell, the Second Continental Congress assembled, again in Philadelphia. But while the First Continental Congress had been limited to sending petitions to the British authorities on the other side of the Atlantic Ocean and to organizing in secret a government to put financial pressure on the British, the Second Continental Congress was faced with the problems of conducting a revolution. The tasks faced by the congressional delegates were those of controlling, organizing and supplying a steadily growing American military effort.

Increased Activity in Boston

In Boston, the militia forces that had taken the British garrison under siege were swiftly replaced by the volunteers of what may be called a New England army. Each of the contributing colonies provided a contingent of men under its own commander and undertook to supply its contingent. As far as it went, this plan was adequate, but there was no organized chain of command, and Ward was overall leader only because the other commanders chose to support him. Even so, all important decisions had to be made in council, and this inevitably caused delays. By mid-June, volunteers assisted by militiamen made up the American siege force. But, the enlistment period of the Connecticut volunteers was due to end on December 10, and the other contingents' terms of service would run out at the end of the year. The Americans would probably be unable to force the British to surrender since they could not stop supply ships from entering Boston. Other factors also worked against the Americans: lack of training, lack of uniforms and other military supplies, shortages of ammunition and bayonets, and the use of many different kinds of muskets which all required different ammunition.

Meanwhile, the British position was steadily improving. On May 25 Gage received reinforcements from England that boosted his strength to 6,500 regulars, and at the same time three generals of very high military reputation arrived. Major Generals Sir John Burgoyne, Sir Henry Clinton, and Sir William Howe were each destined to play

Above: Major General Sir William Howe arrived from Great Britain after the start of the war and commanded the entire British effort.
Opposite, top: Major General Sir Henry Clinton arrived with Howe and also rose to prominence.
Opposite, bottom: Ethan Allen summons Captain de la Place of the 26th Regiment of Foot to surrender Fort Ticonderoga on May 10, 1775.

REVOLUTIONARY AND EARLY AMERICAN WARS

an important part in the Revolutionary War. The three newly arrived generals quickly came to the conclusion that the British garrison of Boston needed more room to maneuver, for only thus could the superior firepower and discipline of its regulars be used effectively against the Americans. The British generals therefore planned to move forces to Dorchester Heights on the peninsula south of Boston. This position had previously been ignored by both sides, but offered the possibility that artillery on its heights would allow the controlling side to dominate Boston and its approaches.

The Battle of Bunker Hill

News of the British plan reached the Americans, who countered on June 15 by ordering a force of 1,200 men under Colonel William Prescott to move to a position north of the city on the Charlestown peninsula. The American commanders wished to establish a position on Bunker Hill, a rise commanding

Riflemen, armed with accurate, long-range weapons, gave the Americans a small advantage over the British. Robert Magaw describes service in the elite rifle regiment during the Siege of Boston on August 13, 1775

You will Think me Vain should I tell you how much the Riffle men are esteemed their Dress their Arms their Size Strength & activity but Above all their Great eagerness to Attect the Enemy entitle them to the first Rank. the hunting Shirt there is like a full suit at S.t James.s a Riffle man in his Dress may pass Centinels & Go Almost where he pleases while officers of the Other Regiments are Stoped. since we Cam here the Enemy Dare not show their heads. it was Diverting some Days Ago to stand on our Ramparts on prospect Hill and see half a Dozen Riffle men go Down to the Water side & from behind stone walls Chimneys & pop at their floating Batterys at About 300 Yeards Distance tissaid we Killed several. a few shotts from the Riffles always brot on a fire from the flooting Batterys & bunkers Hill where the Enemy are intrenched: but Without any other Effect than to Afford us Amusement

Riflemen led by Daniel Morgan had become skilled killers. Several of the Americans placed themselves in high trees, and, as often as they could distinguish a British officer's uniform, took him off by deliberately aiming at his person. Firing from concealed positions, they took a terrible toll. A British survivor wrote

"Our army," "abounded with young officers, in the subaltern line, and in the course of this unpleasant duty (the burial of the dead) three of the 20th regiment were interred together, the age of the eldest not exceeding seventeen. - In the course of the last action, Lieutenant Hervey, of the 62nd, a youth of sixteen, and nephew of the Adjutant-General of the same name, received several wounds, and was repeatedly ordered off the field by Colonel Anstruther; but his heroic ardor would not allow him to quit the battle, while he could stand and see his brave lads fighting beside him. A ball striking one of his legs, his removal became absolutely necessary, and while they were conveying him away, another wounded him mortally. In this situation the surgeon recommended him to take a powerful dose of opium, to avoid a seven or eight hours' life of most exquisite torture; this he immediately consented to, and when the Colonel entered the tent with Major Harnage, who were both wounded, they asked whether he had any affairs they could settle for him? his reply was, 'that being a minor, everything was already adjusted;' but he had one request, which he had just life enough to utter, "Tell my uncle I died like a soldier."

REVOLUTIONARY AND EARLY AMERICAN WARS

Left: This somewhat romanticized illustration of a Virginia rifleman in 1775 reveals the main features of this very effective American fighting man.
Below left: A drawing from Harper's Magazine of 1886 shows militiamen bringing gunpowder to the Americans for the Battle of Bunker Hill.
Below right: Americans strengthen their position on Breed's Hill, a 62-ft. height that had been occupied and fortified instead of the 110-ft. Bunker Hill which the American commander, Major General Artemas Ward, had ordered as the main American position on the Charlestown peninsula.

the narrow isthmus connecting the peninsula to the mainland. But on June 16 Prescott's force decided instead to construct a position on Breed's Hill, just outside Charlestown. This position commanded Boston better, but could also be cut off by any British move onto the isthmus behind it. The British were confident that their regulars could not be effectively opposed by the Americans, and after a naval bombardment of the earthworks on the low and vulnerable Breed's Hill at dawn on June 17 an amphibious landing was made by 2,200 men under Howe. The British command felt that the Americans were a "rabble in arms," too poorly led and equipped to warrant anything as formal as a siege. So during the afternoon of June 17 Howe launched a frontal attack against the American redoubt on Breed's Hill, now manned by about 2,200 Americans. The Americans held their fire until the last minute, and then poured down a rain of projectiles that forced the British to pull back. Howe advanced once more against the Americans' front and flanks, and was again pushed back with heavy losses. British reinforcements arrived in time for a third effort, and this time the Americans were short of ammunition and almost wholly lacking in bayonets needed for hand-to-hand fighting. The British thus secured Breed's Hill in this third act of the Battle of Bunker Hill, but to their surprise the Americans managed to pull back in relatively good order. The British losses

25

THE MILITARY HISTORY OF THE UNITED STATES

REVOLUTIONARY AND EARLY AMERICAN WARS

The Battle of Bunker Hill was the most important engagement in the first phase of the Revolutionary War. Even though they were supported by the fire of warships, the British were unable to drive the Americans from Breed's Hill. The Americans finally pulled back as they ran out of ammunition.

The Cambridge or the Grand Union Flag was the first official American flag.

27

THE MILITARY HISTORY OF THE UNITED STATES

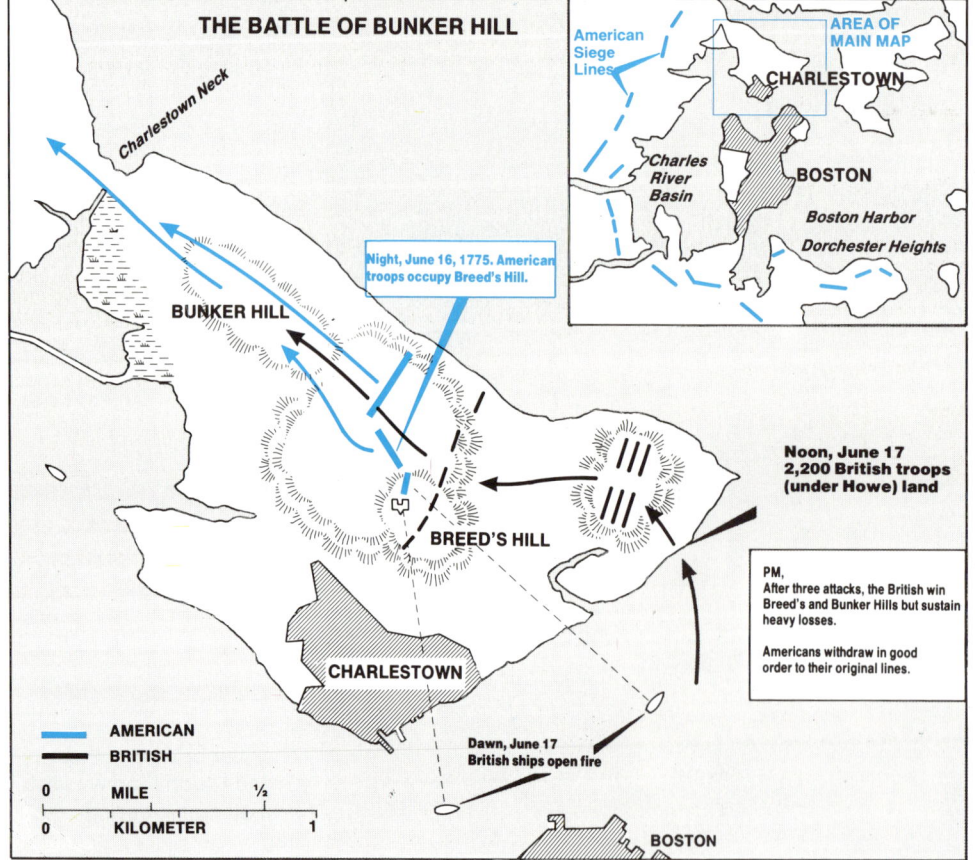

The Battle of Bunker Hill, June 17, 1775. A contemporary illustration reveals how the "heights" of Breed's and Bunker Hills command Boston, and therefore why they were so attractive to the British.

REVOLUTIONARY AND EARLY AMERICAN WARS

War has always produced events that lend themselves to glamorization, and a classic example in the Revolutionary War is the death of Joseph Warren in the Battle of Bunker Hill.

were 1,054, while the American casualties of 440 included 140 dead, 270 wounded and 30 captured.

This was the bloodiest single engagement of the Revolutionary War, and while the result was a tactical victory for the British it was also another boost to American morale. The importance of earthworks in defensive fighting was ignored, and emphasis was placed on the fact that American volunteers had beaten British regulars in two attacks and then been forced back in a third attack only when their ammunition was exhausted. Oddly enough, the long-term results of the Battle of Bunker Hill favored the British rather than the Americans. The British now had a healthy respect for the American soldier, while the Americans built up too optimistic a picture of the abilities of the citizen-soldier against the regular soldier.

Minuteman, Massachusetts Militia (1775)

The Minutemen were the private soldiers of the Alarm Companies formed within provincial militia units to turn out, fully clothed and equipped, "on a minute's notice." The minutemen had no uniform as such, and therefore fought in their civilian clothes, presumably of the type they would wear for hunting. Each man was required to furnish his own musket, together with a bayonet or short sword.

REVOLUTIONARY AND EARLY AMERICAN WARS

The single most important figure of the American effort in the Revolutionary War is George Washington. Born at Bridges Creek, Virginia, on February 22, 1732, Washington served in the Virginia militia and acquired considerable experience of irregular warfare in the French and Indian War. In June 1775, he was unanimously appointed to command of the Continental Army, a position he held until 1783. In 1789, Washington became the first President of the United States and retired to private life in 1797. He died in his home at Mount Vernon, Virginia, on December 14, 1799.

George Washington
For further references see pages
33, *34*, 36-38, 40, 44, 45, 48, 50-53, *54*, 56-57, *58*, 59, *61-62*, 63, *64-65*, 66, *67*, 68, *70*, 71, 72, 73, 85, *86-87*, 88-89, *92*, 93-95, 100-1, 104-5, 107, 109, 121-4, *127*, 130, *131-2*, *136*, 137, 139, 140-1, 145-7, 152, 154, 156, 158, 161, 174, 181, *186-7*, 221, 223, 232.

Revitalized British Effort

After Bunker Hill the British government realized that to retain its American empire a great military effort would be needed. Nearly a year passed before effective plans could be laid and brought into action. Meanwhile the Continental Congress had come to a better understanding of the situation. It realized that it had been forced by matters in New England to assume the leadership of an armed rebellion that could be won only by the concerted action of the 13 colonies. In overall terms, the Americans still expected a negotiated settlement with Great Britain and hoped that reconciliation was possible, but now saw that armed struggle would also be necessary before any agreement could be reached. The Continental Congress knew that it would take the British several months to lay their plans and send in additional troops. Therefore, they had the time available for the creation of a national army, the consolidation of their slight hold on the government of the 13

31

Private, Warner's Battalion of the "Green Mountain Boys" (1775)

The "Green Mountain Boys" originated as military companies raised in various New Hampshire and Vermont towns as a result of the disputes between the settlers of the New Hampshire Grants and colonial officials of New York. In June 1775, the Continental Congress combined the companies into a 500-man battalion commanded by Seth Warner. The battalion suffered severely in the Quebec operation and was then re-formed as Warner's Regiment. Like two similar Canadian regiments, the "Green Mountain Boys" were classed separately from the Continental Army's regiments. The illustration shows the standard uniform, to which were often added Indian items such as a wampum pouch and belt, and a tomahawk.

colonies, and the implementation of plans to force the British out of Boston and to invade Quebec. The Americans believed that peace could be re-established by the end of 1776, so they did not plan for a long war.

The Creation of an American Army

The greatest achievement of the Continental Congress was the creation of an American army in the form of the Continental Army. After receiving an appeal from the Massachusetts Provincial Congress, on June 14 the Continental Congress recognized the forces besieging the British in Boston as the Continental Army. At the same time, it decided to raise ten companies of riflemen in Maryland, Pennsylvania, and Virginia as the first soldiers enlisted directly into Continental service. One day later, Colonel George Washington of Virginia was chosen as commander-in-chief of the Continental Army and commissioned in the rank of major general. The reason for the selection of Washington for the position was not purely military. The Continental Congress knew that the choice of a southerner would help to cement the southern colonies into an alliance for a war then being fought only in a northern colony. On June 16 Washington departed for Boston to assume command of the forces there, which were to be reinforced as soon as possible by six of the new companies of riflemen.

In addition to laying these foundations for the Continental Army, the Continental Congress also began to establish the command structure for a regular army, creating four other major generals and eight brigadier generals to serve under Washington, and establishing staff departments, scales of pay and rations, and articles of war. The choice of the

The Americans based the organization of their army on the European pattern, and thus used the spear as the distinguishing mark and official weapon of junior commissioned officers and senior non-commissioned officers. These weapons are halberds, the variety of spear carrying an axblade on one side, a peak or point (sometimes another axblade) opposite it, and a long spike or blade at the end.

THE MILITARY HISTORY OF THE UNITED STATES

other major generals and the brigadier generals reflected the colonies current situation, so two-thirds of them were New Englanders to acknowledge the fact that the existing army was basically a New England army. Three other officers, Horatio Gates, Charles Lee and Richard Montgomery, were chosen because of their experience in British service. Lee had arrived in America during 1773, and as he was thought to be the ablest officer available he was made Washington's first assistant.

Washington to Supreme Military Command

Washington assumed command of the Continental Army at Cambridge Common on July 3, 1775. At that time, he described his command as a "mixed multitude of people...under very little discipline, order, or government." Washington saw as his most important task the creation of a more formally organized and disciplined army modeled on the British army of the French and Indian War, in which Washington had fought. As Washington put it: "Discipline is the soul of an army. It makes small numbers formidable; procures success for the weak, and esteem to all." Gates, the adjutant general, was responsible for the preparation of orders and regulations, leaving Washington free for the development of discipline, which took the form of regular roll calls and strength returns, and also the discouragement of the tendency of officers and men to come and go as they pleased. Washington did not agree with the "leveling" tendencies of the New Englanders, and because of his belief in the need to distinguish officers from men and to instill a sense of discipline, several types of punishment (pillory, lash, wooden horse and drumming out of camp) were used after the unfortunately large numbers of courts-martial.

These measures were aimed mainly at the existing army. At the same time,

> **Charles Lee**
> For further references see pages
> 53, 54, 61, *62*, 63, 88, *89*, 107, 308.

> **The Continental Army**
> For further references see pages
> *32*, 33, *38*, 42, 49, 51-53, *60*, 62, 63, 66-68, 71, 72, 74, 78, 85-87, 89, 97, 105, *106*, 107, 108, 110, 116, *119*, 122, *137*, 138, 141, 152, 181, 186.

Major General George Washington arrives to take command of the Continental Army at Cambridge Common, Massachusetts, on July 3, 1775.

34

REVOLUTIONARY AND EARLY AMERICAN WARS

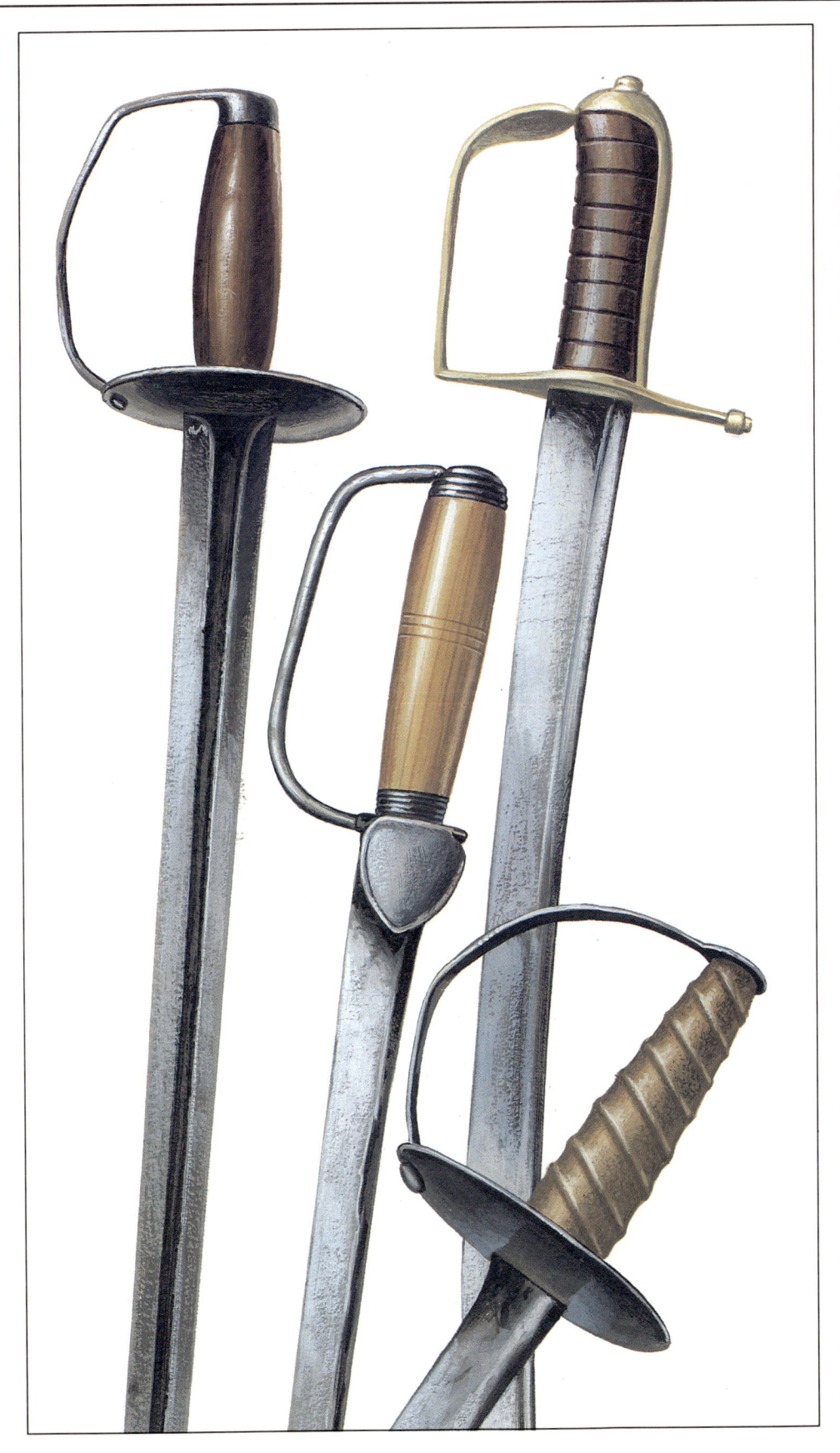

American swords of the Revolutionary War were not as elaborate as those used by the British (see page 47), but were just as effective in a period of change when the sword was losing its importance on the battlefield.

AN APPEAL TO HEAVEN

The ensign of "Washington's Cruisers." This design was at one time a candidate for the official American flag.

35

THE MILITARY HISTORY OF THE UNITED STATES

Major General Horatio Gates had served with the British army in the French and Indian War. He was chosen as one of Washington's senior subordinates because of the high reputation he had secured in that war.

The Continental Congress
For further references see pages
15, *16*, 22, 31-33, 38, 40, 49, 50, 51-53, 56, 62, 70, 71, 79, 85, 90, 96, *98*, 104, 105, 107, *125*, 137, 141, 181, 182, 186, 187, *220*, 221, 222.

Washington had to create the new army being enlisted directly into Continental service. In September 1775, a Congressional committee visited Washington's camp. As a result of several meetings the scheme for the new army was set at 26 infantry regiments each containing 728 men, as well as single rifle and artillery regiments. The overall strength of this army was 20,372 men, to be administered, supplied and paid by the Continental Congress up to the end of 1776. With

REVOLUTIONARY AND EARLY AMERICAN WARS

The most successful American naval captain of the Revolutionary War was John Paul Jones. On December 3, 1775, this outstanding naval officer hoisted on his ship *Alfred* the first U.S. flag flown by an American warship. The flag, the Grand Union (or Cambridge) Flag, contained 13 American stripes with the Union flag in the field. Jones later wrote: "We cannot be parted in life or death. So long as we can float, we shall float together. If we must sink, we shall go down as one."

John Paul Jones
For further references see pages 90, 92, 93.

the exception of the hopelessly underestimated term of enlistment, the scheme was workable - at least on paper. In practice, however, Washington found that the officers as much as the men resisted all efforts to create an army that interfered with locally formed units. They were also unwilling to enlist for another year when their first loyalties were with their families and farms. Despite all the pressures that could be brought to bear, on December 10 most of the Connecticut contingent set off for home, and militia from Massachusetts and New Hampshire had to be brought in to plug the gap in the line besieging the British in Boston. Three weeks later the enlistments of several other contingents expired, and many more men left.

The Importance of Militia Units

So on January 1, 1776, when the army formally became "Continental in every respect," Washington found that instead of 20,000 men under command he had only 8,000, a number that increased to only 9,000 by early March. This meant that the shortfall had to be made up with militia units. By now it had become clear that the initial enlistment of the Continental Army for one year only meant that the whole distressing, disrupting process would have to be repeated at the end of the year.

At this time, Washington was pressing ahead with the siege of Boston. his administrative and personal leadership skills began to show strongly as the army slowly overcame all types of supply failings. The commander-in-chief put small parties of men on board American ships which then succeeded in capturing a useful number of British supply vessels.

October 13, 1775, can be regarded as the birthday of the modern U.S. Navy. On that day, the Continental Congress authorized the fitting out of two ships to intercept vessels carrying stores to the British forces in North America. Precursors of this Continental Navy were "Washington's Cruisers." The first was commissioned on September 5, 1775, as the initial regularly commissioned warship in American service, the schooner *Hannah*. She sailed on the day she was commissioned and, two days later, took the *Unity*, the first naval prize taken in the Revolutionary War. The *Hannah* was soon joined by one brigantine and five more schooners. All flew a variation on the "Liberty Tree" ensign, one of the candidates as the first official American flag. On December 13, 1775, the Continental Congress authorized the construction of 13 frigates (five of 32 guns each, five of 28 guns each and three of 24 guns each) for the Continental Navy. Only seven were completed, and all of them were lost in the Revolutionary War. The first commander of the Continental Navy was Esek Hopkins (left), who was appointed on December 22, 1775 but cashiered less than two years later for failure to follow the orders of the Continental Navy.

REVOLUTIONARY AND EARLY AMERICAN WARS

By the beginning of the fourth quarter of the 18th century the spear was out of date as a first-line military weapon, but still retained a small niche in the British army. In this force the spear (in a number of forms with a variety of names such as pike, half-pike and spontoon) was used as an emblem of the rank and function. The visibility of the tall weapon was supposed to allow soldiers, even in the haze and tumult of battle, to find both the commissioned and senior non-commissioned officers who carried them. In fact the spears were seldom carried in the Revolutionary War.

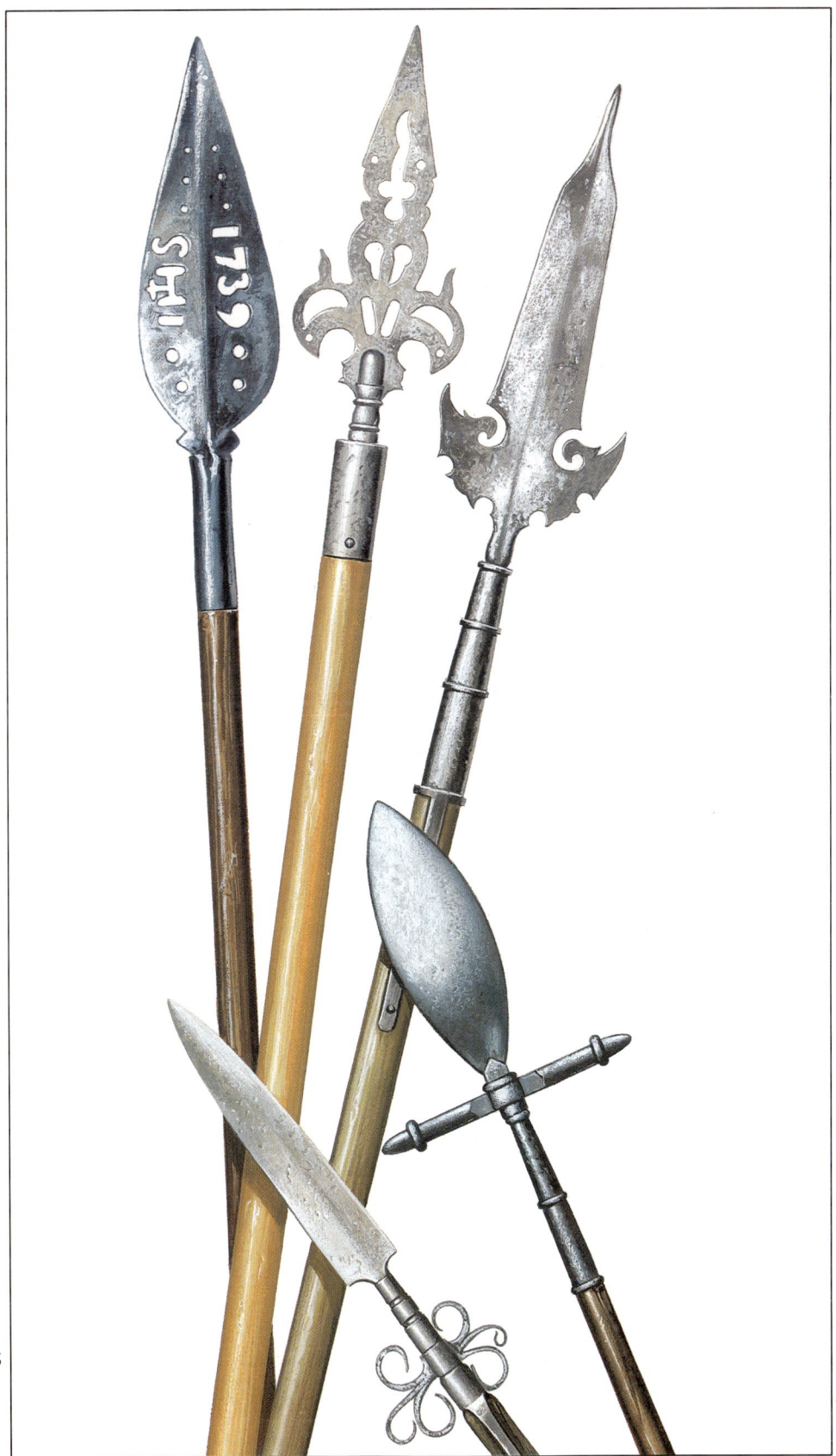

An American merchant flag, used until the 1790s; the colors could vary.

The most successful of these raiding groups was that of Commodore Esek Hopkins. He led six converted merchantmen from Philadelphia, on February 17. They sailed to the Bahamas, where New Providence was attacked and men put ashore to capture cannon and ammunition before the ships returned to Providence, Rhode Island. On March 19 the Continental Congress authorized privateering, and this became a major feature of the Revolutionary War as American ships attacked British shipping on the vital Atlantic routes and elsewhere. At about the same time the Continental Congress and several colonies sponsored purchasing missions to the Dutch and French possessions in the West Indies, where significant amounts of war material were bought. In 1776, Spain also began to sell munitions to the Americans.

Washington also dispatched Colonel Henry Knox, later his Chief of Artillery, to the captured Fort Ticonderoga, and during the winter of 1775-76 Knox returned to Cambridge, Massachusetts over icebound or even nonexistent roads with about 50 pieces of artillery. By March 1776 Washington was well enough equipped to push forward against the British defenders of Boston.

The Invasion of Quebec

In many respects, the siege of Boston was only a sideshow to the main American effort of the period. This took the form of an invasion of Quebec, which the Americans saw as a fourteenth British colony that might rebel. It was an apparently vulnerable target whose loss would deprive the British of its major overland invasion route along the line of rivers and lakes between Montreal and New York. The Continental Congress got nowhere with its appeal for the inhabitants of Quebec to join the American cause, and in June 1775, ordered Major General Philip Schuyler of New York to seize Quebec if it was "practicable" and "not disagreeable" to the inhabitants.

Schuyler managed to create a 2,000-man core for what later became known as the Northern Army. In September 1775, he departed at the head of this force from Fort Ticonderoga with the object of taking Montreal before advancing down the St. Lawrence toward the city of Quebec. To provide a second prong to this invasion, Washington dispatched Benedict Arnold and a force of 1,100 men, including a rifle contingent under Captain Daniel Morgan of Virginia, for an extremely imaginative parallel stroke. Arnold left Cambridge on September 12 for an advance that was to take his force up the Kennebec River and across the wilds of Maine before moving down the Chaudiere River to link up with Schuyler's force outside Quebec.

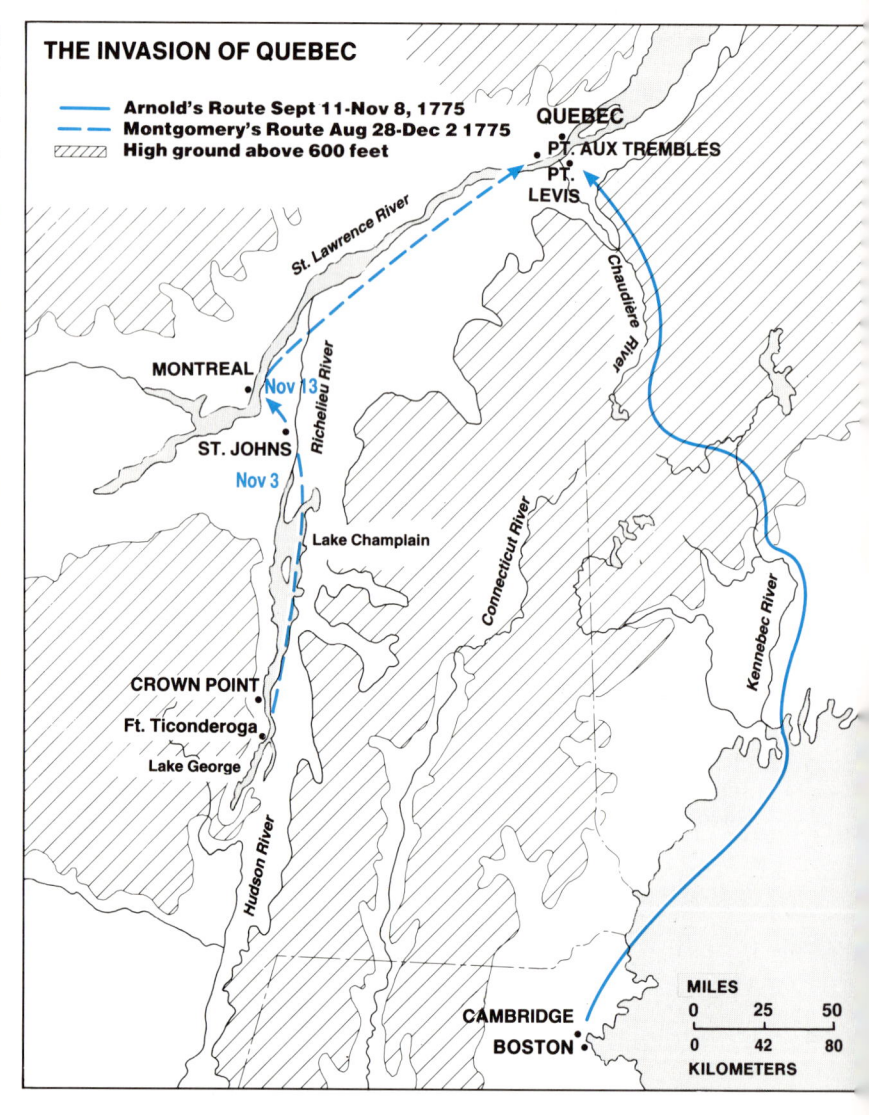

Schuyler made good progress at first, but was then delayed by the stubborn 600-man British defense of Fort St. Johns where the Americans had to leave the

The American attack on Quebec in the closing months of 1775 was poorly conceived and badly executed. It was notable, however, for the classic march through the Maine wilderness by Benedict Arnold's detachment.

Richelieu River and strike northwest to Montreal. Fort St. Johns was taken under siege on September 6, and when Schuyler became ill on September 13, his place was taken by Brigadier General Richard Montgomery. Fort St. Johns finally surrendered on November 2, and Montgomery's force advanced to Montreal. Ethan Allen had already made a disastrous effort to take Montreal and been captured in the process, but on November 13 Montgomery took the city and captured a British river flotilla. The British governor general, Sir Guy Carleton, pulled back to Quebec.

Brigadier General Richard Montgomery headed the main American force involved in the abortive invasion of Canada in the fall and early winter of 1775.

A Classic March through the Maine Wilderness

Five days earlier, Arnold had reached Levis at the mouth of the Chaudiere River opposite Quebec. Arnold's approach march remains one of military history's classics of endurance and determination under adverse geographical and climatic conditions. One part of his force turned back, and Arnold's force was further reduced by starvation, disease, drowning, and desertion. On November 13 Arnold's remaining 600 men crossed the St. Lawrence and, copying General James Wolfe's 1759 maneuver that led to the British capture of Quebec from the French, scaled the cliffs and camped on the Heights of Abraham. As the French had done in 1759, the British regulars and Quebec militia retired into the city. The American force was too small even to consider an assault when the British refused to fight on open ground.

Arnold finally pulled back up the St. Lawrence to Point aux Trembles, where he was joined on December 3 by Montgomery and 300 men, all that could be spared from the American garrison at Montreal. Montgomery then assumed overall command. The American commander was faced by total indifference on the part of the French and by steady loyalty to the crown on the part of the British. He also had to take into consideration the fact that the enlistment of about half his force was due to expire. In an attempt to win a decisive victory while he could, Montgomery launched a desperate attack on Quebec during the night of December 30. The attack was made in a raging snowstorm and was defeated by the numerically superior British, who could call on 1,800 men. In the fight Montgomery was killed and Arnold wounded, and American losses totaled 100 killed and wounded in addition to 300 captured.

The Americans Are Driven Back

Despite his wound and lack of numbers, Arnold tried to keep up the illusion of a

THE MILITARY HISTORY OF THE UNITED STATES

This heroic painting of Montgomery's death in the disastrous American attack on Quebec during December 30, 1775, provides little indication of the real conditions: of bitter cold and driving snow as the outnumbered Americans sought vainly to oust a well prepared and ably led British garrison.

General John Burgoyne
For further references see pages
22, 43, 44, 67, 72, *73*, 74, 76, 78, *79*, 80, *81*, *83*, 85, 109, 119.

siege to buy time for the arrival of reinforcements, which appeared in the form of Continental Army regiments from New Jersey, New York and Pennsylvania. But they arrived by the handful rather than as a single force. Decimated by smallpox and several other diseases, and never adequately supplied with ammunition, clothing and food over their dreadful lines of communication, the 8,000 Americans eventually committed to the Quebec campaign were never in any real position to take the offensive. The British too were reinforced, but on an altogether more sensible basis. Burgoyne arrived on May 6 with forces that were large by local standards. In June 1776 Burgoyne went on the offensive against an American force that was now under the command of Major General John Sullivan, but already beginning to disintegrate. Sullivan attempted to stabilize the American position with an attack on Trois Rivieres during June 6, but the 2,000 Americans under Brigadier General John Thomas had been deceived by faulty intelligence and instead of a 600-man garrison found Burgoyne with 8,000 men. The Americans were utterly dispersed, and Sullivan, realizing that his position was no longer tenable, abandoned Montreal and fell back first to Crown Point and by mid-July to Ticonderoga. In the north, the strategic initiative had passed firmly to the British.

Lake Champlain, the Key

Both sides knew that control of Lake Champlain would decide the outcome of the obvious next move for the British, an advance into New York. Each side therefore rushed to create a small flotilla of warships, with the American effort

Major General John Sullivan was one of the senior American commanders in the New York campaign.

coordinated by Arnold. The British flotilla was manned by sailors from the transport ships that had brought Burgoyne's force up the St. Lawrence River, and its ships were more heavily armed than their American counterparts. On October 28, the Battle of Valcour Island occurred. The British ships attacked the American flotilla and sank or destroyed most of them. Arnold managed to slip away with the survivors, but was caught at Split Rock where the rest of the American flotilla was destroyed. Yet Arnold's effort had saved the day for the Americans: the campaign for control of Lake Champlain had so delayed the British that winter overtook them. The British did briefly occupy Crown Point at the southern end of Lake Champlain, but then pulled back into Quebec for the winter.

Farther east, the Americans had enjoyed better fortunes in the first half of 1776. By spring 1776 Washington felt that his forces were in a position to move against the British garrison of Boston. The American commander-in-chief launched his effort on March 4 with a move onto the Dorchester Heights. The reinforced American artillery was emplaced to threaten the city, and a few days later Washington ordered the fortification of Nook's Hill, a point even closer to Boston. The British had already realized the impossibility of holding Boston for much longer. Howe, Gage's successor as British commander, had also concluded

Major General Sir William Howe
For further references see pages
22, 25, 45, 48, 53, 55-59, 61-63, 66-68, 70-72, *73*, 76, 85, 87, 89, 119.

Above: A map of New York during the Revolutionary War provides striking evidence of how small all American cities were at the time. The city was vitally important, but occupied only the southernmost tip of Manhattan Island.

Right: The American siege of Boston was not pressed with great severity even under Washington's personal command, but Howe still decided that the city was a poor base for American operations and completed the evacuation of his force by March 17, 1776.

that Boston was a poor strategic base from which to retain the American colonies. Howe had been holding Boston only until the arrival of the transports needed for the British evacuation to Halifax in Nova Scotia, but finally pulled out under the increasing American pressure. In Halifax, Howe intended to await reinforcement as he planned the capture of a new British base of operations in the 13 colonies.

American Advantages From the British Loss of Boston

Despite the fact that the British had planned their evacuation of Boston, the Americans did benefit materially from their seizure of the city, for Washington's forces gladly accepted the artillery and ammunition that the British had been unable to remove. More important,

Captain George Pausch was a German soldier hired by the British to fight in North America. He and his men left their homes in 1776. Many never returned.

Pausch's Journal: 1776 May 15,

In conformity to the order of our Gracious Prince the roll-call was beaten at half-past three P. M., and the company marched out of the Mill-fortification to the Parade-ground, where all the necessary accountrements for my men were found in readiness. A quarter of an hour afterwards, the signal was given by the tap of the drum for a forward movement; and, the lines being formed, we at once marched through the hospital Gate of the old town to the wood-warehouses. Here the company immediately embarked on the ships, which had been designated for our transportation, in the presence of our most gracious sovereigns.

Pausch and his men crossed the Atlantic aboard a leaky, unseaworthy ship that formerly had been a slave trading ship. It was a miserable journey.

Toward 4 o'clock in the morning of the 15th this gale was succeeded by a favorable wind which lasted till the 17th, when by 4 o'clock in the morning it threatened to change into a most furious gale. Indeed, it soon became so violent, that the Captain, who was generally a most courageous man and a daring mariner, lost his courage. So, also, did the sailors. All the sails which were hoisted were torn by the wind into tatters, and the main mast (the strongest) was broken short off. Each successive wave following the other swept over the deck or rather the ship; and so much water came into the vessel, that those who slept in the lowest bunk under the forward deck with their baggage, were flooded; and this, too although all the openings and air-holes (dead lights) were covered. Now the ship would lay on one side, and now on the other - her masts touching the waters, which now rose around the ship higher than the masts. At times we seemed to be in a deep abyss between the walls of water. Every one of us, including the Captain himself, expected every moment would be our last; and each one appeared reconciled to the inevitable, giving up all hope of ever seeing America, or his fatherland again.

Pausch and his artillerymen eventually arrived in Canada where they joined Burgoyne's invasion of New York. Pausch's cannon, along with the Hessian infantry, saved the hard pressed British forces at the Battle of Freeman's Farm, 19 September, 1777.

The firing seemed to draw nearer; from which one might infer that our right wing was retreating. Accordingly, we left our position, and marched for about a quarter of an hour in the direction of the firing. We then formed in line of battle, I placing the two cannon in the road which led into the woods. The fences, which lay to my left, I had already quickly thrown down in order that the enemy, on his approach, might not hide behind them.

Meanwhile, Major von Geismar, who was yet on the staff of Gen. Riedesel, was sent by the latter to see if there was any possibility of reaching Gen. Burgoyne and informing him that he stood here in readiness with his own Regiment, two companies of the Regiment Rhetz and two 6 pound cannon, and that he was only waiting for orders to reinforce him. In the meantime, the patrols returned one after the other. The second patrol having reported that the communication between us and the troops in action was open, the General (Riedesel) marched at once toward the right.

He choose this way, in order to make a division on the right flank of the enemy. He also ordered the march to be beaten on the drums, which caused the men to cheer repeatedly. After descending the hill we met von Geismar on his return with orders from Gen. Burgoyne directing Gen. Riedesel to attack the enemy on their right flank, and, if possible, to follow them up. This, however, we were prevented from doing both by the woods and the swamps behind which the enemy were hidden. I was also to go to the right wing of the 21st English regiment.

Under a shower of the enemy's bullets, I safely reached the hill just as the 21st and 9th Regiments were about to abandon it.

REVOLUTIONARY AND EARLY AMERICAN WARS

Nevertheless, I continued to drag my two cannon up the hill, while Gen. Phillips exhorted the English Regiments, and the officers their men, to face the enemy. English captains and other officers and privates and also the Brunswick Chasseurs, which happened to be detailed here, grasped the ropes. The entire line of these regiments faced about, and by this faithful assistance, my cannon were soon on top of the hill. I had shells Rev 3-4 brought up and placed by the side of the cannon; and as soon as I go the range, I fired twelve or fourteen shots in quick succession into the foe who were within good pistol shot distance.

The firing from muskets was at once renewed, and assumed lively proportions particularly the platoon fire from the left wing of Riedesel. Presently, the enemy's fire, though very lively at one time, suddenly ceased. I advanced about sixty paces sending a few shells after the flying enemy, and firing from twelve to fifteen shots more into the woods into which they had retreated. Everything then became quiet; and about fifteen minutes afterwards darkness set in.

A fine pair of English hangers.

47

THE MILITARY HISTORY OF THE UNITED STATES

however, was the boost to American morale at a time when it was being battered by the news from the Quebec front. Washington expected that the British would now move against New York and started to move his forces into this area. This was what Howe was planning, and the British forces in Halifax were reinforced for the effort, which was to be supported by a fleet commanded by Howe's brother, Admiral Sir Richard Howe.

For the immensely difficult task of subduing the American colonies 3,000 miles across the Atlantic Ocean, Sir William Howe requested reinforcement to a strength of 50,000 men. Such a figure was impossibly large for the British government to find, yet during 1776 Howe's strength rose to more than 30,000 men. These troops included an increasingly large number of German mercenaries recruited largely from Hesse-Kassel, which during the course of the Revolutionary War provided about 30,000 men including officers up to the rank of major general.

Though there was in general a uniformity of pattern in the swords of each regiment, officers often carried their own swords. These German weapons show great variation in overall design as well as in detail of decoration, and some of the more ingenious had features such as a saw-back.

Richtige Abbildung der von den amerikanischen Provinzialisten belagerten und wiedereroberten Hauptstadt und Festung Boston in Amerika, im Monat Merz 1776.

A German illustration of the British seaborne retreat from Boston considerably overemphasizes the heights overlooking the city.

The Declaration of Independence

It was now clear that the British were not prepared to accommodate American desires for greater liberty and rights within the British empire. A great British effort was clearly underway to reduce the American colonies to their original status, and the only other possibility open to the Americans was complete independence from Great Britain. The Declaration of Independence on July 4, 1776, thus established the new nation. At the same time, it turned the limited rebellion to secure rights for the Americans under the British flag into a war for independence. All sensible men now saw that a major and sustained national effort would be required. The tasks facing the new nation were enormous. With a population of perhaps 2.5 million, the 13 new states had a pool of manpower greater than the British could hope to maintain in any practical manner on the western side of the Atlantic. However, about 20 percent of this population were black and in general slaves not eligible for service, about 35 percent of the rest remained loyal to the British, and there was also a sizeable percentage of fence-sitters. Of those able to serve in the army, most were farmers with large families to support and land to tend, a fact that made long-term recruitment all but impossible. Other factors against American independence were lack of any real industrial base and poor communications. Lack of an industrial base meant that the Continental Army had to rely on captured British equipment or supplies from friendly European powers brought in through a tightening British blockade. American communications generally ran up and down rivers, and along the coast: the former made transportation very difficult between what had now become different states, especially when the British blockade effectively prevented coastal movement.

Another factor that made it difficult for the Americans to fight a successful war against the British was the nature of the government that came into being in 1776. The very limited central government had only the smallest power, whereas each state government jealously retained its already extensive powers. The Continental Congress continued as a meeting place for states' delegates, but lacked any powers

THE MILITARY HISTORY OF THE UNITED STATES

The single most decisive episode in American history was the signing of the Declaration of Independence on July 4, 1776. This declared that the United States of America was "free and independent ... absolved from any allegiance to the British Crown."

of its own or an executive to carry out its enactments. Shortly after the Declaration of Independence, in an effort to provide the Continental Congress with limited but specific powers, Articles of Confederation were drawn up. However it was only in 1781 that the Articles were ratified by the states, which remained extremely jealous of their rights despite the near disasters that had overtaken the fledgling United States because of its lack of a workable central government. The Continental Congress meanwhile exercised many of the powers granted by the Articles, but lacked the power to tax or to raise military forces. All the Continental Congress could do, therefore, was set quotas for the states to meet on the basis of their wealth and population. The Continental Congress lacked the power to compel the individual states to meet their quota requirements, which were almost never met.

Washington's Problem

In these circumstances, it is not surprising that Washington never got the army he needed, in either size or composition. Numbers of men and equipment were always below the requirement, and state militia units often had to be used to bolster the strength of the Continental Army. This put Washington in a vicious circle of declining numbers: when the Continental Army needed militia reinforcement at dire moments, the militiamen were less willing to serve and the position of the Continental Army was worsened, making it even less likely that militia reinforcement would be forthcoming. Even when militia forces were made available to the Continental Army, the system was highly inefficient in terms of appointments, supplies, and lines of communication.

Washington remained opposed to the concept of reinforcing the Continental Army with state militia and by early 1776 had decided that success could be provided only by an enlarged Continental Army enlisted for the duration of the war. The commander-in-chief finally persuaded the Continental Congress that his idea was right, and in October 1776, it voted for a new Continental Army establishment of 88 infantry battalions totaling about 60,000 men, enlisted for three years or "during the present war" with each state to provide men in accordance with the quota established in the Articles. After the November 1776 retreat across New Jersey the Continental Congress voted an additional 22 battalions to be recruited

An illustration of 1876 provides portraits and autograph signatures of the men who formulated and signed the Declaration of Independence in Philadelphia on July 4, 1776.

directly by the Continental Army. This 110-battalion establishment remained in force until 1781, when it was trimmed to a 59-battalion establishment.

But this was all on paper. In practice Washington never had more than 30,000 men under command. In only a few battles was Washington ever able to field as many as 15,000 men. This was a very serious limitation on the commander-in-chief's ability to wage the war for independence. It must be admitted, however, that the Americans would have been very hard pressed to equip a Continental Army at full establishment strength, and that the small size of the Continental Army placed less strain on an already overburdened supply system.

Washington's Greatest Achievement

Almost certainly Washington's greatest Achievements were the creation of any type of Continental Army at all and then its maintenance in the field. The result was a peculiarly American army that never developed into the image of the British army as Washington originally desired, but which ultimately proved effective for the type of war in which it evolved.

The Continental Army lived and fought in three territorial divisions or departments under the overall leadership of Washington. The main army was that under Washington himself in the middle states, while the Northern Army operated in northern New York and the Southern Army in the Carolinas and Georgia. Washington was in many respects a commander in name only as far as the Northern and Southern Armies were concerned, for the Continental Congress appointed their commanders and issued orders directly to them. Up to 1777 the Northern Army was more important by far than the Southern Army, which existed only on paper. By 1780 the situation was completely reversed as the British shifted their main effort to the south.

The Continental Army consisted mainly

U.S. Army Campaign Streamers of the Revolutionary War

Lexington: April 19, 1775
Ticonderoga: May 10, 1775
Boston: June 17, 1775 -
   March 17, 1776
Quebec: August 28, 1775 -
   July 1776.
Charleston: June 28-29, 1776
Long Island: August 26-29, 1776
Trenton: December 26, 1776
Princeton: January 3, 1777
Saratoga: July 2, 1777 -
   October 17, 1777
Brandywine: September 11, 1777
Germantown: October 4, 1777
Monmouth: June 28, 1778
Savannah: December 29, 1778;
   September 16, 1779 - October 10, 1779
Charleston: March 29, 1780 -
   May 12, 1780
Cowpens: January 17, 1781
Guildford Court House:
   March 15, 1781
Yorktown: September 28 -
   October 19, 1781

Charleston
For further references see pages *55*, 56, 96, 97, *99*, 100-102, 108, 110, 117, 118, 120, 131, 132, 136.

Major General Sir Henry Clinton
For further references see pages *22*, *55*, 63, 79, 87, 88, 93, 95, 96, 100, 101, 107, 108, *109*, 110, 117, 119, 120, 122-124, 127, 131, 134.

of infantry and artillery, and possessed virtually no cavalry. The basic infantry unit was the regiment or battalion of eight companies. Such units were grouped in differing numbers into a brigade commanded by a brigadier general. Several brigades formed a division commanded by a major general. The four regiments of artillery constituted the artillery brigade commanded by Brigadier General Henry Knox, but for tactical purposes the artillery companies were distributed among the infantry units.

At the same time that the Continental Army was beginning to take shape, the Continental Congress was trying to provide an American navy. The building of 13 frigates was authorized in 1776, but the strength of the British navy was overwhelming and completely dominated maritime matters until the advent of French sea power later in the war.

Lack of British Strategy

The British failed to develop a consistent strategy throughout the war, which meant that they operated on a year-to-year basis. Washington could not develop a comprehensive strategy either, but, he did develop an operational plan, a consistent line of action, that successfully exploited British weakness. He kept his main force in a central position to block any British advance into the American interior, he considered very carefully whether or not to offer battle for limited objectives, he always made sure that his army could not be destroyed in its entirety, and he always tried to find a method of concentrating his forces for the decisive moment when the British were spread too thin. Ironically, Washington understood more fully than the British the importance of naval power. In the long term this allowed Washington to exploit a naval victory by his French allies to strike the decisive blow.

The nearest that the British came to a consistent strategic objective throughout the war was the securing of the Lake Champlain/Hudson River line as a means of dividing the colonies. The British expected that this would allow them to reach agreement with the less inflamed Americans in the middle and southern colonies and then concentrate their military effort against the New Englanders who had started the war. For the 1776 campaign, therefore, Howe decided to use Great Britain's undisputed mastery of the sea to move the British strength from Halifax to New York, where a base would be secured before the British advanced up the Hudson River/Lake Champlain line. With commendable military sense, Howe felt that the full British strength should be used for the New York operation. In a manner typical of the divided British control of the war, however, the authorities in London had already sent a substantial number of men for operations in Quebec. Howe decided on another division of strength, for according to ex-governors of southern colonies taking refuge in British ships off the coast of the southern states, loyalists in this region needed only limited support before they would rise and reinstate British rule.

War in the South

This last adventure was entrusted to Admiral Sir Peter Parker. His squadron was so delayed in its arrival from England toward the end of May that loyalist uprisings in the Carolinas and Virginia had already been defeated. In December 1775, Virginia rebels had defeated loyalists in a minor engagement at Great Bridge near Norfolk, and the British governor had fled to the safety of a British warship lying offshore, from which he sent reports to London of the willingness of the loyalists to oust the rebels. More significantly, on February 27, 1776 a force of 1,100 North Carolinians had defeated about 1,800 loyalists in the Battle of Moores Creek Bridge as the loyalists were marching on Wilmington in the hope of establishing a British coastal base.

Despite such failures, Parker decided to attack Charleston, the largest city in the south, using Clinton's force which had been earmarked for the proposed base at Wilmington. The vulnerability of Charleston was fully appreciated by Washington, who sent Lee south to organize the defenses of the city with the South

Officer, Corps of Light Infantry (1777)

In the summer of 1777, Washington created a regimental-size Corps of Light Infantry using men detached from existing regiments. This illustration shows an officer of the corps (distinguishable by his spontoon, crimson sash, and silver rather than white worsted epaulets) with the red facings that distinguished men of the southern group of mid-Atlantic states (Delaware, Maryland, Pennsylvania, and Virginia).

Colonel William Moultrie was the commander of the seaward defense of Charleston, South Carolina, on June 28, 1776. On this date, the American fort on Sullivan's Island, constructed of palmetto logs and sand, soaked up the British cannon fire without suffering major damage, and then used its artillery to severely damage the ships of Admiral Sir Peter Parker's squadron. The result was the withdrawal of Major General Sir Henry Clinton's force, which had been entrusted with the capture of Charleston.

Carolina militia and newly raised Continental forces. Against Lee's advice, the South Carolinians based their defense on Fort Moultrie, a palmetto fort built on Sullivan's Island commanding the approach to Charleston harbor. In purely tactical sense, this was the wrong place to locate the main defense of the city, but the American error was remedied by the faulty British assault, which was planned and executed too hastily. Clinton's troops landed on neighboring Long Island, but could not take any active part in the Battle of Sullivan's Island on June 28 because the water was too deep for them to wade across to Sullivan's Island. So when Parker's ships tried to pass Sullivan's Island and enter Charleston harbor they were devastated by the American artillery under Colonel William Moultrie. Parker sensibly extracted his squadron, and shortly afterward, Clinton's men were lifted off Long Island for transport to New York, where they came under Howe's command.

For the next three years, the British ignored the southern states. Yet there were undoubtedly many southern loyalists who would have supported a British effort in the region.

There has long been a tendency to depict the more famous historical figures of the Revolutionary War as ordinary men responding to challenge. Israel Putnam had acquired a considerable reputation as a middle-ranking officer in the British colonial forces involved in the French and Indian War, but this idealized picture shows him leaving his plow to become one of Washington's most important subordinates with the rank of major general.

The British Invade New York

Between March and June Howe had waited at Halifax for his reinforcements, which were severely delayed by the weather. Toward the end of June, Howe decided that he could wait no longer and embarked in his brother's fleet for New York. On July 2, Howe's army landed on Staten Island, where it waited for reinforcement. Ordered by the Continental Congress to hold New York, Washington had only 19,000 men and was faced with the problems of countering a land attack, a naval attack, or both. Here Washington made the same mistake as the South Carolinians at Charleston: he concentrated his defense as far forward as possible. Major earthworks were thrown up on the Brooklyn Heights, and batteries of artillery were established on Governor's Island and Staten Island. While half of Washington's army held Manhattan Island, the other half under Major General Nathanael Greene took up positions across the Flatbush area of Long Island. Greene succumbed to malaria and was replaced by Major General John Sullivan, but at the last moment Washington installed Major General Israel Putnam over Sullivan. Washington's command was too far forward and also divided. The only land communication to Manhattan Island from the mainland was over the Kingsbridge at the northern tip of the island, farthest from the settlement of New York at the southern end. Here, though, the British did not make the tactical mistake that defeated them at Sullivan's Island.

By mid-August, Howe had been reinforced to a strength of 32,000 men, including 9,000 Hessians, but knew that the campaigning season was too advanced for his full Hudson River/Lake Champlain operation. The British commander decided to take New York to provide his force with adequate winter quarters as well as a base for the Hudson River/Lake Champlain operation to be undertaken in the following year.

REVOLUTIONARY AND EARLY AMERICAN WARS

Above: British movement up the Hudson River by boat was barred by a chainlink barrier across the river near West Point.
Above right: Another of Washington's most important subordinates in the New York campaign was Major General Nathanael Greene.

On August 22, the British started to land on Long Island after crossing The Narrows and by August 25 had pushed 20,000 men onto Long Island. Knowing that Putnam was positioned to defend the approaches to the shore of Long Island offering the shortest crossing to New York, Howe pinned the American left and right wings (commanded respectively by Sullivan and Brigadier General William Alexander). His main strength passed across the American front to outflank and attack the Americans' left wing in the Battle of Long Island on August 27. The American forward positions crumpled, and they fled back to their main position on the Brooklyn Heights: American losses were 200 killed and 1,000 taken prisoner while the British suffered 400 casualties. Half of Washington's army would probably have been destroyed if Howe had pursued vigorously, but in the military fashion of the period, he halted at nightfall, camped and prepared for a methodical assault over the next few days. Washington did not wait for the British assault to develop, and during the night of August 29-30, he evacuated the Long Island force, which crossed the East River to New York in boats manned by the fishermen of Colonel John Glover's Marblehead Regiment. It was a brilliantly planned and executed evacuation, but could have ended in disaster if the British naval forces had intervened. According to some sources, the wind was against them,

57

THE MILITARY HISTORY OF THE UNITED STATES

Above: Brigadier General William Stirling's American left-flank force withdraws across Cowann's Creek toward Brooklyn in the closing stages of the Battle of Long Island on August 27, 1776. The retreat was typical of American reverses at a time when Major General Sir William Howe was showing an astute tactical skill in his leadership of the British.
Left: Artillery was vitally important to each side in the Revolutionary War. After the Battle of Long Island, the American guns were carefully evacuated as Washington's army moved south to New York.

The evacuation of the American forces from Long Island to New York on August 29-30, 1776, was planned with great skill and carried out brilliantly. Washington, seen here directing operations from his horse, was the last American to leave the Brooklyn shore.

but others reported that the Americans put obstacles in the river.

The Battle of White Plains

Washington now had two weeks to complete his defenses of Manhattan Island as Howe prepared his next move, a landing in Kip's Bay on September 15. The Connecticut militia holding this area broke and ran, and if Howe had quickly pressed ahead he could have reached the western shore of Manhattan Island without difficulty and so divided the American force in two. But on reaching the middle of the island Howe paused until the rest of his force had landed. This gave Putnam just enough time to pull his men out of New York and slip up the west side of the island into the main defensive position. Here the Battle of Harlem Heights was fought on September 16, and Washington checked Howe's advance.

Washington knew that the Harlem Heights position was dangerously exposed to a British outflanking movement by water. This became clear on October 18 when four British brigades began to land at Pell's Point on the western shore of Long Island Sound, northeast of Washington's position and well in its rear. Washington pulled his men back to White Plains, but left 6,000 men in Fort Washington on the northern end of Manhattan Island and in Fort Lee just across the Hudson River.

On October 28 Howe launched a probing attack on Washington's latest position, but was initially repulsed in this so-called Battle of White Plains. As the day wore on, the determination of the American resistance began to flag, and the British regular troops finally drove the Americans from the field. Washington had already foreseen the futility of continued resistance against the militarily superior British, and thus the Americans were already pulling back up the eastern bank of the Hudson River toward the New York highlands. Washington expected that the British would press hard on his heels, but Howe again outmaneuvered the American commander-in-chief. The British commander felt that there was little value in pursuing the remnant of the American army more than 20 miles north of New York, and instead turned southwest to Dobb's Ferry on the eastern bank of the Hudson River and thereby isolated Fort Washington from any chance of overland retreat to the north.

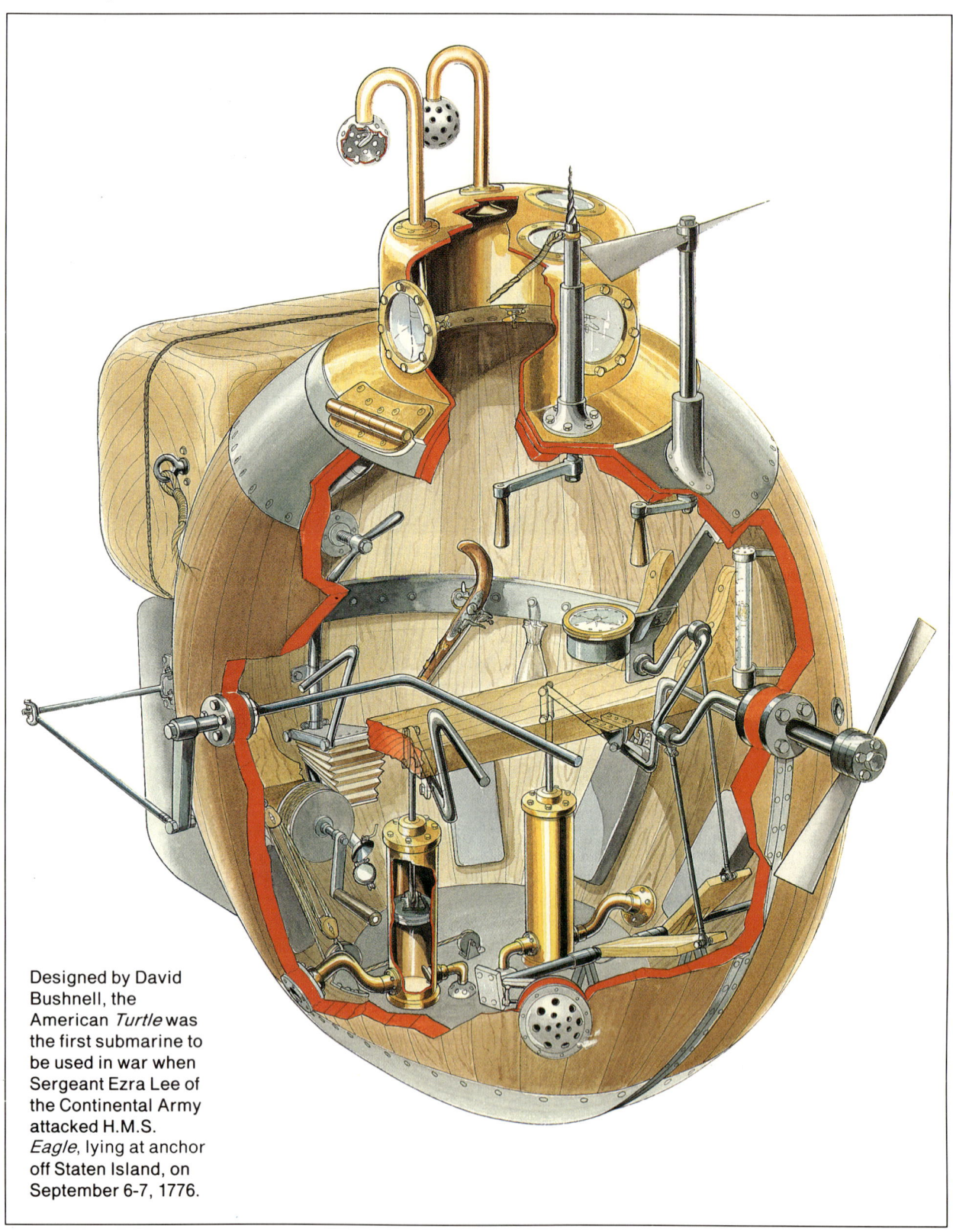

Designed by David Bushnell, the American *Turtle* was the first submarine to be used in war when Sergeant Ezra Lee of the Continental Army attacked H.M.S. *Eagle*, lying at anchor off Staten Island, on September 6-7, 1776.

The New York campaign of 1776 was a major failure for American arms, and led to Washington's retreat through New Jersey to the Delaware River and the temporary safety of Pennsylvania.

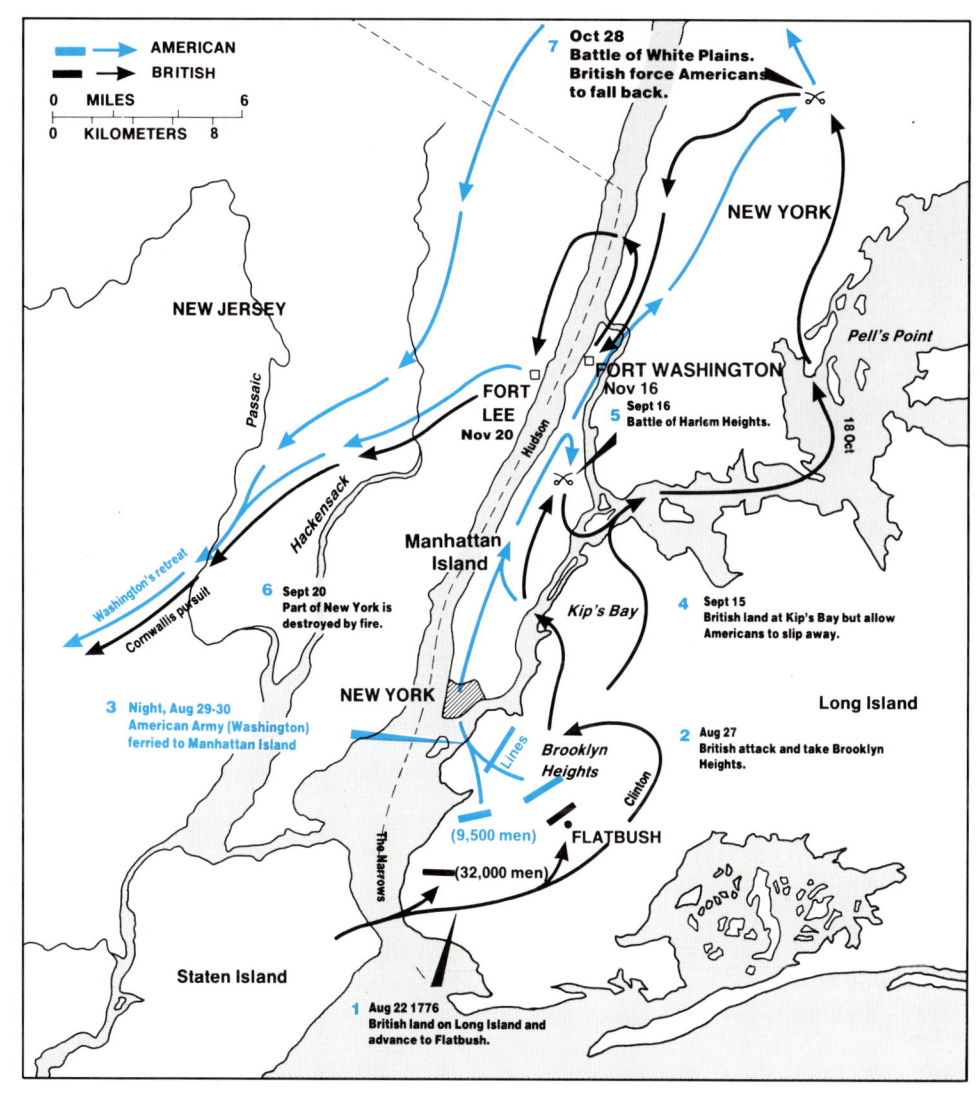

Washington Retreats From New York

Greene had now recovered from his bout of malaria and advised Washington to maintain a defense in the two Hudson River forts. Washington agreed and also decided to split his command. Major Generals Lee and William Heath were left on the New York side of the Hudson River with about 8,000 men to prevent any British advance into the New York highlands by holding the passes at North Castle and Peekskill. Washington himself led the remaining 5,000 American fighting men across the Hudson River into New Jersey.

Howe was biding his time, and on November 16, he made his effort against Fort Washington. With the aid of a bombardment from British warships on the river, the British infantry successfully stormed the fort, capturing 3,000 Americans and large quantities of materiel. Greene decided that it was no longer worth defending Fort Lee, which was evacuated on November 18. The Americans could not take the artillery, ammunition and stores held in the fort with them, and everything that could not be destroyed fell into the hands of the grateful British.

Washington Crosses the Delaware

Pressure on the Americans falling back

THE MILITARY HISTORY OF THE UNITED STATES

through New Jersey was maintained by a detachment under Major General Lord Cornwallis, who had been detached by Howe with the specific purpose of harrying Washington. By the end of November, the American forces were in full retreat south across New Jersey toward the Delaware River. Cornwallis's detachment pressed them from river barrier to river barrier - first the Hackensack, then the Passaic and Raritan, and finally the Millstone. Lee and his 4,000 men had been ordered to join Washington south of the Delaware River in Pennsylvania, and thus constituted a rearguard for Washington's force. An experienced ex-British colonel, Lee was becoming increasingly concerned with Washington's handling of strategic matters, writing to Gates that "...a certain great man is most damnably deficient..." Lee deliberately delayed his retreat in the belief that his force could operate within New Jersey, worrying the British so seriously with raids that the American position would be restored. But Lee was quickly trapped at Morristown, and after a short delay, he surrendered on December 12 with about half of his men. The one useful result of Lee's ambition was the additional breathing space it gave to Washington in his retreat to the Delaware River. He halted in early December to regroup and rest his surviving 2,000 men as he tried to decide what to do next. On the day that Lee surrendered near Morristown, the Continental Congress decided that Pennsylvania would probably be the next target of the British, and hurriedly left Philadelphia for Baltimore, Maryland. The Continental Congress also decided that the desperate state of American affairs called for desperate measures, and on the same day, Washington was voted almost dictatorial powers in an effort to keep the revolution alive.

It was not just the British who were causing trouble for Washington. During this period, his army was also melting away around him. Whole companies of attached militia forces left together, and the Continental Army was hard hit by desertions. The same applied to the 8,000-man force left to guard against a British push into the New York highlands, where the American commanders were becoming increasingly concerned that the enlistment of their men would expire at the end of the year, giving them every legal right to return home regardless of the desperate military situation.

The British were fully aware of Washington's problems and confidently expected that the arrival of the new year would see the total disintegration of the American forces and the collapse of the "American rebellion." Howe therefore or-

Above: Major General Charles Lee had been ordered to pull back across the Delaware River to join Washington, but delayed in the hope of catching the British unawares in New Jersey. He was trapped at Morristown on December 12, 1776, and surrendered to Lieutenant Colonel Harcourt.

Right: A stern Washington supervises the Continental Army's crossing of the Delaware River.

REVOLUTIONARY AND EARLY AMERICAN WARS

dered Cornwallis to halt his pursuit of Washington. Instead, the British seized Newport, Rhode Island, in an amphibious assault by a detachment under Clinton with naval support. Before pulling back most of his forces to winter quarters in New York, Howe established an outpost line in New Jersey between Trenton and Bordentown on the northern bank of the Delaware River, with the line of communications back to the Hudson River and New York guarded by further outposts at Princeton, New Brunswick, and Perth Amboy. Howe could be pleased with his efforts of the year. Despite a late start, the British had seized a base area for operations in the following year, which might not even be needed, as it appeared that the American rebellion was about to collapse.

The Battle of Trenton

South of the Delaware River, Washington knew that a bold stroke was needed. Only a major success would salvage the American position by restoring national morale and, more important in the short term, boosting enlistment in the Continental Army and persuading its existing soldiers to re-enlist. On the Pennsylvanian side of the Delaware River, Washington's strength was slowly rising as the surviving 2,000 men of Lee's command, eight understrength regiments of the Northern Army, and some Pennsylvania militia units arrived. By the last week in December, Washington could muster about 7,000 men, who would have to be used before their enlistments expired on December 31.

In a move of extraordinary courage, Washington decided to strike the Hessian garrisons of Trenton and Bordentown, which were likely to be at a low state of capability when the attacks were launched on Christmas night. Washington's plan was based on movements by three separate forces. The first was made up of 2,400 men of the Continental Army led by Washington himself, which was to cross the Delaware River nine miles above Trenton at McConkey's Ferry and then advance in two columns to arrive at opposite ends of Trenton's main street early in the morning of December 26. The

The Battle of Trenton on December 26, 1776, was a turning point of the Revolutionary War. Before the battle, the Americans were close to defeat, and the revolution was dying. After the battle, the Americans were revived, and poised on the British line of communication from New York.

General Charles Cornwallis
For further references see pages 62, 64-66, 71, 101, 104, 108, *109*, 110, 116, 117, 119, 120, 122, *123*, 124, 127, *128*, 130, 131, *132*.

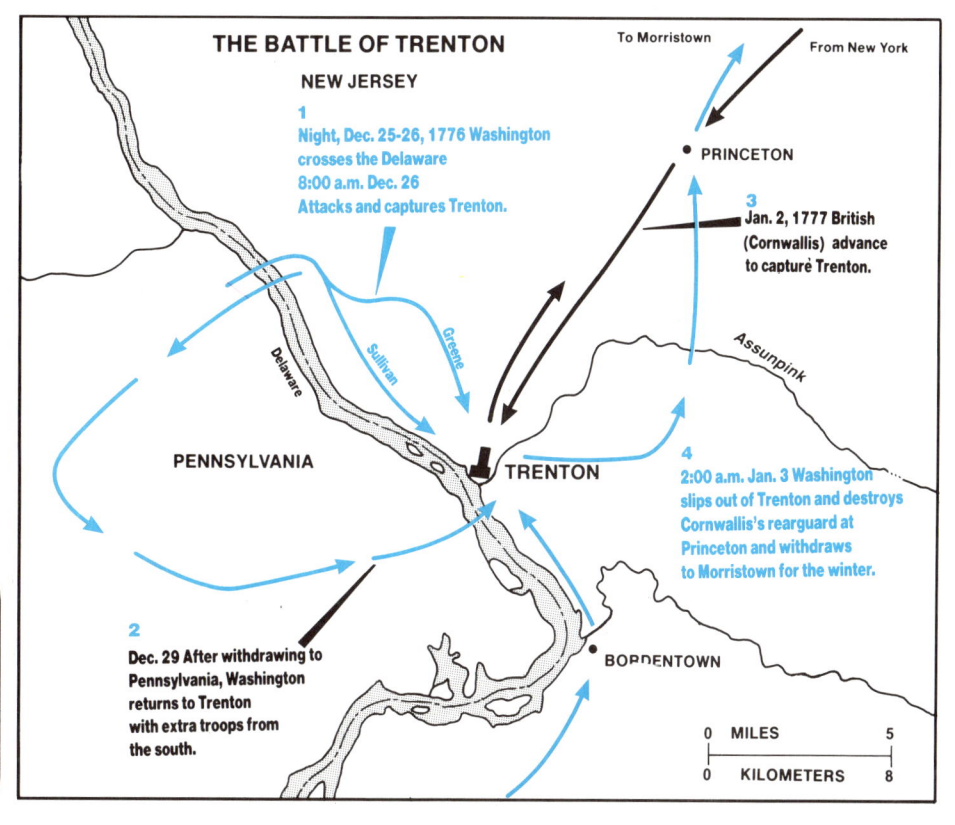

THE BATTLE OF TRENTON
NEW JERSEY

1. Night, Dec. 25-26, 1776 Washington crosses the Delaware 8:00 a.m. Dec. 26 Attacks and captures Trenton.
2. Dec. 29 After withdrawing to Pennsylvania, Washington returns to Trenton with extra troops from the south.
3. Jan. 2, 1777 British (Cornwallis) advance to capture Trenton.
4. 2:00 a.m. Jan. 3 Washington slips out of Trenton and destroys Cornwallis's rearguard at Princeton and withdraws to Morristown for the winter.

Washington's planning and execution of the Battle of Trenton remain superb examples of their type of strategy. They also delivered an all-important psychological blow to the British.

second force was to be provided by Pennsylvania militiamen who, under the control of Brigadier General James Ewing, were to cross the Delaware opposite Trenton to cut the garrison's escape route across Assunpink Creek. The third force was also to be made up mainly of militiamen who, under the command of Colonel James Cadwalader, were to cross the Delaware below Bordentown before falling on the garrison.

The night chosen for the attack was cold and windy, and flying snow made visibility very poor. The Delaware was filled with blocks of drifting ice, and neither Ewing's nor Cadwalader's forces were able to cross. But spurred on by the commander-in-chief's total determination, the main force managed to reach the northern bank of the river and divided into the planned two columns under Greene and Sullivan. They reached their planned starting points outside Trenton after Sullivan's column advanced along the river road and Greene's on the inland road.

The Hessian garrison of 1,400 men under Colonel Johann Rall was taken completely by surprise. For the loss of four dead (including two frozen to death) and four wounded, Washington's force killed 40 of the garrison including the commander, and captured 918 more. About 40 Hessians escaped to Bordentown across Assunpink Creek, which should have been held by Ewing's force. The Americans also captured a large quantity of materiel including cannons, small arms, and ammunition of huge importance to the Continental Army.

The Battle of Trenton was a great boost to American morale, reflected strongly in the fact that Washington was then able to persuade many of his men to extend their enlistment by six weeks. The commander used a full appeal to the patriotism of his men, but also had to offer $10 per man in hard money. On the night of December 30-31 Washington again crossed the Delaware and occupied Trenton, this time with about 5,000 men. Cornwallis had been stung by the defeat at Trenton and had responded by calling in his detachments scattered throughout New Jersey to create a force of about 8,000 men. With them he intended to box Washington in

Washington accepts the Hessian surrender after the Battle of Trenton. Particularly important to the American effort was the capture of many small arms and cannon, and other useful equipment and supplies.

between the Delaware and the Atlantic Ocean.

Another British Delay

After a forced march, Cornwallis' initial force of 5,000 troops reached Trenton on January 2, 1777, and took up position outside the town. Cornwallis was sure that he had Washington trapped and postponed the start of his attack to the following day. He hoped that this would allow his men to rest before fighting and give the follow-up force of 2,500 more men the chance to travel the 12 miles from Princeton. Washington had 5,200 men, but was becoming increasingly worried about the reliability of the 3,600 militiamen among them. During that night, therefore, the Americans slipped away to the east along the disused old road to Princeton, deceiving the British by leaving their camp fires burning.

On January 3, Washington fell on the British regiments that were just leaving Princeton to reinforce Cornwallis and in the Battle of Princeton inflicted heavy losses on them. On hearing the news of this latest reverse Cornwallis became increasingly worried about his comparatively long and vulnerable lines of communication. He decided not to pursue Washington as the latter led his men toward Morristown, but instead made for winter quarters at New Brunswick and Perth Amboy at the mouth of the Raritan River. Washington had achieved what he had intended, and his forces established their own winter quarters in the hills around Morristown.

In a period of 10 days, Washington, "fanning dying embers into a lively flame," had put new heart into the American Revolution and its war for independence. Frederick the Great of Prussia, one of the few undisputed "great captains," said that Washington's Trenton campaign was one of the most brilliant campaigns in history. The American victories at Trenton and Princeton were in themselves comparatively small, but they meant that Washington would have an army for the new year's campaigning season. On the

THE MILITARY HISTORY OF THE UNITED STATES

other side, Cornwallis' withdrawal to the Raritan meant that Howe's base area was reduced from a viable launch point for next year's offensive to just the city of New York, a foothold in New Jersey and the port of Newport.

Those Americans with political and strategic sense now knew that throwing off British rule would be no easy matter, and Washington remained more than ever convinced that his best course was maintaining the Continental Army without risking battle in order to eventually wear down the British. The British were currently faced with a great strategic problem: for they had to put down the rebellion so crushingly that the French would not dare to enter the war openly on the side of the Americans. So 1777 was the year in which the British could make or break the American Revolution, and this fact should have been reflected in a tight strategy under a single commander. In fact it was the year in which British planning was most confused and the resulting operations least coordinated.

Britain's Only Coherent Plan of the War

As early as November 30, 1776, Howe had put forward an overall plan that was the most far-sighted and comprehensive devised by any British commander during the war. From his base area in New York, New Jersey and Rhode Island, Howe planned an early start to the campaigning season such as he had been denied earlier in the year. Howe's plan was to leave garrisons totaling 15,000 men (8,000 in New Jersey to check Washington and 7,000 as garrison of New York), while using the rest of his army for offensive operations. One force of 10,000 men was to be launched from Newport into New England while a second force of 10,000 men would advance up the Hudson River to meet a British force advancing from Quebec via Lake Champlain. Assuming that these spring and summer moves were successful, Howe proposed to take Philadelphia in the fall and then advance

The death of Brigadier General Mercer in the Battle of Princeton on January 3, 1777. The battle was small, but fought with great determination, and it had important strategic consequences.

REVOLUTIONARY AND EARLY AMERICAN WARS

Washington's headquarters during the winter of 1777. After victory at Princeton the American army went into winter quarters at Morristown, New Jersey.

The first Stars and Stripes which was adopted by the Continental Congress, 14 June, 1777.

into the southern states during the winter. Howe estimated that he needed 35,000 men for the year's campaign, yet he had only 20,000 men in America. The request for 15,000 more men went to London, which countered with an offer of 8,000 men. But even before he received London's answer, Howe had begun to alter his plan in the light of Washington's successes in New Jersey and now planned to make Philadelphia the main objective of his 1777 campaign. On March 3, 1777 this revised plan was approved in London, together with a reinforcement of 5,500 men and the suggestion that Howe launch a diversionary move in New England. Meanwhile Burgoyne had succeeded in having the Quebec command made independent of Howe, so creating the dangerous situation of divided commands in North America. Burgoyne proposed that his forces should advance south to link up with those of Howe. This plan was approved in London on March 29, though no real thought was given to exactly how Burgoyne and Howe should link up. The only two possibilities were a junction of Burgoyne's advance and Howe's New England diversion, or an early success against Philadelphia by Howe so that he could return to New York and then advance north. The British thus entered the campaigning season of 1777 with two commanders and two strategic plans. Even when he learned on August 3 that he could expect no cooperation from Howe, the ambitious Burgoyne refused to alter his own scheme.

The need to have these plans confirmed in London combined with delays in the arrival of reinforcements and supplies meant that many of the campaigning season's earlier months were lost. The sole episode of note was a raid on April 25 launched under Major General William Tryon, British governor of New York. This attack destroyed the American depot at Danbury, Connecticut but was then harried all the way back to the British lines by a militia force under Arnold.

Support From the French

The British loss of time was Washington's gain. Men to form the new Continental Army were arriving slowly. It was June before Washington could call on 8,000 men in New Jersey, and the Northern Army was in an even poorer state. The situation was made worse still by a lack of all types of equipment, food, and even clothing. All were in desperately short supply until the secret arrival of three French ships. They carried many of the items which the Americans could not produce for themselves. An American mission in France was meanwhile working to bring France into the war as an open ally of the Continentals. The French agreed in principle, but decided to wait until the Americans proved their determination and capability with a major victory. With the foreign supplies, a number of

THE MILITARY HISTORY OF THE UNITED STATES

The Marquis de Lafayette occupies a special place in American military history as the Frenchman who arrived in a time of crisis to offer practical help. It is therefore not surprising, that Americans serving in the French Air Force before the United States entered into World War I were grouped into a unit known as the "Lafayette Escadrille."

European officers began to arrive. Many were adventurers of little real skill, especially in the high ranks they demanded, but they could offer the knowledge of professional soldiers. Among them were several who proved very important to the Continental Army: Louis Du Portail and Thaddeus Kosciuszko were experienced engineers and skilled teachers; Casimir Pulaski raised the Continental Army's first effective cavalry unit; Johann de Kalb and Marie Joseph du Motier le Marquis de Lafayette became good leaders as well as excellent practical teachers; and Friedrich Wilhelm von Steuben proved a superb trainer of men.

Washington Evades the British

Howe spent June 1777 in a series of maneuvers designed to coax Washington into battle before the British commander launched his main offensive toward Philadelphia. Washington's army was based at Middlebrook, New Jersey, so that the American commander-in-chief could respond to a British move southwest against Philadelphia or north up the Hudson River. Washington was not to be tempted, however, for he knew he must avoid battle to keep his army intact. Yet he also understood the importance of keep-

Marquis de Lafayette
For further references see pages 88, 92, 121, *122*, 123, 127, 128, 130.

Gunner, Hesse-Kassel Artillery Company (1776)

Hesse-Kassel sent three companies of artillery (two of them specially raised for the purpose) to serve with the British in America, and this was the German state's complete corps of artillery. The three companies arrived on Long Island in 1776, and took part in nearly every major engagement of the Revolutionary War. Each company was made up of five officers, 14 non-commissioned officers, three drummers and 129 gunners, and the weapon used was mainly the light 4-pounder field gun. The gunner's uniform was similar to that of most artillerymen except that the facings were nearer crimson than scarlet, and the vest and breeches were a yellow-buff color.

THE STARS AND STRIPES
WASHINGTON DESCRIBING THE FLAG TO LAFAYETTE AND OTHER FRENCH AND AMERICAN OFFICERS

ing at least some of his forces in front of the British. American senior officers generally agreed with Washington that the main British effort would take place on the Hudson River/Lake Champlain line, probably in the form of an advance to the north by Howe and to the south by Burgoyne. Washington detached part of his force under Putnam to garrison four forts on the west bank of the Hudson River between 30 and 40 miles north of New York, and later he detached another small force to aid the Northern Army against Burgoyne's advance.

Washington kept the bulk of his army ready to intercept any movement by Howe's forces directly toward Philadelphia, the American capital which was protected by a series of forts along the Delaware River and by obstacles to the sea approaches. For two months, Howe kept up his effort to tempt Washington into a pitched battle. Then he switched plans. On August 23 he embarked 18,000 soldiers on transports for the short voyage into Chesapeake Bay, where the troops were landed on August 25 at Head of Elk (now Elkton) on the Elk River. This effective use of sea power put the British in the Americans' rear, and on the correct side of the Delaware River for an overland advance to Philadelphia. Washington rapidly moved south with 10,500 men to take up a defensive position on the east bank of Brandywine Creek, barring the British move on Philadelphia.

The Battle of the Brandywine

The American forward positions at Cooch's Bridge were swept aside on September 2 by the advance of Howe's main force. The British then pushed forward to the Americans' main position on the Brandywine between Chad's Ford and a point opposite Parkerville. On September 11, the Battle of the Brandywine was fought. Washington had deployed his army well forward in two parts, the left wing under his own command and the right wing under Sullivan. Howe repeated the tactic that had proved successful on Long Island: the British right, in the form of General Wilhelm von Knyphausen's Hessian contingent, demonstrated in front of the American left while Cornwallis took the British left on a long march to the ford at Sconneltown above the American right

George Washington shows the Stars and Stripes to the Marquis de Lafayette and other French and American officers. Adopted by the Continental Congress on June 14, 1777, this flag was composed of seven red stripes separated by six white stripes and, in the field, a blue rectangle containing a circlet of 13 white stars, one for each new state.

The Chew House was the key to the Battle of Germantown on October 4, 1777. The advancing American columns were checked by concentrated British fire from the house, which had been turned into an effective strongpoint.

flank. Lacking cavalry for reconnaissance Sullivan learned of Cornwallis' approach only at the last minute and was caught as he tried to change fronts to meet the British attack. Sullivan's wing broke in disorder, and Cornwallis' men advanced to cut Washington's line of retreat at Dilworth. The American commander sent Greene with two brigades to check this threatening move, weakening his own front so much that he had to retreat before the Hessian advance. But Greene's effort had saved the Continental Army, which pulled back to Chester after losing 1,000 men; the British lost 526 men.

Howe moved skillfully forward to Philadelphia in a series of pinning and flanking movements, and the way was finally cleared on September 21 when a British night attack on Paoli routed Brigadier General Anthony Wayne's brigade. Philadelphia was quickly evacuated, and the Continental Congress moved first to Lancaster and then to York as once more it decreed dictatorial powers for Washington. The British entered Philadelphia on September 26. Only after combined army and navy operations between October 22 and November 20 did they overcome the stubborn resistance of Forts Mifflin and Mercer lower down the Delaware. Then the British could ship reinforcements and supplies into the captured American capital.

The British Occupation of Philadelphia

Once in Philadelphia, Howe dispersed his forces slightly. Retaining his main strength in the city, he deployed 9,000 men in Germantown north of Philadelphia and another 3,000 in New Jersey, thereby securing his overland line of communications with New York. Just as Howe had repeated his Long Island tactic at the Brandywine, Washington now tried to win a victory with an adaptation of his Trenton tactic, in this instance against the Germantown garrison. Trenton had involved the movement of only two columns of men over short distances. Washington's Germantown plan was on a larger scale involving 13,000 men. The plan called for a converging advance by four columns, two of militiamen on the flanks and two of the Continental Army (commanded on the left by Greene and on the right by Sullivan) on four roads to meet in Germantown at dawn on October 4. The Battle of Germantown was an American

THE BATTLE OF GERMANTOWN

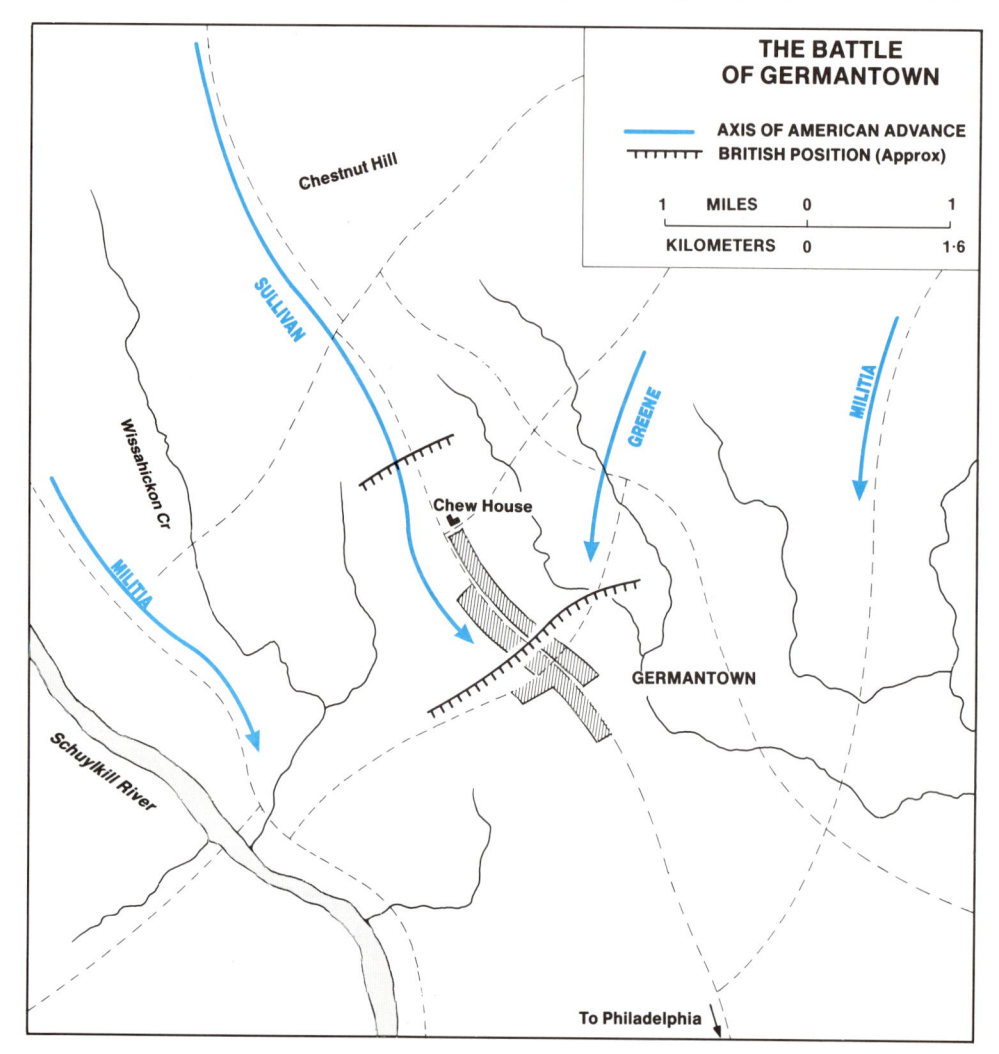

The Battle of Germantown on October 4, 1777, revealed to Washington with great clarity the problems faced by a commander who divided his command into four separate columns, especially when two of them were made up mainly of inexperienced militiamen.

failure: the two militia columns never arrived, and the two Continental Army columns fired on each other as they approached Germantown. The British fell back before Sullivan's column, but left a detachment of sharpshooters in the stone Chew House. The two American generals spent so much time arguing whether or not to take the house that the British had time to re-form and advance, forcing the Americans to retreat after suffering 700 casualties and losing 400 men captured.

Howe brought his army together after Germantown and moved forward to tackle Washington at Whitemarsh. But the British commander then pulled his army back into winter quarters in Philadelphia without forcing a battle, leaving Washington to choose his own winter quarters at Valley Forge, about 20 miles northwest of Philadelphia.

Burgoyne's Invasion of New York

Howe's offensive can only be regarded as ponderous, and it was ultimately of less importance than the other British effort of the year. This was Burgoyne's northern operation, which also began in June 1777 with Albany, New York, as its first objective. Burgoyne divided his command into two parts. At the head of the larger force made up of 7,200 regulars (4,000 British and 3,200 Hessian) supported by 650 loyalists, Canadians, and Indians, Burgoyne was to advance up the Richelieu River, through Lake Champlain, and past Lake George to take Saratoga before advancing on Albany just below the point where the Mohawk River flows into the Hudson River. At the head of the smaller unit of 700 regular troops sup-

Major General Sir John Burgoyne commanded the British forces in Canada. He failed to establish effective coordination of his operations with those of Sir John Howe farther to the south.

ported by 175 loyalists under Sir John Johnson and about 1,000 Iroquois under Thayendanega, also known as Joseph Brant, Lieutenant Colonel Barry St. Leger was to move up the St. Lawrence River and through Lake Ontario to Fort Oswego. From here, he was to advance up the river to Lake Oneida before striking cross-country to the headwaters of the Mohawk River at Fort Stanwix, also known as Fort Schuyler (now Rome), and then advancing down the river to link up with Burgoyne at Albany.

On paper the plan looked workable, but in practice it ignored all the problems of divided commands seeking to meet at a common objective without any effective means of communication between the two forces. Burgoyne reduced his chances still further by forgetting the hard-learned lessons of the French and Indian War and starting a wilderness campaign with 138 pieces of artillery, an enormous amount of baggage and a large number of women.

Burgoyne's progress as far as the southern end of Lake Champlain was completed without difficulty, for the Northern Army under Schuyler mustered only 2,950 men (2,500 at Ticonderoga and 450 at Fort Stanwix). The problems of Schuyler, a New Yorker of aristocratic manner, were made worse by the fact that the New Englanders in his army generally refused to obey his orders and indeed openly argued for replacement of Schuyler by Gates. Inevitably the Americans were unable to offer any effective resistance to Burgoyne, who arrived outside Fort Ticonderoga on July 1 and soon emplaced his artillery on a height overlooking the fort. Brigadier General Arthur St. Clair saw that resistance would serve no purpose but to cost the Americans casualties they could not replace, and on the night of July 5-6, he evacuated the fort and retreated southeast into Vermont, while sending the sick and wounded and his command's baggage by boat south to Skenesborough (now Whitehall).

Burgoyne immediately launched a pursuit, his advance guard by road and the main body by water. Burgoyne overtook the American rearguard on July 7, and in the Battle of Hubbardton, decisively crushed it. The fighting stand of Seth Warner's militia detachment bought enough time for St. Clair to slip away via Rutland to link up with Schuyler at Fort Edward on the upper Hudson north of Saratoga. St. Clair's baggage train was captured at Skenesborough. Burgoyne now decided to deviate from his original plan, which had called for the British army to be floated down Lake George, and instead decided on an overland advance from Skenesborough toward Saratoga, though the heavy equipment still had to use the Lake George route.

American "Scorched Earth" Policy

As they pulled back, the Americans devastated the region's already rough roads, destroyed the bridges over numerous deep ravines, felled trees onto the road and dug ditches to flood dry ground with swamp water. The efforts were aided by torrential rain that swelled creeks and turned dirt into thick mud. It took Burgoyne three weeks to reach Fort Edward, where on July 29 he found that Schuyler had pulled back to Stillwater. American strength was now increasing, though still not to the point at which Schuyler could seriously contemplate giving battle to a considerably weakened Burgoyne. Washington sent

Daniel Morgan, who rose to the rank of brigadier general, was one of several Americans who showed great tactical skill in the Revolutionary War. He was also the officer largely responsible for proving that riflemen could be very effective in spite of the slow rate of their fire.

Major Generals Arnold and Benjamin Lincoln to support Schuyler, the latter a Massachusetts officer possessing considerable influence over the New Englanders who were still a thorn in Schuyler's side. Schuyler was also bolstered by the arrival of 1,600 militiamen, as well as 3,000 men of the Continental Army, including 500 men of Colonel Daniel Morgan's rifle regiment and 750 men supplied by Putnam in New York.

Schuyler's most important new strength was the manpower of the local militia units, which had become increasingly angry with the terrorization of their home areas by Burgoyne's virtually uncontrolled Indians. The single most important event was the murder and scalping of Jane McCrea, after which many more men came forward for militia service. These units still refused to serve under Schuyler, and command of these units was therefore entrusted to John Stark, who was commissioned as a brigadier general by New Hampshire. Stark raised a 2,000-man force and took up position at Bennington in southern Vermont to block any advance which may be planned by Burgoyne into New England and thus on to further secure positions.

Private, Morgan's Rifle Corps (1777)

Volunteers from the frontier of Virginia, the men of Morgan's Rifle Corps were extremely capable skirmishers and scouts, and also proved themselves notably self-reliant and used their own Pennsylvania rifles, powder horns and leather bullet bags. The fringed hunting shirt and trousers were made of white linen.

Burgoyne Checked at Saratoga

As the Americans grew in strength, Burgoyne learned on August 3 that Howe would not be making any northern diversion that could lead to a link-up of two major British forces. By now the British were very short of supplies and all types of transportation, and on August 11, Burgoyne ordered Colonel Friedrich Baum to take 650 Brunswickers to forage in the Bennington area. On August 16 the German force was surrounded and destroyed by Stark's force in the Battle of Bennington. Arriving later in the same day to reinforce Baum, the 650 Brunswickers of Colonel Heidrich von Breymann were in turn destroyed. Von Breymann escaped with less than two-thirds of his men. The American militiamen, supported by Warner's "Green Mountain Boys" after a forced march from Manchester, suffered only 70 casualties (30 dead and 40 wounded), but killed 207 of the enemy and captured another 700. The Americans also captured a useful quantity of small arms, light artillery, and wagons. It was an important reverse for Burgoyne, who was deprived not only of much needed food and transportation, but also, about one-tenth of his strength.

Like that of Burgoyne, St. Leger's initial movement had been completed without difficulty, and the combined British, German, loyalist and Iroquois force assembled at Fort Oswego on July 25. St. Leger then moved up the Oswego River to Lake Oneida, continued by water to the eastern end of the lake, and struck out overland again to Fort Stanwix. The British force arrived on August 2 and on the following day laid siege to the American garrison, whose men decided to hold out to the bitter end as they anticipated an Indian massacre if they tried to retreat.

The Battle of Fort Stanwix

As soon as news of the British siege reached him on August 4, Brigadier General Nicholas Herkimer of the Tryon County militia set off with a relief force of 800 local militiamen. On August 6 the relief

---

Burgoyne sent two Hessian columns to invade Vermont. American militia gathered under popular leaders such as John Stock to resist the Hessians. The Militia defeated and captured the Hessians at the Battle of Bennington, 16th August, 1777. An American Militia man recalls the battle.

"I enlisted at Francestown, N.H., in Colonel Stickney's regiment and Captain Clark's company, as soon as I learned that Stark would accept the command of the State troops; six or seven others from the same town joined the army at the same time. We marched forthwith to Number Four, and stayed there a week. Meantime I received a horn of powder and run two or three hundred bullets; I had brought my own gun. Then my company went on to Manchester; soon after I went, with a hundred others, under Colonel Emerson, down the valley of Otter Creek; on this excursion we lived like lords, on pigs and chickens, in the houses of tories who had fled. When we returned to Manchester, bringing two hogsheads of West India rum, we heard that the Hessians were on their way to invade Vermont. Late in the afternoon of rainy Friday, we were ordered off for Bennington in spite of rain, mud and darkness. We pushed on all night, making the best progress we could; about day-break I, with Lieut. Miltimore, came near Bennington, and slept a little while on a hay-mow, when the barn-yard fowls waked us; we went for bread and milk to the sign of the 'wolf,' and then hurried three miles west to Stark's main body.

Stark and ****** rode up near the enemy to reconnoitre; were fired at by the cannon, and came galloping back. Stark rode with shoulders bent forward, and cried out to his men: 'Those rascals know that I am an officer; don't you see they honor me with a big gun as a salute.' We were marched round and round a circular hill till we were tired. Stark said it was to amuse the Germans. All the while a cannonade was kept up upon us from their breast-works; it hurst no body, and it lessened our fear of the great guns. After a while I was sent, with twelve others, to lie in ambush, on a knoll a little north, and watch for tories on their way to join Baum. Presently we saw six coming toward us who, mistrusting us for tories, came too near us to escape. We disarmed and sent them, under a guard of three, to Stark.

Between two and three o'clock the battle began. The Germans fired by platoons, and were soon hidden by the smoke. Our men fired each on his own hook, aiming wherever he saw a flash; few on our side had either bayonets or cartridges. At last I stole away from my post and ran down to the battle. The first time I fired I put three balls in my gun; before I had time to fire many rounds our men rushed over the breast-works, but I and many others chased straggling Hessians in the woods; we pursued until we met Breyman with 800 fresh troops and larger cannon, which opened a fire of grape shot; some of the grape shot riddled a Virginia fence near me; one shot struck a small white oak behind which I stood; though it hit higher than my head I fled from the tree, thinking it might be aimed at again. We skirmishers ran back till we met a large body of Stark's men and then faced about. I soon started for a brook I saw a few rods behind, for I had drank and forgot my thirst. But the enemy outflanked us, and I said to a comrade, 'we must run, or they will have us.' He said: 'I will have one fire first.' At that moment, a major, on a black horse, rode along behind us, shouting 'fight on boys, reinforcements close by.' While he was yet speaking, a grape shot went through his horse's head; it bled a good deal, but the major kept his seat, and rode on to encourage others. In a few minutes we saw Warner's men hurrying to help us; they opened right and left of us, and one half of them attacked each flank of the enemy, and beat back those who were just closing round us. Stark's men now took heart and stood their ground. My gun barrel was at this time too hot to hold, so I seized the musket of a dead Hessian, in which my bullets went down easier than in my own. Right in front were the cannon, and seeing an officer on horse-back waving his sword to the artillery, I fired at him twice; his horse fell; he cut the traces of an artillery horse, mounted him and rode off. I afterward heard that the officer was Major Skene. Soon the Germans ran, and we followed; many of them threw down their guns on the ground, or offered them to us, or kneeled, some in puddles of water. One said to me, 'Wir sind ein bruder!' I pushed him behind me and rushed on. The enemy beat a parley, minded to give up, but our men did not understand it. I came to one wounded man flat on the ground, crying water or quarter. I snatched the sword out of his scabbard, and while I ran on and fired, carried it in my mouth, thinking I might need it. The Germans fled by the road and in a wood each side of it; many of their scabbards caught in the brush and held the fugitives till we seized them. We chased them till dark, Colonel Johnston, of Haverhill, wanted to chase them all night. We might have mastered them all, as they stopped within three miles of the battle field; but Stark, saying 'he would run no risk of spoiling a good day's work, ordered a halt, and return to quarters.

I was coming back, when I was ordered by Stark himself, who knew me, as I had been one of his body gaurds in Canada, to help draw off a field-piece. I told him 'I was worn out.' his answer was, 'don't seem to disobey; take hold, and if you can't hold out, slip away in the dark.' Before we had dragged the gun far, Warner rode near us. Some one pointing to a dead man by the road-side, said, 'Your brother is killed', 'Is it Jesse?' asked Warner. And when the answer was 'yes', he jumped off his horse, stooped and gazed in the dead man's face, and then rode away without saying a word."

force was ambushed by the Iroquois in a wooded ravine near Oriskany about 6 miles from Fort Stanwix, and after a bloody battle fought during a thunderstorm, the mortally wounded Herkimer ordered the remnants of his command to scatter into the woods. Casualties were heavy on both sides, and while the loss of nearly half their strength meant that the militiamen could not relieve Fort Stanwix, their own losses further worried the Indians, who were already unhappy with the static nature of the Fort Stanwix operation. Insult was added to injury as the garrison made a sortie during the Battle of Oriskany and devastated St. Leger's camp.

Despite the fact that Burgoyne was only 24 miles away from his position at Stillwater, Schuyler decided that Fort Stanwix had to be relieved and allowed the detachment of 950 Continental Army volunteers under Arnold, who moved as rapidly as possible up the Mohawk River, to set out. Arnold cleverly sent ahead a half-witted Dutchman, his clothes full of holes, together with an Oneida Indian guide, to tell the Iroquois that the Continental Army was advancing "as numerous as the leaves on the trees." Believing that such a man could only be telling the truth, the Iroquois decamped after scalping a number of loyalists. This left St. Leger seriously exposed, and on August 22, the British commander abandoned the siege, and his camp, to fall back to Fort Oswego leaving the Americans his artillery and supplies.

Early in September, the news of St. Leger's failure reached Burgoyne, who now understood that he would receive help from neither Howe nor St. Leger. Burgoyne's report to London provides a telling indication of the strengths of the Americans: "The great bulk of the country is undoubtedly with Congress in principle and zeal; and their measures are executed with a secrecy and dispatch that are not to be equalled. Wherever the King's forces point, militia in the amount of three or four thousand assemble in twenty-four hours; they bring with them their subsi-

The Battle of Bennington on August 16, 1777, was a major tactical success for the Americans. In the battle, the "Green Mountain Boys" deprived the British of about one-tenth of their overall strength and, by destroying and capturing much of their wheeled transport, effectively removed from them any real chance of living off the land.

Burgoyne meets with his Indian allies at Saratoga. The Indians provided the British with an effective capability for skirmishing and reconnaissance. But reports of their atrocities so inflamed local Americans that many joined the Continental Army under Gates.

stence, etc., and the alarm over, they return to their farms..."

Burgoyne's Fatal Gamble

But Burgoyne was not deterred from pushing forward, and having occupied Saratoga he now gambled on reaching Albany or losing his army. Despite the fact that the increasing number of deserters from his Indian allies had left him with no effective means of gathering tactical intelligence, Burgoyne crossed to the western bank of the Hudson River on September 13 and prepared to advance along the riverbank road. The British commander also sent a request for aid to Clinton in New York. On August 19, the Continental Congress had at last yielded to New England pressure and replaced Schuyler with Gates. Gates was a clever commander who fully understood Burgoyne's problems. He therefore advanced four miles from Schuyler's Stillwater position to the Bemis Heights, where the technical skills of Brigadier General Kosciuszko created an entrenched position around Neilson's Barn to command the riverbank road.

The 1st Battle of Saratoga, or the Battle of Freeman's Farm, took place on September 19. Advancing with 6,000 men against 7,000, Burgoyne saw that a frontal effort could stand little chance. Therefore, he detached 4,200 men in three columns commanded by von Riedesel, Hamilton, and Fraser in an attempt to outflank the Americans' left with a turning movement past Freeman's Farm. Gates detached 3,000 of his men under Arnold to deal with this British attack, which was beaten back. Particular damage was done by the riflemen under Morgan. After suffering 600 casualties to the Americans' 300 the British halted. Arnold asked Gates for reinforcements so that he could counterattack, but Gates refused, and the lines of the two armies stabilized. For the next three weeks, skirmishing occurred as the British dug in and waited for the help promised by Clinton.

Its arrival amounted to no more than a gesture. With a force of only 7,000 men available to him in the New York area, Clinton advanced with 4,000 men up the Hudson River and on October 4 stormed Forts Clinton and Montgomery in the New York highlands. Clinton was a cautious commander and was now satisfied that his effort had materially aided Burgoyne. Sending his advance guard farther forward by ship to burn Esopus (now Kingston), Clinton pulled back to New York. Burgoyne was on his own and now had to prepare to face Gates.

The New York campaign of 1777 and the Battles of Saratoga ended any British hope of splitting New England from the other "rebellious colonies."

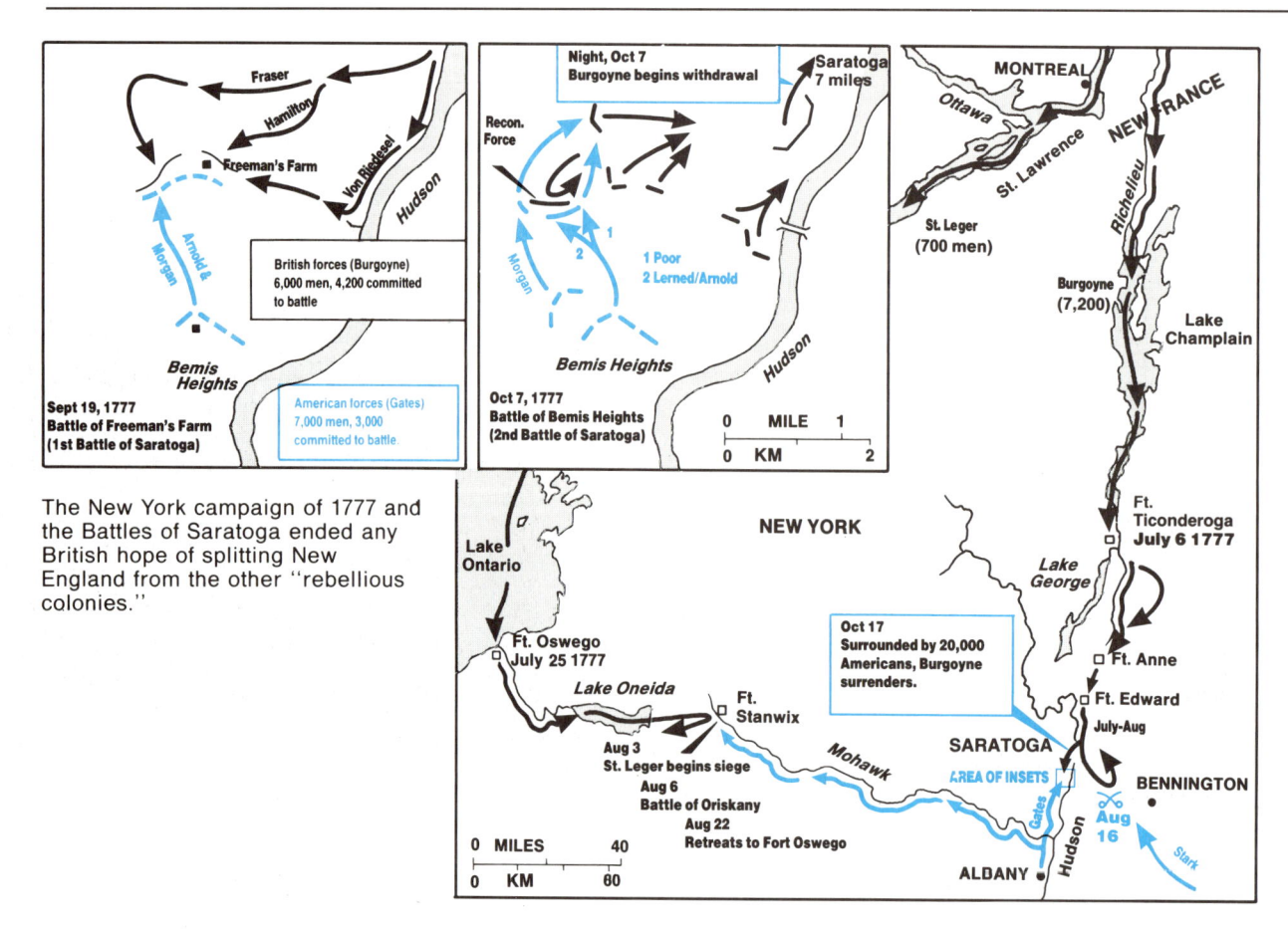

The Second Battle of Saratoga

Gates knew that he had only to wait. The British had to try to break through to Albany as they were desperately short of all supplies, food was running out, the animals had exhausted all possible grazing, and desertion was becoming an acute problem. Meanwhile, American strength was increasing as militia units continued to arrive. By October 7, Gates had more than 10,000 men under his command. On this day, Burgoyne sent out a "reconnaissance in force" to test the American position and hopefully to turn the Americans' left flank. So the Second Battle of Saratoga, otherwise known as the Battle of Bemis Heights began. Gates responded to the British "reconnaissance in force" by dispatching a force containing Morgan's riflemen. They drove the British back to their fortified position. Arnold had been at loggerheads with Gates and was confined to his tent, but he could not sit idly while the battles were being fought.

REVOLUTIONARY AND EARLY AMERICAN WARS

Above: A British cartoon summarizes the feeling in Great Britain when news of Burgoyne's surrender at Saratoga arrived.

Left: Severe fighting was the order of the day on and around the earthworks in the Second Battle of Saratoga (the Battle of Bemis Heights) October 7, 1777.

Arnold rushed out to take part in the American counterattack and was wounded in the attack on Breymann's Redoubt. By nightfall, the British had been forced back to their defense line on the river, having suffered 600 casualties to the Americans' 150.

With only 5,700 men left, Burgoyne fell back toward Saratoga two days later. The American militia worked their way around the British flanks and cut Burgoyne's already inadequate supply lines. Faced with more than 18,000 better supplied Americans who were in a superior position, Burgoyne had no alternative but to surrender on October 17. All his men passed into captivity, and large quantities of arms, ammunition and yet more supplies fell into American hands. The "Convention of Saratoga" established that the disarmed British soldiers should be marched to Boston for evacuation under parole to Great Britain. In a shameful repudiation of these terms, the Continental Congress later decided that the prisoners should not be allowed to return home.

THE MILITARY HISTORY OF THE UNITED STATES

REVOLUTIONARY AND EARLY AMERICAN WARS

The surrender of General Burgoyne at Saratoga on October 16, 1777. This was a major blow to British plans for the defeat of the American "rebellion."

Private, Pennsylvania State Regiment (1777)

State troops were organized for defense of their parent states and were not part of the Continental Army or the state militia. By the early part of 1777, Pennsylvania possessed, in addition to units of Continental service, a state artillery regiment and a state infantry regiment. These were taken into Continental service in June and November 1777 respectively. The Pennsylvania State Regiment contained both rifle and musket men, the latter wearing blue coats with red or white facings depending on cloth availability when the coat was made. A blanket roll was often carried in place of a regular knapsack.

Turning Point in the Revolutionary War

The American victory at Saratoga was a major turning point of the Revolutionary War. For the Americans this triumph more than balanced the failure of Washington against Howe. As for the British, the failure of Burgoyne meant that their positions in America had to be reviewed, with the result that Ticonderoga and Crown Point were abandoned to leave the British in control only of New York, Philadelphia and part of Rhode Island. Most important of all, it persuaded France to recognize the United States. On February 6, 1778, a Franco-American alliance was sealed by the signature of two agreements. The first was a treaty of friendship and commerce, the other a military alliance to become effective if and when war broke out between France and Great Britain.

The Ordeal at Valley Forge

This, however, was in the future. The ordeal of the Continental Army at Valley Forge during the savage winter of 1777-78 still had to be faced.

Valley Forge has since become a symbol of patriotic suffering, bravery, and endurance. When Washington retired to winter quarters at Valley Forge during October 1777, he had with him the 6,000-man core of the Continental Army. At first, the men had only tattered tents with which to keep at bay the increasingly bitter wind. At the beginning of the Valley Forge winter, some men lacked blankets shoes, and even pants. As the snows came, the supply position became much more difficult: for weeks, there was no meat. The men were at times forced to boil shoes and eat the only slightly softened leather.

It was not that there were no supplies, in various depots spoiled food, and clothing was unissued. The problem lay with the failure of the Continental supply system, which had been hamstrung since mid-1777 by the resignations of the quartermaster general and commissary general, who saw that there was more money to be made in civilian life than in the army. Established in York, Pennsylvania, the Continental Congress was split by factional intrigue and could not appoint men to either of these immensely important posts. The result was that the existing supply services tried, but only half-heartedly, to resolve the physical difficulties of supplying the army at Valley Forge, and in the process caused their own men immense hardship. The position was complicated by the activities of the Conway cabal, which from September 25, 1777, tried to oust Washington from supreme command in favor of Gates. In 1777, Gates was appointed president of the new Board of War, which numbered among its members at least two enemies of Washington. The leader of the movement to oust Washington was Colonel Thomas Conway, an Irish mercenary who had left French service to join the American cause. Conway had many American supporters in his

The Continental Army's ordeal at Valley Forge was caused not so much by a lack of supplies as by the difficulty of obtaining available supplies out of the bureaucratic system and then moving them with inadequate transportation.

THE MILITARY HISTORY OF THE UNITED STATES

effort to elevate Gates over Washington, but when Conway was unsuccessful and resigned on December 23, the scale of the attack on Washington quickly declined.

From the ordeal of Valley Forge, there emerged a more effective army. Washington persuaded his ablest lieutenant to accept the position of quartermaster general. From then on, the supply situation of the Continental Army improved quite considerably.

Top left: Washington explains matters to a Congressional committee at Valley Forge. By then, the winter had become so bitter than the soldiers had built a virtual town of log cabins to replace their tents.
Above: Only after his men had built their log cabins did Washington occupy this house as his headquarters.
Left: Von Steuben at Valley Forge, where his moves toward true discipline began to create an effective Continental Army.

86

Von Steuben Revives the Continental Army

Another event of major importance at Valley Forge was the appearance in February 1778 of von Steuben. He claimed to have been created a baron for services to a small German state and to have been a lieutcnant general on the staff of Frederick the Great. In reality von Steuben had been only a captain, but he was well versed in the military discipline of the Prussian army. Washington had long wanted to improve the discipline of the Continental Army, and in von Steuben he had the man to achieve this task. Appointed inspector general in charge of training, von Steuben proved to be a superb trainer of men, and one who never failed to know the difference between the American volunteer soldier and the European professional soldier. Von Steuben's training program in the late winter and early spring of 1778 was geared exactly to combining the needs of the Continental Army and the capabilities of the American soldier. Officers were taught the responsibility of looking after their men. The men were drilled in a simplified version of the complex formations and movements of European armies, the care of their equipment, and the effective use of the bayonet. Von Steuben also convinced the Americans of the importance of light infantry. The first steps to creating such troops for scouting and skirmishing were taken under the German's inspiration. After von Steuben's training program the American soldier was increasingly a match for the British soldier on the open field of battle.

Even as spring began and von Steuben forged ahead with his training program, Howe remained inactive and so lost his last real chance of catching and defeating Washington. Howe was weary of the war and asked to be replaced. His successor was Clinton. As Washington began to prepare for the emergence of the Continental Army from Valley Forge, Clinton was preparing the British evacuation of the American capital in accordance with orders he had received from London. With a French involvement on the side of the Americans becoming inevitable, the British had to consider the defense of their other possessions in the western hemisphere. This was the main reason for Clinton's retirement to New York after the detachment of 5,000 men to the West Indies and 3,000 more to Florida. In New York, Clinton was to consolidate his forces for a vigorous summer offensive. Because he lacked the ships to move 3,000 horses as well as his men, Clinton decided to take the overland route to New York. On June 18, Clinton's army left Philadelphia,

Above: Washington in prayer at Valley Forge.
Above left: Washington at Valley Forge, where the men of the Continental Army endured terrible hardship.

THE MILITARY HISTORY OF THE UNITED STATES

the Americans - somewhat unexpectedly - made contact with the British rear guard Clinton reacted with more speed than Lee, maneuvering to envelop the American right. Lee pulled his force back in circumstances that soon became very confused. This retreat angered Washington. The American commander-in-chief assumed personal command in what had now become a defense against a powerful British counterattack. Both armies became fully involved in this Battle of Monmouth Court House. It lasted until nightfall as a stalemate in which the Americans for the first time matched the British in battlefield skills. Each side admitted to 350 casualties, but the losses

Left: Frederick William Augustus von Steuben, the ex-Prussian army officer who became the Continental Army's disciplinarian task master.
Below: Washington took personal command in the Battle of Monmouth Court House.
Bottom: "The Heroine of Monmouth" was Molly Pitcher, who took her dead husband's place at an American cannon and served throughout the battle.

which was immediately reoccupied by Washington.

Washington then followed in the tracks of the British with his full strength of 12,000 and looked for an opportunity to bring Clinton to battle under favorable circumstances. How to do this presented problems. None of Washington's subordinate generals supported a general action. Wayne and de Lafayette suggested a partial attack to tackle a portion of the British army as it straggled in a long column along the road, while the same Lee who had been captured at Morristown (but later exchanged in a swap of prisoners) thought that the best course would be guerrilla action to harass the British.

The Battle of Monmouth Court House

On June 26 Washington settled on a bold approach and decided to launch his advance guard against the rear of the British column once Clinton had set off from his overnight halt at Monmouth Court House on June 27. Command was initially entrusted to de Lafayette, but Lee successfully demanded the command when he learned how large the American force was to be. Lee's advance took American force over rough, unreconnoitered ground. When

88

REVOLUTIONARY AND EARLY AMERICAN WARS

Major General Charles Lee must have been a man of odd appearance, for many acquaintances said that this contemporary caricature was, in fact, a good likeness.

were undoubtedly much higher.

During the night, the British slipped away and a few days later reached New York, where they were put under blockade when the Continental Army reached White Plains on June 30. Lee demanded a court martial to review his actions at Monmouth Court House, and was somewhat harshly judged guilty of disobedience to orders, poor conduct of the retreat, and disrespect of Washington. As a result Lee resigned.

France Enters the War

War between France and Great Britain broke out on June 17, but in far-sighted anticipation, the French had sent Admiral Jean Baptiste le Comte d'Estaing from France in May with a force of 11 ships of the line and transports carrying 4,000 men. Admiral Howe lacked British naval strength to challenge this French fleet. Thus, the strategic initiative thus passed to the Americans and their French allies during the late summer of 1778. Washington was determined to take full advantage of all that this offered.

The French fleet arrived in American waters on July 8 off Sandy Hook and immediately implemented a naval blockade of New York to match that of Washington on land. The American and French commanders then decided on a combined land and sea assault on New York until d'Estaing called off the French naval attack. The admiral feared that his deeply laden ships would be stranded on the bar running between Staten Island and Sandy Hook. The allied commanders switched their attentions to the weaker British toehold in the area at Newport.

Lying as it does on an island with difficult approaches, Newport presented considerable problems for d'Estaing and Sullivan, the local commander with whom d'Estaing worked after arriving in Narragansett Bay. The plan finally adopted had serious flaws: the French ships were to force the passage on the western side of the island, and the Americans were to cross over and attack the British from the east. The French arrived off Newport on July 29 and forced their passage. Sullivan's forces began to cross to the island on August 8, and d'Estaing began to disembark the French troops. Unfortunately for the allies, Admiral Howe arrived from New York with a reinforced fleet, forcing d'Estaing to re-embark his soldiers and put out to sea to engage Howe. As the two naval forces maneuvered for position off Newport, both fleets were dispersed by a great storm on August 12. Howe's ships fell back to New York to refit, and those of d'Estaing went to Boston for the same purpose. Sullivan was left with no option but to call off the attack on Newport and try to extricate his forces from their untenable position as best he could.

An Early Failure for Franco-American Cooperation

This first effort at allied cooperation therefore ended as a total fiasco. Then, d'Estaing decided that matters in the West Indies were more important to French interests. On November 4 the French weighed anchor and sailed for the West Indies. This failure of cooperation dashed all Washington's hopes for a decisive American victory in 1778. In 1779, the French were forced by British activities to

Admiral Jean Baptiste le Comte d'Estaing
For further references see pages *99*, 100.

89

focus their attention on the West Indies, so the British were able to regain the initiative on the American mainland. The following years saw the Revolutionary War increasingly caught up in complex European affairs. In June 1779 Spain declared war on Great Britain. In December 1780 the Netherlands also became involved following a British declaration of war in exasperation about Dutch trade with the United States. Neither of these European powers actually allied themselves with the fledgling United States. Nevertheless, Great Britain had to guard against the possibility of an invasion of England, and she undertook operations on a global scale against her three adversaries. Smaller forces were therefore available for American operations.

Yet the Americans were not able to take any real advantage of this British weakening, for their own war effort was made increasingly difficult by war weariness, insufficient finance, poor central administration and the absence of any strong direction of the war effort. The British were determined to hold onto their American possessions. Although they were unable to match the numbers of men available in earlier campaigns, they were generally able to field in America an army larger than that which Washington could muster.

Development of American Sea Power

During this period, there was a marked increase in American seafaring activity. Lacking a navy with which to challenge the British in a conventional naval war, the Continental Congress had already authorized the construction of 13 frigates. It also issued letters of marque that allowed up to 2,000 merchant ships to be fitted as privateers manned by up to 70,000 men. The privateers never reached this number, peaking at 449 ships during 1781, but their efforts were a serious worry to the British, especially with their raids in the sea lanes connecting Great Britain with the West Indies. In 1778, the first of America's great naval heroes emerged in John Paul Jones, who had been born in Scotland and learned his

These fine ships were built by the Honourable East India Company for the valuable trade with India and the Far East, and before the Revolutionary War often sailed into American ports as part of Great Britain's pattern of global trade. The Indiamen were built to the highest standards of structural strength, but were also very well equipped for the carriage of wealthy and important passengers. They were also armed and manned to warship standards so that they could fight off pirates and privateers, and even small warships. The *Bonhomme Richard*, commanded by John Paul Jones, was the French East Indiaman *Duc de Duras* before her conversion into an American heavy frigate. Built in 1766, this 900-ton ship mounted 40 guns.

REVOLUTIONARY AND EARLY AMERICAN WARS

THE MILITARY HISTORY OF THE UNITED STATES

seafaring as a slave trader and smuggler. In his first cruise, between April and May 1778, Jones took his Ranger from the French port of Brest into British waters. After terrorizing shipping in the Irish Sea, he landed at Whitehaven on the northwest coast of England to spike the guns of the local fort. He then crossed to St. Mary's Island in the Scilly Isles to capture the home of the Earl of Selkirk. Jones then cruised off northern Ireland, captured H.M.S. *Drake* off Carrickfergus and took her into Brest.

Triumph of the *Bonhomme Richard*

During his second cruise, in the *Bonhomme Richard* converted from a French East Indiaman, Jones sailed again into British waters. On September 23, 1779 off Flamborough Head he attacked a British convoy sailing on the Baltic route and was heavily engaged by the escorting frigate, H.M.S. *Serapis*. The two ships fought one of the most remarkable single-ship actions of all time. The *Serapis* set the *Bonhomme Richard* on fire before the British captain called on Jones to surrender. Responding "I have not yet begun to fight!," Jones breathed new hope into his men. They boarded the British frigate after shooting away her mainmast and finally forced a British surrender after the *Serapis* gun deck had been swept by an explosion touched off by an American grenade. Jones transferred his crew from the sinking *Bonhomme Richard* and sailed the *Serapis* into Brest.

While these events were on the horizon, Washington was consolidating his blockade of New York. Monmouth Court House was the last general battle fought in the northern theater. Washington was determined to prevent any further British eruption from New York. The American

Above left: Brigadier General Anthony Wayne agreed with de Lafayette that a more cautious plan should have been adopted in the approach to the British before the Battle of Monmouth Court House. Such a strategy would have resulted in an attack on the British rear instead of the general engagement that took place.

REVOLUTIONARY AND EARLY AMERICAN WARS

Above: The single-ship action between the *Bonhomme Richard* and *Serapis* remains a classic of its type.
Above right: John Paul Jones was the first U.S. naval hero. In his first commission, he captured eight British ships and destroyed another eight.

defensive line was centered on West Point, on the western bank of the Hudson River. Clinton made no concerted effort to breach or even attack it. Instead, Clinton hoped to tempt the Americans forward of their line with major raids on May 31, 1779 against the unfinished forts at Verplanck's Point and Stony Point. Washington was too clever to take the British bait. Seeing that Washington had avoided the trap, Clinton pulled back his main body to New York. Then Washington responded by launching Major General Wayne with a force of the new light infantry against the British garrison of Stony Point. Delivered with the bayonet after a stealthy approach, the American recapture of Stony Point on the night of July 15-16 achieved the useful military result of removing the British threat to West Point. It was more significant as an indication that the Americans were well on the way to mastering the skills of light infantry and bayonet fighting. Wayne was unsuccessful in his attempt to recapture Verplanck's Point, and the British soon retook Stony Point.

Static Warfare in New York

The war around New York had now taken on the character of a strictly limited war involving skirmishes and raids designed to test each side's watchfulness. A typical raid took place on August 18, when a small force under Major Henry "Lighthorse Harry" Lee recaptured Paulus Hook on the New Jersey side of New York harbor.

The Battle of Saratoga had removed any real threat of a British invasion of New York from Canada. The British sought to exploit their good relations with the Indian tribes in order to stir up trouble for

Left: The storming of Stony Point on July 15-16, 1779, by Major General Anthony Wayne's light infantry.

Below: American success in the Battle of Stony Point removed the British threat to West Point and confirmed the fighting abilities of the newly created light infantry arm.

REVOLUTIONARY AND EARLY AMERICAN WARS

Henry Lee played a modest but useful part in the Revolutionary War. He is best remembered as the major general who in 1794 commanded the militia force sent to western Pennsylvania to deal with the "Whiskey Rebellion."

the Americans all along the frontier, and to tie down American forces in duties far from the main centers of the war. Wherever possible, the activities of the pro-British Iroquois were aided by loyalist groups, and considerable disturbance was achieved in the frontier regions.

However, Clinton's relative inactivity in New York gave Washington the chance to deal with the Indian attacks. The main bases for these loyalist-led raids were Fort Niagara and Detroit. From here, the Indians swept through the Mohawk valley of New York (notably on November 11, 1778), the Wyoming valley of Pennysylvania (notably on July 3, 1778), and the new American settlements in Kentucky. Other massacres were perpetrated by the Johnson family, a notoriously bloodthirsty group, and by John and Walter Butler. In August 1778, Washington launched a punitive expedition into Pennsylvania and northwest New York under the command of Sullivan with Lee as his deputy. The expedition laid waste the villages of the Iroquois and finally trimmed this British operation to manageable size by defeating the Indians plus a number of loyalists in the Battle of Newtown on August 29. The expedition then returned in September 1778 after mopping up some last pockets of resistance.

THE MILITARY HISTORY OF THE UNITED STATES

The expedition of Lieutenant Colonel George Rogers Clark crosses the Wabash River while approaching Vincennes, which was captured for the United States on February 25, 1779.

American Successes in Virginia

Similar in its effect was the expedition launched by the state of Virginia in the winter of 1778-79. A force of 175 militiamen, supposedly raised for the defense of Kentucky, was led by Lieutenant Colonel George Rogers Clark. He conducted a small campaign of great tactical skill that overran all the British outposts in the areas of what are today Illinois and Indiana, culminating in the capture of Vincennes on February 25, 1779. Neither Sullivan nor Clark had been able to tackle the main British positions at Fort Niagara and Detroit, but the effect of the two expeditions was to limit the scope of the Indian raids. Clark's capture of Vincennes also allowed the United States, during negotiations for the Treaty of Paris in 1783, to put in a successful claim for the region between the Allegheny Mountains and the Mississippi River, an area much greater than that of the original 13 states.

As the revised nature of the war began to become clear to the British, late in 1778 they decided to switch the focus of the main effort farther to the south. Here loyalists had kept the southern colonies in a state of ferment for two years. Small-scale operations between loyalists and American patriots had been frequent, but no major operations had been attempted by either side. In the Carolinas and Georgia, loyalist strength was higher than in the middle and northern colonies. The British felt that loyalist operations would be easier to support, as the regions were relatively close to the British bases in the West Indies, where major naval forces were stationed to guard against French ambitions. The British plan was to return the three southern states to British rule one by one and use the area as the major base from which to attack northward and reconquer the other 10 colonies.

The British Invasion of Georgia

Moving forward from the British colony of East Florida, a small British force under Major General Augustine Prevost began to overrun Georgia in the winter of 1778-79. This southernmost of the rebellious states had become a British colony only in 1733 and was still very sparsely populated. On November 8, 1778 Lieutenant Colonel Archibald Campbell was moved by sea from New York with 3,500 men of Clinton's army. On December 29, he captured Savannah at the mouth of the Savannah River, crushing the defense of 1,000 American militiamen commanded by Brigadier General Robert Howe. In January 1779 Prevost arrived in Savannah after his advance through Georgia, and Campbell advanced up the Savannah to take Augusta on January 29. An American force under Ashe was sent from Charleston, South Carolina, in February to handle Campbell's detachment. But south of Augusta, in the Battle of Briar Creek, the British decisively beat back the Americans on March 3.

Alarmed by the obvious implications of this revised British strategy, the Continental Congress sent Major General Benjamin Lincoln to Charleston in December 1778 as commander of the Southern Army, which also received reinforcements

Savannah
For further references see pages 97, 100, 101, *102*, 118, 136.

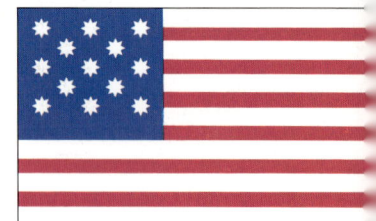

The Naval flag flown by the U.S. Navy ship *Alliance* in European waters, October, 1799.

96

REVOLUTIONARY AND EARLY AMERICAN WARS

In the campaign in the south, the British hoped to exploit the availability of many loyalists to bolster their own strength while pitting the American

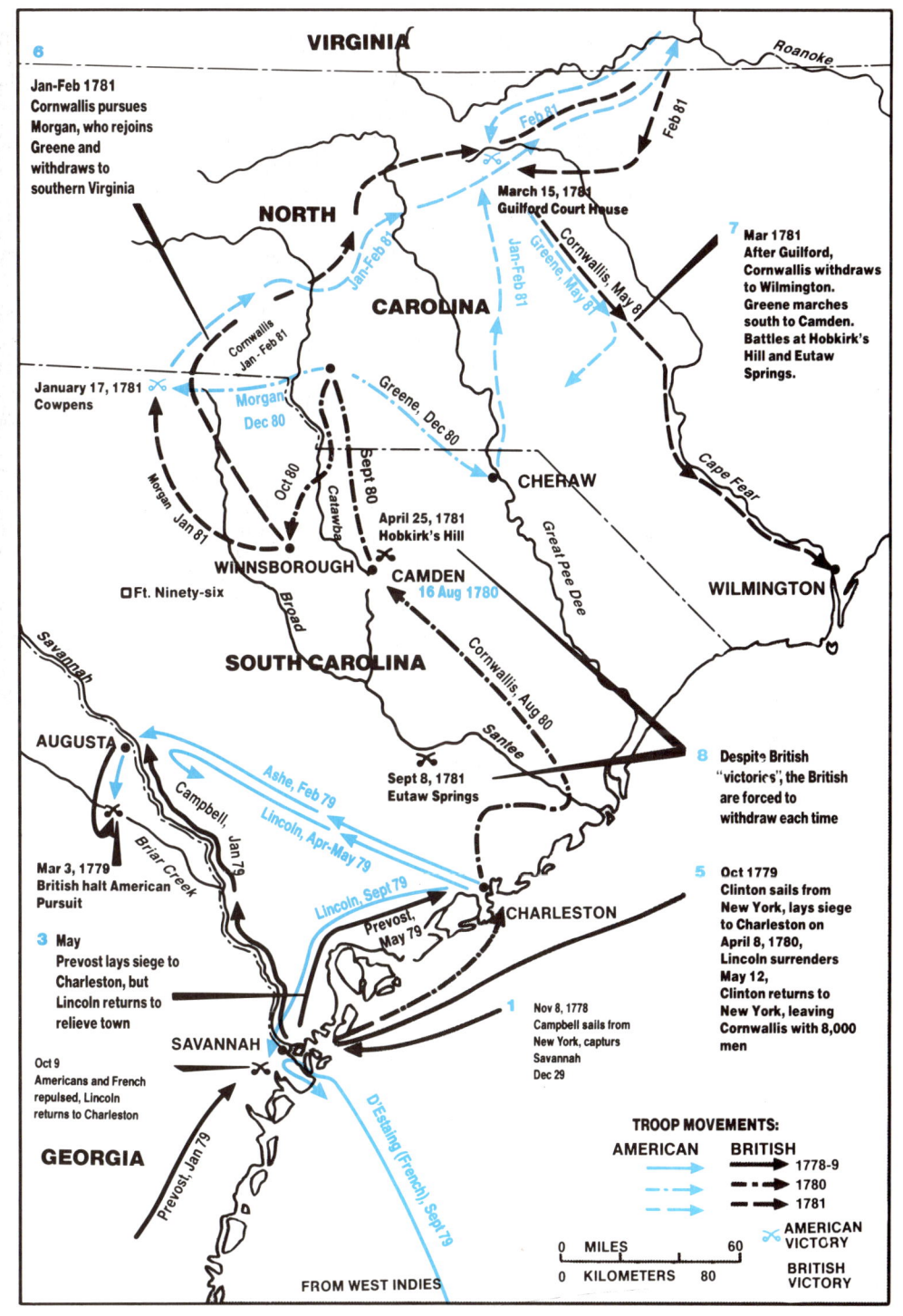

6 Jan-Feb 1781 Cornwallis pursues Morgan, who rejoins Greene and withdraws to southern Virginia

March 15, 1781 Guilford Court House

7 Mar 1781 After Guilford, Cornwallis withdraws to Wilmington. Greene marches south to Camden. Battles at Hobkirk's Hill and Eutaw Springs.

January 17, 1781 Cowpens

April 25, 1781 Hobkirk's Hill

CAMDEN 16 Aug 1780

Sept 8, 1781 Eutaw Springs

8 Despite British "victories", the British are forced to withdraw each time

5 Oct 1779 Clinton sails from New York, lays siege to Charleston on April 8, 1780, Lincoln surrenders May 12, Clinton returns to New York, leaving Cornwallis with 8,000 men

Mar 3, 1779 British halt American Pursuit

3 May Prevost lays siege to Charleston, but Lincoln returns to relieve town

1 Nov 8, 1778 Campbell sails from New York, captures Savannah Dec 29

Oct 9 Americans and French repulsed, Lincoln returns to Charleston

TROOP MOVEMENTS:

AMERICAN	BRITISH
→	→ 1778-9
–→	–→ 1780
→→	→→ 1781

✗ AMERICAN VICTORY
✗ BRITISH VICTORY

from the Continental Army. Lincoln's orders were to build up American strength and then to strike against the British in Georgia and, by logical extension, South Carolina,. In April, Lincoln decided on another overland advance from Charleston for the recapture of Augusta. As he was approaching the town he received news of British moves on the coast and headed back to Charleston. On the coast an effort was made by Prevost to take Port Royal halfway between Savannah and Charleston, but it had been repulsed February 3 by American forces commanded by William Moultrie. Prevost moved against Charleston again in May,

97

Private, Continental Marines (1779)

Although marines are known to have been in existence since May 1775, when they are mentioned in the payroll of the *Enterprise*, the official birthday of the US Marine Corps is November 10, 1775, when the Continental Congress ordered the raising of two marine battalions. The first recruiting center for the Continental Marines was in Philadelphia at the Tun Tavern, whose landlord was commissioned into the Marine Committee of the Continental Congress. A marine uniform was approved by Congress that consisted of a green coat with white facings, and for officers a silver epaulet on the right shoulder. In 1779, the color of the facings was changed to red, probably because of the shortage of white material in Philadelphia, which was the depot for the Continental Marines. The Continental Marines were disbanded at the end of the Revolutionary War and then raised once more in July 1798 as the Marine Corps.

REVOLUTIONARY AND EARLY AMERICAN WARS

but he was forced to pull back once more by the arrival of Lincoln's force from Augusta. Prevost fought off an attack by Lincoln at Stone Ferry on June 19 and returned safely to Savannah.

Warfare between Patriots and American "Tories"

While these more formal military operations were proceeding, the small-scale warfare between loyalists and American patriots continued. On February 14, a loyalist brigade was defeated by Colonel Andrew Pickens's militia at Kettle Creek. North Carolina and Virginia militia units raided the villages of the troublesome Chickamauga Indians in Tennessee. In May Admiral Sir George Collier's British squadron burned Portsmouth and other towns on the coast of Virginia.

Meanwhile d'Estaing's French squadron had been operating in the West Indies. On July 6, 1779, the French met Admiral John Byron's British force in the

Above: The largest single American reverse in the Revolutionary War was the loss of Charleston, which was surrendered by Major General Benjamin Lincoln on May 12, 1780.

Right: French support for the American cause was linked directly to their opposition to the British in control of the western hemisphere. In July 1779, the French under Admiral d'Estaing took Grenada. This scene depicts French officers cutting off their epaulets to decorate the shoulders of grenadiers who had fought with distinction.

Battle of Grenada. Although the French fared better in the inconclusive engagement, d'Estaing decided to return to American waters. On September 3, the French ships appeared off Savannah and captured two British warships as well as two transports. The French fleet then landed 6,000 troops to take Savannah under siege on September 12. Lincoln moved south with 1,350 Americans to take part in the siege, giving the allies a total strength of 7,350 men against the 3,500 under Prevost's command. But the defenses of Savannah were formidable, and the allies made very limited progress. D'Estaing was worried that his fleet, unable to use Savannah harbor, might fall prey to seasonal storms and ordered a general assault in an effort to speed progress. The French warships attempted a bombardment of the British positions with no success. On October 8, the allies advanced for the general assault in five columns. The British had been warned of the planned attack by a deserter and were fully prepared. Fighting from behind their prepared defenses, the British were able to push back each allied attack in the hardest fighting of the war since the Battle of Bunker Hill. The British suffered 150 casualties, but the allies lost more than 800 men, including the invaluable Pulaski. D'Estaing broke off the siege, re-embarked his men and sailed once more for the West Indies. This second attempt at allied cooperation had failed as dismally as the first at Newport, and the result was a serious American loss of faith in the French. The British and loyalists, on the other hand, were delighted with their victory, which seemed to offer great hope for continued success in the south.

Clinton Moves to Savannah

In New York, Clinton had come under increasing pressure from the British government to push the southern campaign as hard as possible. The departure of d'Estaing for the West Indies had restored command of the sea to the British. This offered the possibility for operations that would benefit from greater strategic mobility than Washington could hope to achieve. On October 11, the British garrison of Newport was evacuated. Soon, Clinton began to pull back his New York outposts and, leaving von Knyphausen in command of a New York garrison much reduced in responsibilities and numbers, sailed with 8,000 men for Savannah. The British left New York on December 26 and, after a stopover on the Virginia coast, arrived off South Carolina. With the arrival of Clinton and his army, the British could now put into the field some 14,000 men, a number far superior to that of Lincoln, who could be reinforced only slowly and in smaller numbers by the difficult overland routes available to Washington.

The British attack on Charleston was planned with great care as a combined operation involving the army and the navy. It began on February 11, 1780, when British troops cautiously surrounded the city. Clinton landed his forces on John's Island south of the city and moved up the west bank of the Ashley River until he was at a point north of Charleston on its promontory between the Ashley and Cooper Rivers. At the insistence of the South Carolina authorities, Lincoln had prepared his defenses across the promontory just north of the city. On March 29, Clinton's force crossed the Ashley and deployed across the promontory, cutting off the city and its defenders. The British action was completed on April 8, when British warships brushed aside the limited defense of Fort Moultrie south of the city and sealed the city off from the sea.

The Americans Lose Charleston

Clinton decided that tried and true measures were best. The British used the traditional system of advancing trench lines in siege of Charleston, which was also bombarded by the ships of Admiral Marriot Arbuthnot's squadron. On May 12, Lincoln bowed to the inevitable and surrendered his command. A total of 5,466 fighting men were captured, together with large quantities of artillery, small arms, and ammunition, to make the fall of Charleston the single greatest American disaster of the war.

Men of Lieutenant Colonel Francis Marion's guerrilla outfit cross the Pee Dee River during their campaign against loyalists in 1778.

His task complete, Clinton sailed for New York again, leaving Cornwallis and a force of 8,000 men in the south to "pacify" South Carolina. Cornwallis went about his task with a ruthless determination. The free hand given to the cavalry regiment commanded by the loyalist Lieutenant Colonel Sir Banastre Tarleton resulted in levels of brutality that turned most American opinion decisively against the British. The worst of Tarleton's excesses took place in the Battle of Waxhaw Creek on May 29, when a regiment of 350 Virginians under Colonel Abraham Buford was trapped just after crossing from North into South Carolina. Buford tried to surrender, but Tarleton's men massacred most of the Americans. News of such massacres inflamed American feeling still more against the British. This led to a further increase in guerrilla operations against the British occupation by bands under the command of men such as Lieutenant Colonel Francis Marion (the "Swamp Fox"), Brigadier General Thomas Sumter, and Brigadier General Andrew Pickens.

From his main bases at Beaufort, Charleston, Georgetown, and Savannah, Cornwallis and his regulars, supported by a large numbers of loyalists, tried to hold down an area that stretched as far west as Fort Ninety-Six. It was an impossible task. In effect, a civil war raged through South Carolina, with the British completely unable to pick the fruit of their purely military victory at Charleston in the face of steadily increasing grassroots opposition. To this extent, the Charleston campaign echoed the Saratoga campaign of three years earlier.

Washington sent south additional American forces. On June 22, Major General de Kalb arrived in Hillsboro, North Carolina, with the 900 men of two very understrength brigades as the core of a new Southern Army. The American commander-in-chief knew that by itself

THE Military HISTORY OF THE UNITED STATES

Top: The British used traditional methods of advancing trench lines in the siege of Charleston, which was also bombarded by the ships of Admiral Arbuthnot's squadron.

Center: The death of Brigadier General Johann de Kalb in the Battle of Camden on August 16, 1780.

Bottom: On October 9, 1779, the Americans and French launched a combined attack on the British base at Savannah, but were driven back after severe fighting.

Sergeant, New York Regiment (1779)

French influence is evident in this uniform of a sergeant in comparatively light combat order rather than heavier marching order. Apart from his musket, the most interesting features are the crossbelts supporting ammunition pouches that are tucked far enough toward the back to leave the man's front clear for easy movement of the weapon, and the leather harness supporting the man's pack of field equipment, probably a blanket, clothes, and food. The musket is a typical flintlock of the period, either a French Charleville model of 1763 or an American copy of it. Comparatively large numbers of these weapons were supplied by France, and variations on the basic model were reproduced by more than 200 gunsmiths in Maryland, Massachusetts, Pennsylvania, and Rhode Island in calibers ranging from 0·72 to 0·80 inch.

this force could achieve virtually nothing, but hoped that, around this nucleus of regular forces, a growing number of militia units would gather. But without consulting Washington, the Continental Congress in July appointed the hero of Saratoga, Gates as commander of the new Southern Army. That this was a poor choice was soon demonstrated. Rather than control and amplify the already successful guerrilla war in South Carolina while he concentrated and trained his forces, Gates opted for an advance with a force of 4,000 men, mainly militiamen, into South Carolina, where he planned to capture the British outpost at Camden.

The Battle of Camden

Cornwallis moved out from Charleston with some 2,200 British regulars and, after crossing the lower reaches of the Santee River hastened northwest to meet Gates outside Camden on August 15. During the early morning of August 16, Gates deployed his militiamen on the left and his Continentals, under de Kalb, on the right. The militia were still moving into position as Cornwallis attacked, and almost immediately broke and fled in total disarray. This left de Kalb's men hopelessly exposed on their left flank. The Battle of Camden was a British victory. The British infantry destroyed de Kalb's command, while Tarleton's cavalry pursued the routed Americans for 30 miles. Gates managed to escape, moving so fast that he covered the 160 miles to Hillsboro in only three days. The American survivors of the battle slowly straggled back to Hillsboro, but only 800 men rejoined the commander. Nine hundred men, including de Kalb, had been killed, and another 1,000 captured. This disastrous American episode was made worse by the fact that Tarleton caught and virtually destroyed Sumter's guerrilla force, sent by Gates to

For his part in the treason of Benedict Arnold, Major John Andre was sentenced to death. The calmness with which he received the sentence impressed all those present. Arnold escaped, receiving 6,315 pounds sterling and a commission in the rank of brigadier general from the British.

American Fortunes at Their Lowest Ebb

August 1780 can perhaps be regarded as the lowest ebb in American fortunes during the Revolutionary War. Matters could only get better. The Continental Congress returned the southern command to Washington, who appointed his "right arm," Greene, to command the Southern Army in place of Gates. This was one of the last appointments in a series of shuffles that went a long way toward removing many of the difficulties under which the Continental Army had been laboring. Supply failings and the decreasing value of Continental currency had hit the Continental Army hard. There had even been a mutiny by the troops at

raid a British wagon train, at Fishing Creek on August 18. South Carolina remained in British hands.

Morristown on May 23, 1780, after a winter in which the army had suffered even worse hardships than at Valley Forge. The mutiny had been quelled without delay, but the problem was still there. The Continental Congress tried to pass the problem to the individual states by demanding that each state provide the clothing for its own contingent and provide a quota of other supplies for the complete army. The system could not and did not work. The states were slow in meeting their quotas, and when supplies were provided, it was almost never at the right time or place. Greene had resigned as quartermaster general early in 1780, and the difficulties of maintaining the Continental Army became impossible as men refused to come forward when they knew that they would receive neither pay nor essential supplies. A militia statistic reveals the severity of the situation: in 1780, less than half the number of men were enlisted for one year's service than

The powder tester was an essential item of kit for proving the effectiveness of the gunpowder in each barrel. Based on a pistol, the tester was loaded with a standard charge and fired. The gases generated by the powder as it was fired then drove the heavy curved lever from the muzzle, and so turned the curved indicator scale. From this the firer could read a powder figure for comparison with those provided by other firings. Because of manufacturing defects and fraud, British powder at the time of the Revolutionary War was much inferior to that made by the French. This resulted in an inquiry which revised the system effectively. British powder was the best in the world by the time of the French Revolutionary and Napoleonic Wars that started only 15 years after the end of the Revolutionary War.

Gunner, Continental Artillery (1780)

Knox's Brigade of Artillery served with the main body of the Continental Army between 1777 and 1783. The brigade was made up of four battalions each of 12 companies, a company from the Regiment of Artillery Artificers, and the civilian drivers. The task of the artificers was maintenance of the brigade's technical equipment. The uniform shown here was adopted in 1779 with a dark blue coat with red facings and yellow lacing. Artillerymen carried full infantry equipment (including a musket for personal defense) and this man is also notable for his striped overall trousers and a drag rope. Non-commissioned officers were distinguished by their two epaulets, those for corporals in yellow worsted and those for sergeants in yellow silk.

De Rochambeau had serious reservations about the willingness of the Americans to sustain a major war effort.

had volunteered in 1776 for three years' service. The May 1780 mutiny at Morristown was an obvious result of the problem. The failure to solve the problem is indicated by further mutinies at Morristown (January 1, 1781 and May 1781) and Pompton (May 1781), all put down with some severity.

The Americans' problems were a source of great satisfaction to the British, who once again came to the conclusion that they would now win the war without undue difficulty. But the Americans' problems were also a major worry for the French. From July 11, 1780 a French army of 4,000 men under General Jean Baptiste de Vimeur le Comte de Rochambeau had been landed at the Newport base evacuated by the British. It was planned that this army, along with its supporting force of seven ships of line under Admiral de Termay, would then cooperate with American forces for an offensive against Clinton's New York army. But the French had been blockaded by British warships and could not seriously plan any offensive with the Americans. De Rochambeau had already warned his government: "Send us troops, ships and money, but do not count on these people or their resources, they have neither money nor credit, their forces exist only momentarily..." Another French commander thought that the British needed to persuade only one highly placed American to turn traitor to secure an easy and victorious end to the war.

The Treason of Benedict Arnold

In fact, Clinton had already found such a traitor in Benedict Arnold, who was offered large sums of money by the British. Feeling that he had been slighted by the Continental Congress and that the Americans were now in effect fighting for France, Arnold accepted the British offer. He managed to secure for himself command of West Point and then schemed to deliver the position to the British. With the capture of a British agent, Major John Andre, on September 21, Washington learned of the traitorous plan and foiled it. Arnold escaped, received a large sum of money from the British, and was commissioned as a brigadier general in the British service. Andre was hanged as a spy.

Despite all these problems, which reached their lowest point with Arnold's treason, the Americans somehow managed to build the foundations for a continued effort in 1781. Finances were put on a sounder footing by Robert Morris, a wealthy Philadelphian who was persuaded by the Continental Congress to become Superintendent of Finance The Continental Army's supply problems were eased by the appointment of Colonel Timothy Pickering to replace Greene, putting an able administrator at the head of the army's supply system. The Board of War was abolished, and a new Secretary of War was found in Lee, who had been exchanged after the Charleston disaster. Lee personally handled with greater speed and skill many of the tasks that had previously been undertaken by committees of the Board of War. Lee also

THE MILITARY HISTORY OF THE UNITED STATES

The oath of allegiance signed by Major General Benedict Arnold at Valley Forge was witnessed on May 30, 1778, by Henry Knox.

worked closely with Pickering to improve the Continental Army's supply situation. Particularly important was Lee's abandonment of devalued paper money and the setting up of a temporary practice of private contracts, backed by his own credit as guarantee that the contractors would eventually be paid in gold.

The Militia Begins to Come of Age

The first concrete evidence that the Americans were recovering from the disasters at Charleston and Camden was provided by the militia, whom the British had come to hold in low esteem. De Rochambeau had even reported: "...when they are about to be attacked in their own homes they assemble...to defend themselves." Clinton had reluctantly agreed by this time to the plan suggested by Cornwallis for an invasion of North Carolina. As a first move, Cornwallis sent Major Patrick Ferguson, who had been very successful in raising loyalist forces in the back country of South Carolina, into North Carolina. Ferguson was to raise loyalist forces that would then meet Cornwallis's main advance at Charlotte, which had begun in September from Camden. News of Ferguson's advance with his 1,100 "American Volunteers" spread immediate alarm among the "over-mountain men" of western North Carolina, southwestern Virginia, and what is now eastern Tennessee.

The Battle of King's Mountain

These three areas combined to create an elite force of 1,400 mounted riflemen. They gathered at the Catawba River in western North Carolina under the command of Colonels Isaac Shelby and Richard Campbell, and then moved forward to tackle Ferguson. The two forces, among whom the only non-American was Ferguson, met at King's Mountain close to the border of North and South Carolina on October 7, 1780. The result was a decisive defeat for the loyalists: Ferguson and many of his men were killed, some while trying to surrender,

REVOLUTIONARY AND EARLY AMERICAN WARS

Major General Lord Cornwallis was the British commander in the southern campaign. The lack of effective cooperation between Cornwallis and Sir Henry Clinton in New York was a major factor in the eventual British defeat.

and most of the survivors were captured.

King's Mountain had the same effect on Cornwallis's plan as Bennington had exercised on Burgoyne's scheme. The North Carolina loyalists were now unwilling to support Cornwallis, who was then forced to begin a rain-sodden withdrawal toward Winnsborough, South Carolina during October. The British retreat was harassed constantly by American militia. So dismal was the prospect for Cornwallis that Clinton was forced to reinforce Cornwallis with 2,500 men who would otherwise have been used to establish a base in Virginia. Having achieved their immediate task, the militiamen then followed their normal, unfortunate practice and returned home. Arriving to assume command of the Southern Army on December 2, Greene found that Charlotte had only 1,482 men, of whom 949 were at Charlottetals, all poorly clothed and equipped. By the middle of the month reinforcements from Washington had reached Greene, bolstering American strength to 3,000 men including 1,400 Continentals. Clinton's reinforcements had meanwhile reached Cornwallis, who had an overall strength of 4,000 better clothed and equipped regulars.

The experienced Greene knew full well the dangers involved in dividing his command in the face of a numerically superior enemy, but also knew that he had no alternative but to do so. His army could not grow in strength on the meager supplies available in Charlotte, but divided into two parts, it could live off the land and grow in capability and mobility. A divided Southern Army could also provide two cores around which militia forces could gather. The American movement began on December 20. Greene himself took half of the army southeast to Cheraw Hill on the Great Pee Dee River in South Carolina. Brigadier General Daniel Morgan took the other half west across the upper reaches of the Catawba River, also in South Carolina. The two parts of the Southern Army were separated by 140 miles, a distance that according to the conventional military wisdom of the day spelled disaster for the Americans.

Continued British Pressure in North Carolina

Cornwallis was still determined to invade and capture North Carolina for the British cause. Ignoring the sensible warnings of Clinton, he virtually stripped the main British base at Charleston by bringing up additional men and nearly all the available supplies. Faced with Greene's divided army, Cornwallis decided to do much the same thing, though in this instance the British force was divided into three parts. One part was sent southeast under Brigadier General Alexander Leslie to Camden with the task of checking Greene at Cheraw Hill. The second part, with 1,100 fast-moving infantry and cavalry under Tarleton was launched northwest to trap Morgan's detachment, The third, under Cornwallis himself paralleled Tarleton slightly farther to the east with the object of intercepting any of Morgan's detachment that escaped from Tarleton.

The British movements started in January 1781, and on January 17, Tarleton caught up with Morgan at a spot west of King's Mountain known as the Cowpens, an open area with scattering of timber about six miles from the Broad River. This ground was not of the Americans' choice, for Morgan had been trying to get his force across the river. But Morgan managed a tactical masterstroke that made best use of his mixed force, only one-quarter of them Continentals. Morgan deployed these regulars on a hill in the center of his position, leaving the flanks completely open. In front of this main position, he located two lines of militia riflemen with instructions that the first line was to fire only two volleys before falling back on the second line. The combined lines were then to fire until pressed by the British and then fall back behind the Continentals and so create a reserve. Behind the hill Morgan placed Lieutenant Colonel William Washington's cavalry with orders to charge the British at the decisive moment. Morgan's tactical plan was excellent, and he made sure that every man knew exactly what he was to do.

The Battle of Cowpens

Immediately after he encountered Morgan, Tarleton ordered the attack. His force moved up in regular order against the forward-deployed militia. They inflicted

The arms of the United States reflect the nation's varied and sometimes bloody origins.

Lieutenant Colonel William Washington, the American cavalry commander, fights with Lieutenant Colonel Sir Banastre Tarleton in the Battle of Cowpens on January 17, 1781. The battle was small in scope, but was a decisive tactical victory for the Americans and a classic example of the double envelopment.

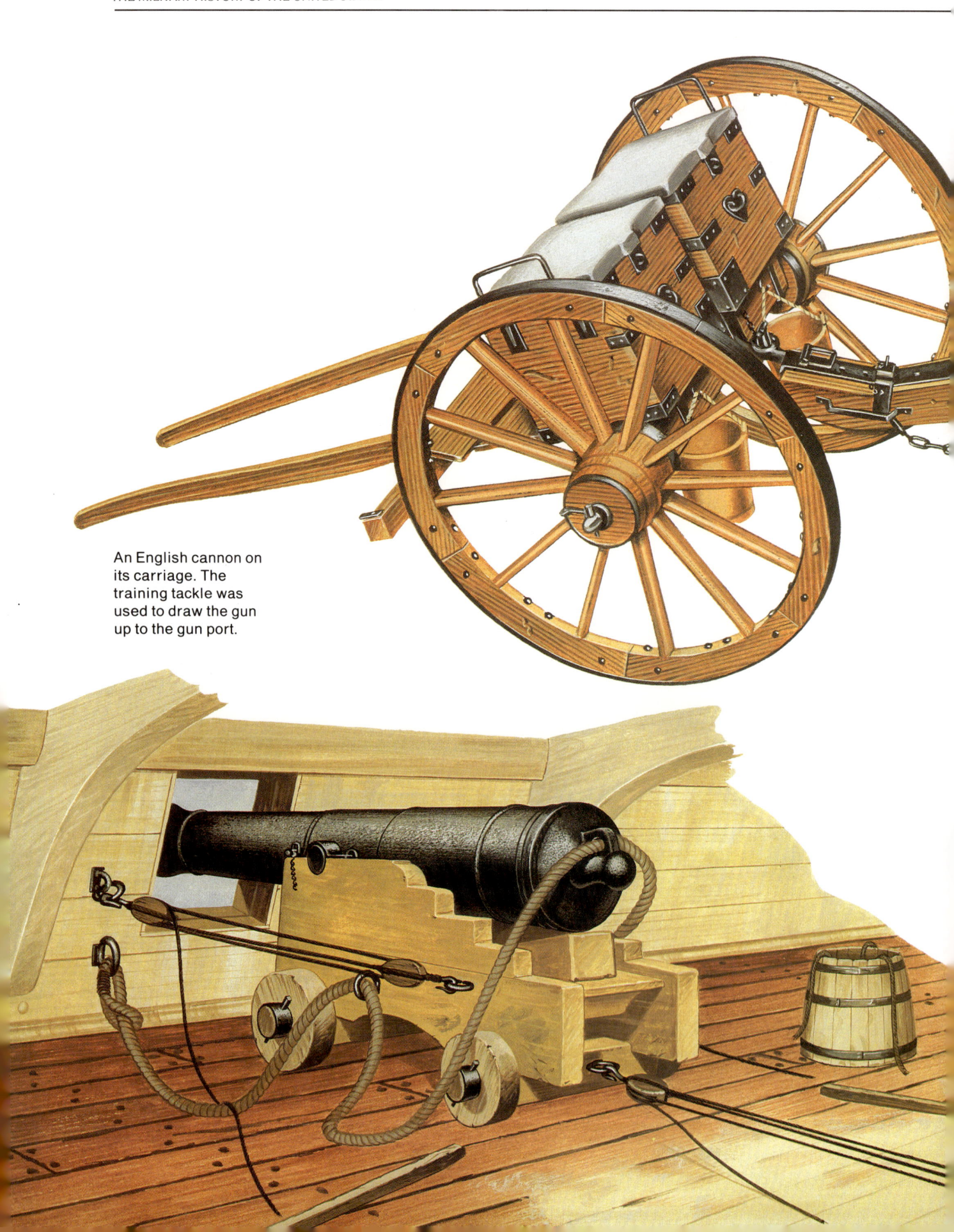

THE MILITARY HISTORY OF THE UNITED STATES

An English cannon on its carriage. The training tackle was used to draw the gun up to the gun port.

REVOLUTIONARY AND EARLY AMERICAN WARS

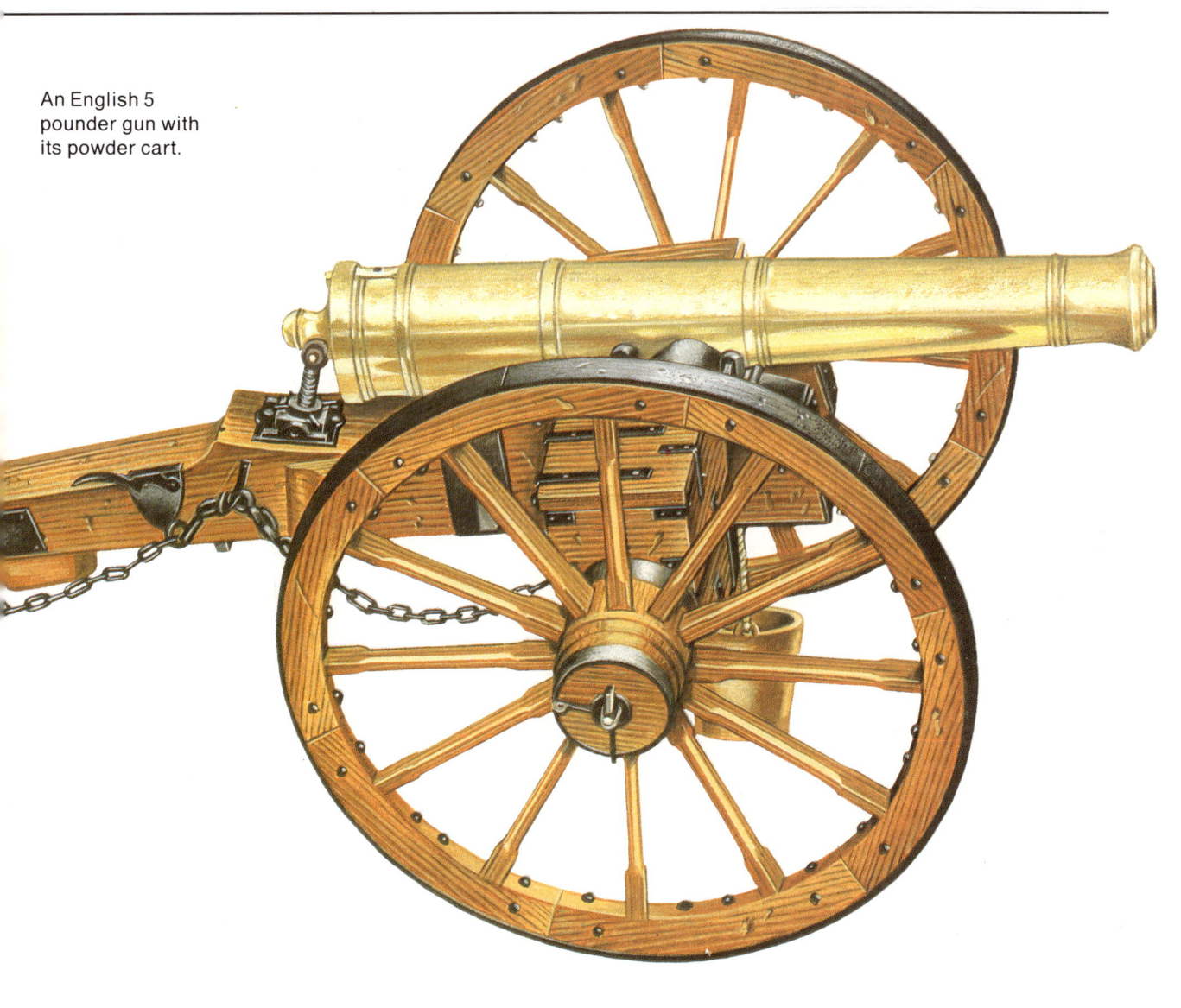

An English 5 pounder gun with its powder cart.

An American mortar surrounded by a section of the chain that was originally strung across the Hudson at West Point.

The Revolution in the South featured bitter civil war between whigs and tories. Sixteen year old Thomas Young fought in many guerrilla actions and served at the important battles of King's Mountain (October 7, 1780) and Cowpens (January 17, 1781).

"I was born in Laurens District, South-Carolina, on the 17th June 1764. My father, Thomas Young, soon after removed to Union District, where I have lived to this day. In the spring of 1780, I think in April, Colonel Brandon was encamped with a party of seventy or eighty whigs, about five miles from Union Court House, where Christopher Young now lives. Their object was to collect forces for the approaching campaign, and to keep a check upon the tories. They had taken prisoner, one Adam Steedham, as vile a tory as ever lived. By some means, Steedham escaped during the night, and notified the tories of Brandon's position. The whigs were attached by a large body of the enemy before day, and completely routed. On that occasion, my brother, John Young, was murdered. I shall never forget my feelings, when told of his death. I do not believe I had ever used an oath before that day, but then I tore open my bosom, and swore that I would never rest until I had avenged his death. Subsequently, many tories felt the weight of my arm, and around Steedham's neck I fastened the rope, as a reward for his cruelties. On the next day, I left home in my shirt sleeves, and joined Brandon's Party. Chr. Brandon and I joined at the same time, and the first engagement we were in was at Stallions', in York District.

We had been told of a party of tories, then stationed at Stallions'; a detachment of about fifty whigs, under Colonel Brandon, moved to attack them. Before we arrived at the house in which they were fortified, we were divided into two parties; Captain Love, with a party of sixteen, of whom I was one, marched to attach the front, while Colonel Brandon, with the remainder, made a circuit to intercept those who should attempt to escape and also to attack the rear. Mrs. Stallions was a sister of Captain Love, and, on the approach of her brother, she ran out and begged him not to fire upon the house. She ran back to the house, and sprang upon the door step, which was pretty high. At this moment, the house was attacked, in the rear, by Colonel Brandon's party, and Mrs. Stallions was killed by a ball shot at random through the opposite door. At the same moment with Brandon's attack, our party raised a shout and rushed forward. We fired several rounds, which were briskly returned. It was not long, however, before the tories ran up a flag, first upon the end of a gun; but, as that did not look exactly peaceful, a ball was put through the fellow's arm, and, in a few minutes, the flag was raised on a ramrod, when we ceased firing. While we were fighting, a man was seen running through an open field, near us. I raised my gun to shoot him, when some of our party exclaimed, "don't shoot, he is one of our own men." I drew down my gun, and in a moment he halted, wheeled round, and fired at us. Old Squire Kennedy, who was an excellent marksman, raised his rifle and brought him down. We had but one wounded, William Kennedy, who was shot by my side, through the wrist and thigh. The loss of the tories was two killed, four wounded, and twenty-eight prisoners, whom we sent to Charlotte, North-Carolina. After the fight, Love and Stallions met and shed bitter tears. Stallions was dismissed, on parole, to bury his wife and arrange his affairs.

The next engagement I was in, was at King's Mountain, South-Carolina, on the 17th October, 1780. When our division came up to the northern base of the mountain, we dismounted, and Colonel Roebuck drew us a little to the left, and commenced the attack. Ben Hollingsworth and myself took right up the side of the mountain, and fought, from tree to tree, our way to the summit. I recollect I stood behind one tree and fired, until the bark was nearly all knocked off, and my eyes pretty well filled with it. One fellow shaved me pretty close, for his bullet took a piece out of my gun-stock. Before I was aware of it, I found myself apparently between my own regiment and the enemy, as I judged, from seeing the paper which the whigs wore in their hats, and the pine knots the tories wore in theirs, these being the badges of distinction. On the top of the mountain, in the thickest of the fight, I saw Colonel Williams fall, and a braver and a better man never died upon a battle-field. I ran to his assistance, for I loved him as a father; he had ever been so kind to me, and almost always carried a cake in his pocket for me and his little son, Joseph. They carried him into a tent, and sprinkled some water into his face. He revived, and his first words were, "For God's sake, boys, don't give up the hill!" He died the next day, and was buried not far from the field of his glory. Daniel and Joseph Williams, his sons, were both massacred by the tories at Hays' Station, where Daniel first threw his father's pistols into the burning house, rather than they should go into the hands of the tories.

We arrived at the field of Cowpens about sunset, and were then told that there we should meet the enemy. It was upon this occasion I was more perfectly convinced of General Morgan's qualifications to command militia, than I had ever before been. He went among the volunteers, helped them to fix their swords, joked with them about their sweethearts, told them to keep in good spirits, and the day would be ours. And long after I laid down, he was going about among the soldiers, encouraging them, and telling them that the old wagoner (Morgan) would crack his whip over Ben (Tarleton) in the morning, as sure as they lived. "Just hold up your heads, boys, give them three fires, and you will be free. And then, when you return to your homes, how the old folks will bless you, and the girls will kiss you for your gallant conduct." About sun-rise the British advanced at a sort of trot, with a loud halloo; it was the most beautiful line I ever say. When they shouted, I heard Morgan say, "They give us the British halloo, boys - give them the Indian whoop;" and he galloped along the lines, cheering the men, and telling them not to fire until they could see the whites of their eyes. The militia fired first, they being in advance. At first, it was pop, pop, pop, and then a whole volley; but when the regulars fired, it seemed like one sheet of flame from right to left! Oh! it was beautiful! I heard old Colonel Fair say that John Savage fired the first gun in this battle.

After the second forming of the militia, the fight became general and unintermitting. In the *hottest of it, I saw Colonel Brandon coming at full speed to the rear, and waving his sword to Colonel Washington. In a moment, the order to charge was given. We made a most furious charge, and cutting through the British cavalry, we wheeled and charged them in the rear. In this charge, I exchanged my tackey for the finest horse I ever rode; it was the quickest swap I ever made in my life. At this moment, the bugle sounded: we made a half circuit at full speed, and came upon the rear of the British line, shouting and charging like madmen. At the same moment, Colonel Howard gave the order, "charge bayonet," and the day was ours - the British line broke - many of them laid down their arms and surrendered, while the rest took to the wagon road, and did their prettiest sort of running away. After this, Major Jolly and seven or eight of us resolved on an excursion to capture some of the baggage. We went about twelve miles, and captured two British soldiers, two negroes, and two horses laden with portmanteaus. One of the portmanteaus belonged to a paymaster in the British service, and contained gold. I rode along some miles with my prisoners and baggage towards our camp, when I met a party which I soon discovered to be British. I attempted to fly, but, my horse being stiff by the severe exercise I had given him, they overtook me. My pistol was empty, so I drew my sword and made battle; I never fought so hard in my life. In a few minutes, one finger on my left hand was split; then I received a cut on my sword arm. In the next instant a cut from a sabre across my forehead (the scar of which I shall carry to my grave); the skin slipped down over my eyes, and the blood blinded me. Then came a thrust in the right shoulder blade, then a cut upon the left shoulder, and a last cut, which you may feel for yourself on the back of my head, and I fell upon my horse's neck. They took me down, bound up my wounds, and replaced me on my horse, a prisoner of war.*

damage on the British, who thought that their planned withdrawal past the left flank of the Continentals was the first sign of an American rout. The British therefore pressed forward right into the fire of the Continentals. Only then did Morgan unleash his double envelopment: the cavalry swept around onto the British right, and the re-formed militiamen onto their left. With his main force trapped and forced to surrender, Tarleton escaped with his small cavalry reserve. The Battle of Cowpens was a classic victory in which, for the loss of 73 casualties (12 killed and 61 wounded) the Americans killed 110 British and captured another 830.

Knowing that Cornwallis was not far away, Morgan moved with great speed to escape the British. In the next five days, he moved 100 miles. He crossed two rivers before he rejoined Greene, who had moved north from Cheraw Hill. The reunited Southern Army pulled back to the Dan River in southern Virginia with the British in pursuit. Cornwallis felt that this was the moment for a supreme effort. To allow his army to move faster, he ordered the destruction of all baggage, wagons, and surplus supplies. Greene kept his forces just in front of the British, swinging back from the unfordable Dan River into North Carolina during February and crossing the upper reaches of the Cape Fear River. During this stage of the campaign Greene lost the services of Morgan, who was forced by arthritis to quit.

On March 15, Greene halted on ground of his own choosing at Guilford Court House and offered battle. The Americans now numbered 4,500 men (1,500 Continentals and 3,000 militiamen) to 1,900 British regulars. The British fought with the utmost determination and, despite their smaller numbers, drove the militiamen off the field and finally gained the upper hand. Greene broke off the battle and retired in good order, leaving the British victorious. But the Battle of Guilford Court House was a Pyrrhic victory for the British: American losses were 78 dead and 183 wounded, while those of the British were 93 dead and 439 wounded. Having lost more than one-quarter of his force and virtually without supplies, Cornwallis had no option but to pull back,

The only non-American on the field during the Battle of Cowpens was the British commander, Lieutenant Colonel Sir Banastre Tarleton.

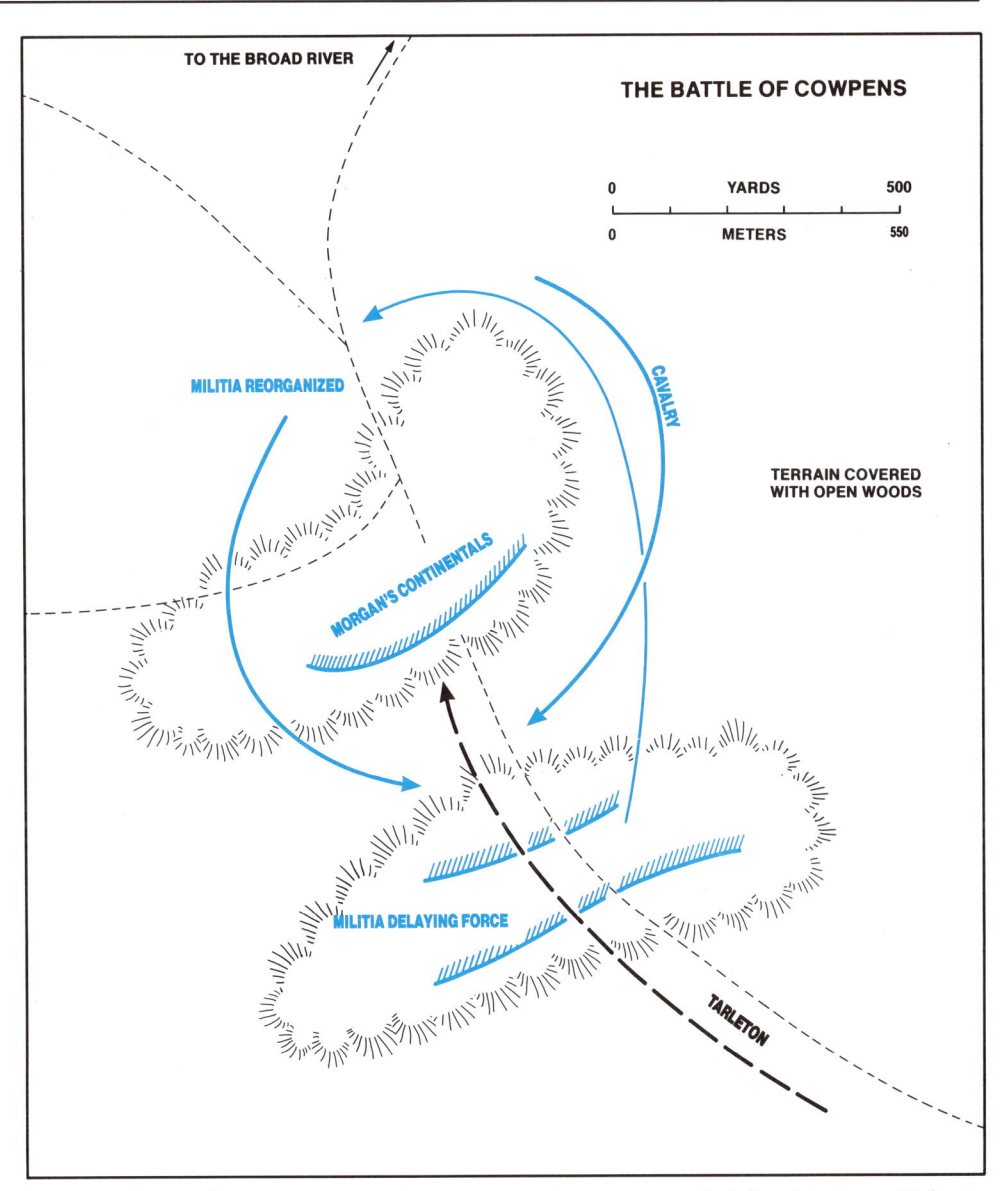

THE BATTLE OF COWPENS

moving down the Cape Fear River to Wilmington. He decided that Georgia and South Carolina could no longer be held, and between April and May 1781, marched with his 1,500 men to join the expedition that Clinton had sent into Virginia.

Despite his tactical defeat at Guilford Court House, Greene knew that his army was in far better shape than it had been only six months earlier and responded rapidly to Cornwallis's withdrawal. The American commander followed Cornwallis most of the way to the Cape Fear River and turned off to the southwest to eliminate the British outposts in South Carolina with the support of the guerrilla units commanded by Marion, Pickens, and Sumter. The first British outpost to be tackled was that of Colonel Francis Rawdon at Camden, and in the Battle of Hobkirk's Hill on April 25, the American forces were firmly checked. One by one, the smaller British outposts fell to detachments of Greene's army or to guerrillas. There were however, other American reverses at Fort Ninety-Six and at Eutaw Springs. Fort Ninety-Six was taken under siege on May 22, but on June 19, a British force relieved the garrison, which fell back with the relief force to Charleston. On September 8, Greene's 2,400-man force attacked the 2,000-man British detachment commanded by Lieutenant Colonel

Left: Lieutenant Colonel Sir Banastre Tarleton was an infamous British leader in the southern campaign.

Below: The Battle of Eutaw Springs on September 8, 1781, was a British tactical victory, but the weakening of the overall British position meant that it was followed by a retreat to Charleston.

Alexander Stewart at Eutaw Springs. After an early success, he was driven back, but Stewart's losses were so heavy that he, too, was forced to retreat to Charleston.

Despite his losses and reverses at the tactical level, in which he had failed to win a single battle, Greene had achieved his strategic objective. By October 1781, the British had lost Georgia and South Carolina with the exception of their garrisons in the ports of Savannah and Charleston.

American Victory in Sight

The way was now set for American victory in the Revolutionary War, especially as the division between Clinton and Cornwallis was now as effective a hindrance to British efforts as the division between Howe and Burgoyne had been in 1777. Clinton was Cornwallis's superior, but Cornwallis had the ear of the government in London and thus felt himself able to conduct his operations without any real regard to Clinton's urgings. For this reason, Cornwallis felt that he was able to strike off into the interior of the Carolinas. Clinton had insisted that all operations should be conducted within reasonable distance of seaborne reinforcement and, by implication, evacuation. When Cornwallis eventually moved to Virginia, he did so without even notifying Clinton.

In 1779, Clinton started an effort to disrupt economic life in Virginia by raiding

Infantrymen of the Continental Army in 1779, with their uniforms set apart by state distinctions. By this time, the men of the Continental Army were a match for the men of the British and German infantry in most of the disciplines of formal warfare.

up its rivers. He knew that such raids would encourage local loyalists and might open the way for the establishment of a British base in the Chesapeake Bay region. This, Clinton hoped, could form one arm of the pincer movement with which he hoped to take Pennsylvania. The other arm would be provided by his currently inactive army in New York. An initial raid in the Hampton Roads area during 1779 had proved highly successful, but a second raid in 1780 had to be diverted to Charleston to provide Cornwallis with reinforcements after the King's Mountain setback. On December 30, 1780, a third raid arrived at Hampton Roads. Under the command of Arnold, this force of 1,600 men had orders to destroy American supplies, prevent the movement of reinforcements for Greene, and

American cavalry under the command of Henry Lee, better known as "Light Horse Harry," at the Battle of Guilford Court House on March 15, 1781. The battle was another British tactical success that was followed by strategic retreat, this time to Wilmington.

Major General Anthony Wayne was nicknamed "Mad Anthony," but was one of the better American commanders in the closing stages of the Revolutionary War.

rally the loyalists. Arnold swept up the James River to seize Richmond on January 5, and after razing the city, he started back toward Portsmouth. Inconclusive operations against American forces commanded by von Steuben followed.

Virginian Coastal Operation

Arnold's presence in Virginia was a magnet to both sides. Washington's response was the dispatch of de Lafayette with 1,200 Continentals, and a plea to the French in Newport for a naval squadron to cut Arnold's seaborne lines of communication and ferry in a number of French troops. The plan was thrown into disarray by the First Battle of the Delaware Capes on March 16. A British squadron of eight line of battle ships under Arbuthnot met Commodore Sochet Destouches's eight French line of battle ships: the British had three ships dismasted, but the French retired to Newport. Clinton sent in another 2,600 men under Major General William Phillips, who assumed command over all the British forces on his arrival

THE MILITARY HISTORY OF THE UNITED STATES

The combined British expeditions then raided further along the Virginia coastal and James River regions before moving south to link up with Clinton's force advancing from Wilmington. Phillips died at Petersburg on May 10, but ten days later, the link-up of ten British forces put Cornwallis in command of Virginia operations, which could call on 8,000 men including the garrison of Portsmouth.

De Lafayette had arrived in Richmond on April 29 and took command of all American forces. This gave him a strength of 3,550 men, including his 1,200 veteran Continentals and von Steuben's largely inexperienced men. Further reinforcement was on its way from Washington in the form of Wayne's brigade of 800 Continentals, which joined de Lafayette on June 10. Between May and July, Cornwallis tried to bring the Americans to battle. But even with militia reinforcement, de

The Marquis de Lafayette leads his men against the British during one of the later campaigns of the Revolutionary War. De Lafayette showed great skill in engaging the British only when he had the advantage. Otherwise he slipped away to avoid battle and conserve his strength.

122

REVOLUTIONARY AND EARLY AMERICAN WARS

Lafayette was still considerably outnumbered and kept slipping away from the British, leading them around large portions of eastern Virginia.

Again, disagreement between the British generals played into the hands of the Americans. Cornwallis thought that Clinton's plan for a pincer offensive against Pennsylvania was militarily poor, while Clinton thought that Cornwallis's attempt to operate deep in Virginia would succeed no better than his operations deep in the Carolinas. Clinton finally gave Cornwallis a direct order to return to the coast, establish a base of operations, and return a part of the British force to New York. Reluctantly, Cornwallis headed for Portsmouth, with de Lafayette following closely. At Jamestown Ford on July 6, the British laid a neat ambush and caught Wayne's brigade. Although taken by surprise, the American veterans fought off the British assault and, despite heavy losses, counterattacked before retiring in good order. The British continued their retreat without further hindrance.

Cornwallis Bottles Himself Up at Yorktown

Cornwallis had been fighting Clinton's demand that part of the Virginia expedition should be returned to New York. On July 20, new orders from Clinton reached Cornwallis: no men need be returned to New York, and Cornwallis was to take and hold the tip of the Virginia peninsula at Yorktown, between the James and York Rivers. Cornwallis had concentrated most of his forces in Yorktown by August 4, giving him a strength of 7,000 men here and in a smaller garrison on the other side of the mouth of the York River estuary at Gloucester Point. De Lafayette had cautiously moved to a covering position with 4,500 men at nearby West Point, at the same time, informing Washington

Cornwallis surrendered at Yorktown on October 19, 1781.

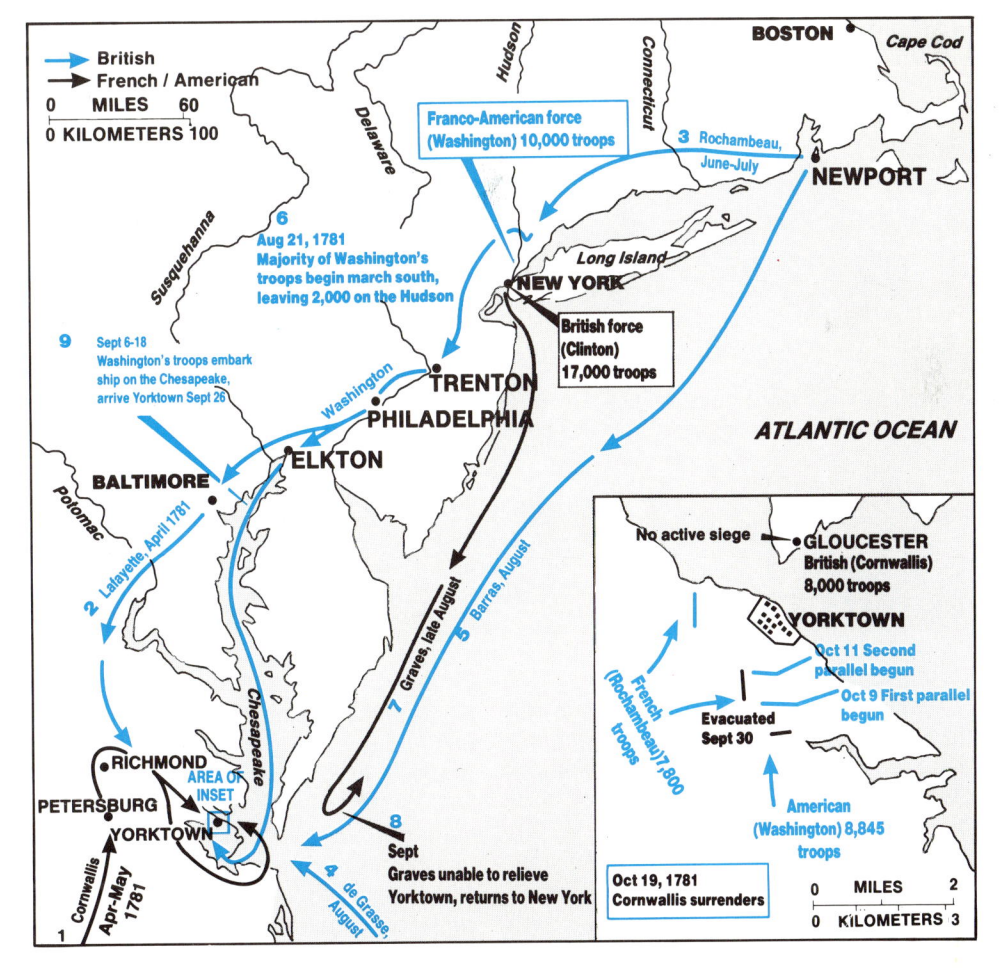

THE MILITARY HISTORY OF THE UNITED STATES

Major General William Heath was the American officer charged with creating the diversion in New York designed to persuade Clinton that the Franco-American allies were planning a northern effort in 1781.

of the latest British move.

Washington had meanwhile been trying to persuade de Rochambeau to commit his French troops to a combined Franco-American assault on Clinton in New York during the summer of 1781. On May 21, Washington and de Rochambeau met near New York to develop a common strategy. The two men agreed that, with British land strength concentrated in two places (New York and the Chesapeake Bay area), the allies' best hope for a victory was to use the growing French naval strength in the West Indies to cut the maritime line of communication between Clinton and Cornwallis. This would allow allied sea and land power to be concentrated against the weaker of the British

Captain, Continental Navy (1780)

As in the Royal Navy, captains of the Continental Navy seldom wore a complete regulation uniform, though a notable exception was Captain Abraham Whipple of Providence, Rhode Island. This officer is thought to have fired the first shot of the Revolutionary War at sea, and had already been involved in the *Gaspee* incident of 1772, when the British revenue cutter of that name ran aground off Narragansett and was burned by local people. Whipple's career ended in 1780, when he surrendered his entire squadron at the fall of Charleston. In March 1777, senior officers of the Continental Navy proposed a new uniform coat of blue lined in white with gold lacing and epaulets, but this was not officially recognized, even though some officers wore it. In 1781, the Continental Congress ordered that no officer was to wear "any gold lace, embroidery or vellum, other than such as Congress of the Commander-in-Chief of the Army or Navy shall direct."

THE MILITARY HISTORY OF THE UNITED STATES

The matched flintlock pistols carried by the American commander-in-chief were a fine pair made in London, and a notably good example of the gunsmith's art in this period.

REVOLUTIONARY AND EARLY AMERICAN WARS

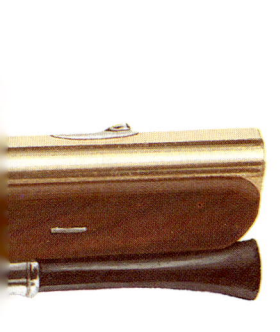

enclaves. A French frigate was dispatched to the West Indies to deliver Washington's request to Admiral Francois-Joseph le Comte de Grasse. During June and July, de Rochambeau moved up from Newport with 4,000 men and put his French army under Washington's command. This gave the American commander-in-chief about 10,000 men, but his prospects were still uncertain as Clinton had at least 17,000 men in New York.

One day after de Grasse had sailed from the West Indies on August 13 with an additional 3,500 French troops collected from Haiti, Washington learned that the French admiral's destination was not to be New York, but Chesapeake Bay, where he should arrive later in the month and be able to stay until mid-October. Washington received this information just after de Lafayette's report about Cornwallis' retirement into the Yorktown peninsula. Here at last was the allies' chance to cut off and destroy a large segment of the British army in America. There was no unified command of inter-allied land and naval forces at the formal level, but in practice, cooperation was now good. Washington decided to move quickly. Admiral Louis le Comte de Barras sailed from Newport with his squadron to link up with de Grasse while de Lafayette was ordered to contain Cornwallis. Major General William Heath was left a force of 2,000 men with which to deceive Clinton that the allies were still planning an attack on New York. On August 21, Washington's combined Franco-American army started to march with the utmost speed and secrecy toward Virginia. The allied army had reached Virginia before Clinton realized that he had been deceived.

The Second Battle of the Delaware Capes

On August 30, de Grasse arrived in Chesapeake Bay with 24 ships of the line, and a few days later 3,500 French troops were disembarked to reinforce de

Right: Each side knew that an American victory at Yorktown in 1781 would decide the outcome of the Revolutionary War in favor of the United States. Here, Washington fires the first shot of the siege during October 3.

127

THE MILITARY HISTORY OF THE UNITED STATES

By an irony typical of history, the decisive battle of the Revolutionary War involved no Americans. The Second Battle of the Delaware Capes was fought on September 5, 1781, between British and French fleets. The tactical result was a tie that left the French in control of Chesapeake Bay when the British pulled back to New York, leaving Cornwallis to his fate in Yorktown.

Lafayette. Late in the month the British naval commander in New York, Admiral Thomas Graves, sailed with 19 ships of the line to intercept de Barras and prevent de Grasse's entry into Chesapeake Bay.

Failing to find de Barras, Graves made for Chesapeake Bay. On reaching Hampton Roads on September 5, he found that the French fleet had already entered the bay. De Grasse sortied against Graves in the

REVOLUTIONARY AND EARLY AMERICAN WARS

Second Battle of the Delaware Capes. The first eight French ships rounded Cape Henry well clear of the rest of the French fleet, but Graves failed to seize the opportunity this offered for piecemeal destruction of the French. The result was inconclusive. For the next four days, the two fleets maneuvered to secure the tactical advantage. This allowed de Barras to slip into Chesapeake Bay unmolested, and

The Franco-American land forces besieging Yorktown knew after the Second Battle of the Delaware Capes that a British defeat was now inevitable. Even so, they planned and executed their effort in the completely scientific manner of contemporary siege warfare.

de Grasse then retired into the bay. Graves then decided that he lacked the strength to force a passage into Chesapeake Bay, so he returned to New York.

This sealed the fate of Yorktown, and with it the British defeat in the Revolutionary War. On September 6, Washington's army reached Head of Elk. Between that day and September 18, they embarked in a flotilla of mainly French ships at Head of Elk, Baltimore and Annapolis for the journey down Chesapeake Bay and around the eastern tip of the Yorktown peninsula. They landed unopposed at Williamsburg, on the southwestern shore of the peninsula, on September 26. De Lafayette's men had meanwhile moved down the peninsula. By September 28, Yorktown had been completely surrounded.

Including some 3,000 Virginian militiamen, Washington had 8,845 American and 7,800 French troops under his command for the siege of 8,000 British. He sensibly left the conduct of the siege to experienced French engineers, who were excellently equipped and could also call on the service of some of France's latest artillery. In a move that greatly aided the allies, Cornwallis abandoned his forward position on September 30, and by October 6, the engineers started digging their first trench 600 yards in front of the British main positions. Three days later, the allied artillery began its bombardment from this trench. On October 11, the engineers had pushed forward about 200 yards of the zigzag trench that extended toward the British position and allowed the start of work on the second trench line. On October 14, American and French infantry stormed two British redoubts that allowed the siege works to be extended to the edge of the York River. On October 16, a major British counterattack was beaten back. Cornwallis now saw that he could not hold Yorktown. He tried to

Washington inspects French artillery in the trenches around Yorktown. The allies used 52 guns to shell the British garrison without respite, and the storming of two British redoubts on October 14 ended all chance that the besieged army might be able to slip away.

evacuate part of his force across the York River to Point Gloucester, where the British beachhead was contained by only small American forces. But a storm prevented the execution of this plan on October 16, and Cornwallis realized that his only hope was relief from New York.

British Surrender at Yorktown

Clinton too had come to this conclusion, but the decision to send Graves with a reinforced fleet and 7,000 troops had taken so long that the fleet did not sail until October 17, the day on which Cornwallis opened surrender negotiations with Washington. The American commander-in-chief allowed two days for written proposals to be prepared, but demanded complete surrender by Cornwallis. On October 19, the British garrison of Yorktown marched out and laid down its arms. On October 24, Graves's fleet arrived with Clinton and his 7,000-man reinforcement, but seeing that the Yorktown garrison had already surrendered it returned to New York. Washington tried to persuade de Grasse to support attacks on the British bases at Charleston and Wilmington, but the French admiral decided that the dangers of the storm season were too great for any further delay. The French sailed for the West Indies.

The American and French victory at Yorktown effectively put an end to the War. When news of the defeat reached London, the government fell, to be replaced by a more realistic administration that decided to end hostilities. More than two years were to pass before the provisions of the Treaty of Paris were implemented and the British completed their evacuation. With the war effectively won, later land operations were undertaken on

THE MILITARY HISTORY OF THE UNITED STATES

GLORIOUS NEWS.

PROVIDENCE, October 25, 1781.

Three o'Clock, P. M.

THIS MOMENT an EXPRESS arrived at his Honour the Deputy-Governor's, from Col. Chriftopher Olney, Commandant on Rhode-Ifland, announcing the important Intelligence of the Surrender of Lord Cornwallis and his Army, an Account of which was printed This Morning at Newport, and is as follows, viz.

Newport, October 25, 1781.

YESTERDAY afternoon arrived in this Harbour Capt. Lovett, of the Schooner Adventure, from York-River, in Chefapeak-Bay (which he left the 20th Inftant) and brought us the glorious News of the Surrender of Lord CORNWALLIS and his Army Prifoners of War to the allied Army, under the Command of our illuftrious General, and the French Fleet, under the Command of his Excellency the Count de GRASSE.

A Ceffation of Arms took Place on Thurfday the 18th Inftant, in Confequence of Propofals from Lord Cornwallis for a Capitulation. His Lordfhip propofed a Ceffation of Twenty-four Hours, but Two only were granted by His Excellency General WASHINGTON. The Articles were completed the fame Day, and the next Day the allied Army took Poffeffion of York-Town.

By this glorious Conqueft, NINE THOUSAND of the Enemy, including Seamen, fell into our Hands, with an immenfe Quantity of Warlike Stores, a forty Gun Ship, a Frigate, an armed Veffel, and about One Hundred Sail of Tranfports.

Above: Cornwallis surrenders to Washington at Yorktown. Surrender negotiations began on October 17, the day that a relief force sailed from New York. On October 19, the British garrison marched out to lay down its arms and effectively ended the Revolutionary War.
Left: Typical of the news broadsheets that confirmed the events at Yorktown for the American people was this example, published in Providence, Rhode Island, on October 25.
Opposite: A. M. Willard's painting "The Spirit of '76" (perhaps better known as "Yankee Doodle") summarizes the patriotism of the Revolutionary War for many people.

only a small scale. In November 1781, Washington marched his men back to the blockade of New York and established his headquarters at Newburgh. De Rochambeau wintered with his forces in Virginia before returning to Rhode Island in the fall of 1782 en route to Boston, where the French army embarked and set sail for France on December 24. The only fighting of the period was the skirmishing around Charleston, where Greene was maintaining his blockade of the British base. Despite the fact that the British had clearly lost the war, the loyalists did not want to abandon the struggle. There were a number of border raids of a particularly bloody nature. Typical was the August 1782 raid from Quebec by loyalists and Indian supporters under the command of an American traitor, Simon Girty. With about 240 men Girty pushed across the Ohio River into what is now Kentuky attacking Bryan's Station on August 15. Driven back here, the raiders prepared an ambush of the type feared by Colonel

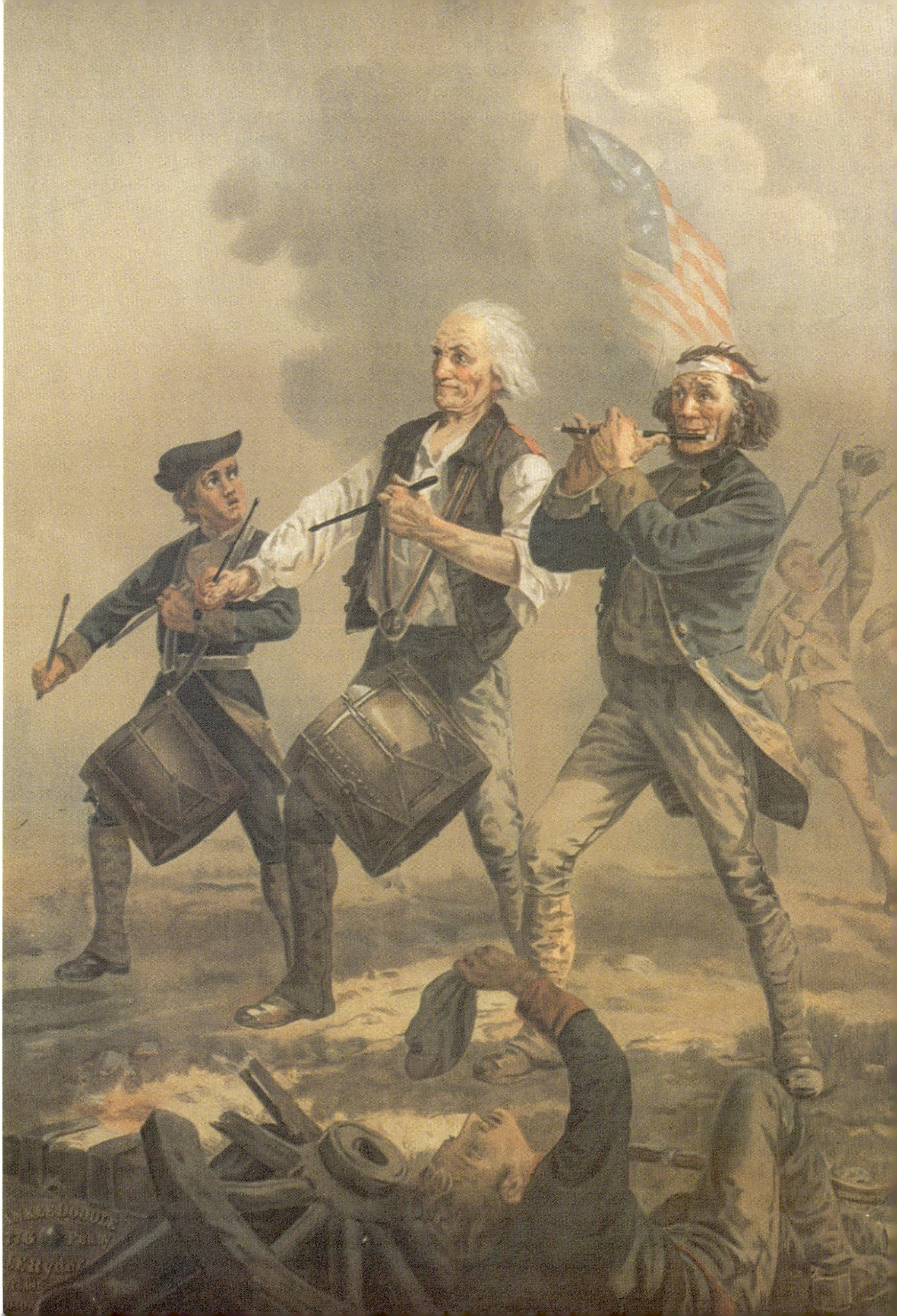

Left: Captain John Barry, commander of the frigate U.S.S. *Alliance* that completed a successful cruise in 1781.

Right: Engraved after George W. Maynard's commemorative painting entitled simply "76," this illustration again reveals the simple nobility with which the Revolutionary War has been characterized by later generations.

Daniel Boone and sprang it on the pursuing force at Blue Licks on August 19 before escaping to safety.

The year 1781 marked the high point in American privateer operations against the British, but the only regular naval action undertaken in this year by the Americans was the cruise of the U.S.S. *Alliance*, a frigate commanded by Captain John Barry. The American warship sailed to France and back, and on the return journey it captured two British sloops, H.M.S. *Atlanta* and H.M.S *Trepassy*, and also took a pair of British privateers.

Formal Independence for the United States

A new British government was formed on March 20, 1782, which began negotiations for peace on April 9. In New York, Sir Guy Carleton took over from Clinton, and

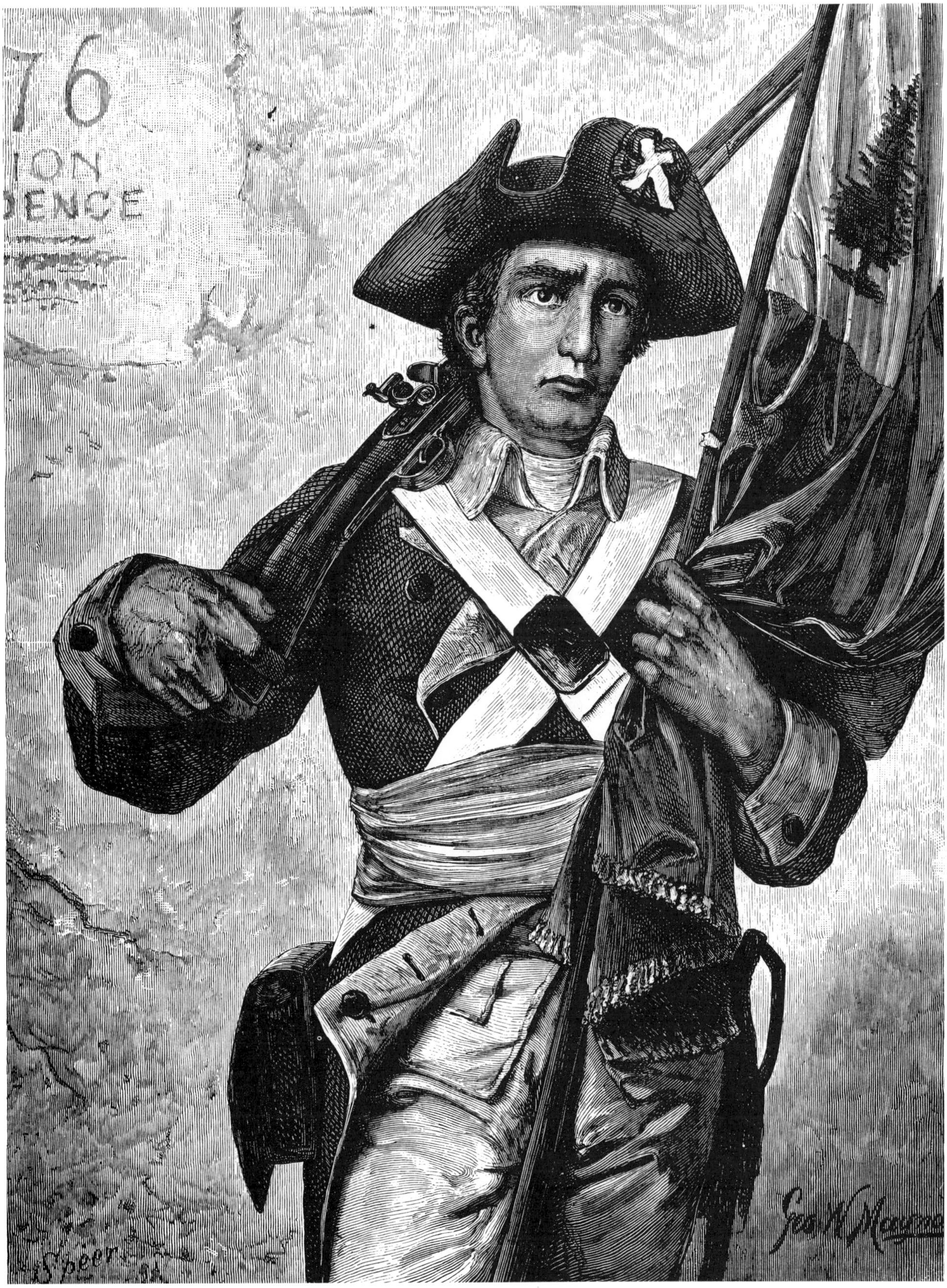
76
ION
DENCE

THE MILITARY HISTORY OF THE UNITED STATES

Below: Washington and his officers at the commander's farewell dinner, held in Fraunces' Tavern on the corner of Pearl and Broad Streets in New York, on December 4, 1783.

Right: Washington resigns as American commander-in-chief on December 23, 1783. Appearing before the Continental Congress in a session in Annapolis, Washington said: "...I retire from the great theater of Action; and bidding an Affectionate farewell to this August body under whose orders I have so long acted, I here offer my Commission and take my leave of all the employments of public life."

the work of evacuating all British troops to New York continued. Wilmington had been evacuated in January, Savannah was cleared on July 11, and troops left Charleston on December 14. On November 30, the Treaty of Paris was signed, to become effective on the conclusion of British hostilities with France and Spain in the Mediterranean, the West Indies, and off the coast of India. The treaty recognized the independence of the United States and ended Great Britain's war with the new country. The Continental Congress ratified the treaty on April 15, and rapid demobilization of the Continental Army followed in June. Starting on November 23, the British evacuated New York, their last American toehold. On December 4, the day on which the last British transport sailed from New York, Washington said farewell to his officers at Fraunces' Tavern. On December 23, 1783, Washington formally resigned his commission at a special Congressional session and retired to private life. The Revolutionary War was finally over, and the United States was a nation with no foreign troops on its soil.

THE MILITARY HISTORY OF THE UNITED STATES

In 1783 the Revolutionary War ended and the United States of America became a sovereign nation as the last British troops were evacuated from New York. Even before the final withdrawal, the Continental Congress had started to demobilize its army, and various state militia units had already returned home.

It was a time for reflection on the reasons why the United States had won the Revolutionary War, and how best to maintain the new country as an independent state. George Washington, looking at the American difficulties throughout the eight years of the Revolutionary War, could explain the American victory only through the intervention of "Divine Providence" on the side of the 13 divided states to defeat Great Britain, at that time the most powerful country in the world. Historical hindsight suggests a number of more practical reasons including British strategic mistakes (especially in 1776-77 and 1780), Washington's leadership and the support provided by the French.

The "Generalship" Factor

All these factors contributed to the American victory, but there are a number of other matters that should be taken into account. Washington, for example, was not responsible for several of the decisive American victories of the war, so the generalship of Benedict Arnold, Nathanael Greene, Henry Knox and Daniel Morgan were also vitally important. The operational and tactical generalship of such leaders would have been useless without the dedication of the average officer and soldier of the Continental Army. Their commitment is shown by the way that the men drove themselves through the hardships of the march on Quebec, the crossing of the

George Washington
For further references see page 31.

The qualities that made George Washington a great general were the same ones that inspired all sixty nine members of the first Electoral College to vote for him in February 1789, to elect him as the first President of the United States of America. In his two terms as president, Washington faced problems as difficult as those he met as commander-in-chief of the Continental Army in the Revolutionary War.

The Continental Congress
For further references see page 36.

> **The Continental Army**
> For further references see page 34.

By the end of the 18th century, the sword had only limited practical use on the battlefield, except in the hands of the cavalry. Even so, the weapon was widely used especially as a distinguishing mark for officers. These European swords are an assortment used in the United States.

Delaware River before the Battle of Trenton, the dire winters at Valley Forge and Morristown, and Greene's forced marches in the southern campaign. The men on the British side often showed great heroism and determination, but they never needed the same degree of dedication that the American soldiers needed and possessed.

This dedication was also displayed by the frequently misunderstood militiamen. Some historians have said that the militia units were useless and that it was the men of the Continental Army who won the war. Others claim that the militiamen were the true citizen-soldiers who won the war. The truth lies somewhere between these two extreme views: the militiamen often made great contributions, though they would have counted for relatively little without the existence of the Continental Army as the permanent core around which the militia units could gather. The fact that militia units could, and did, appear wherever and whenever they were needed often negated the British victories over the Continental Army. This loyalty emphasizes the fact that another key factor in the American victory was the control established over the countryside by patriots before the war had even started. The British were therefore faced with the immensely difficult task of defeating not just an armed enemy in the field. Regardless of the numbers of loyalists that rallied to the British cause, the countryside was filled with those who wanted an independent America.

The Importance of French Support

Even so, only French aid enabled the Americans to win. Most of the small arms, bayonets, and cannon used by the Continental Army came from France. French naval power had diverted British strength to other areas and hampered the British control of the seas that was so important a part of their strategic arsenal. Finally, French manpower and technical skill assured the victory at Yorktown that had been created by Washington's strategic skill.

As the dust of the war began to settle, some far-sighted Americans began to realize that French support had been needed mainly because the American effort lacked any real central direction. Much as Americans in general might not want a strong central government, it was clear that such a government was needed for the control of a major war effort. It is hardly surprising, therefore, that when the Founding Fathers were drafting a new constitution in 1787, most of those who had commanded, or even held high administrative position, during the Revolu-

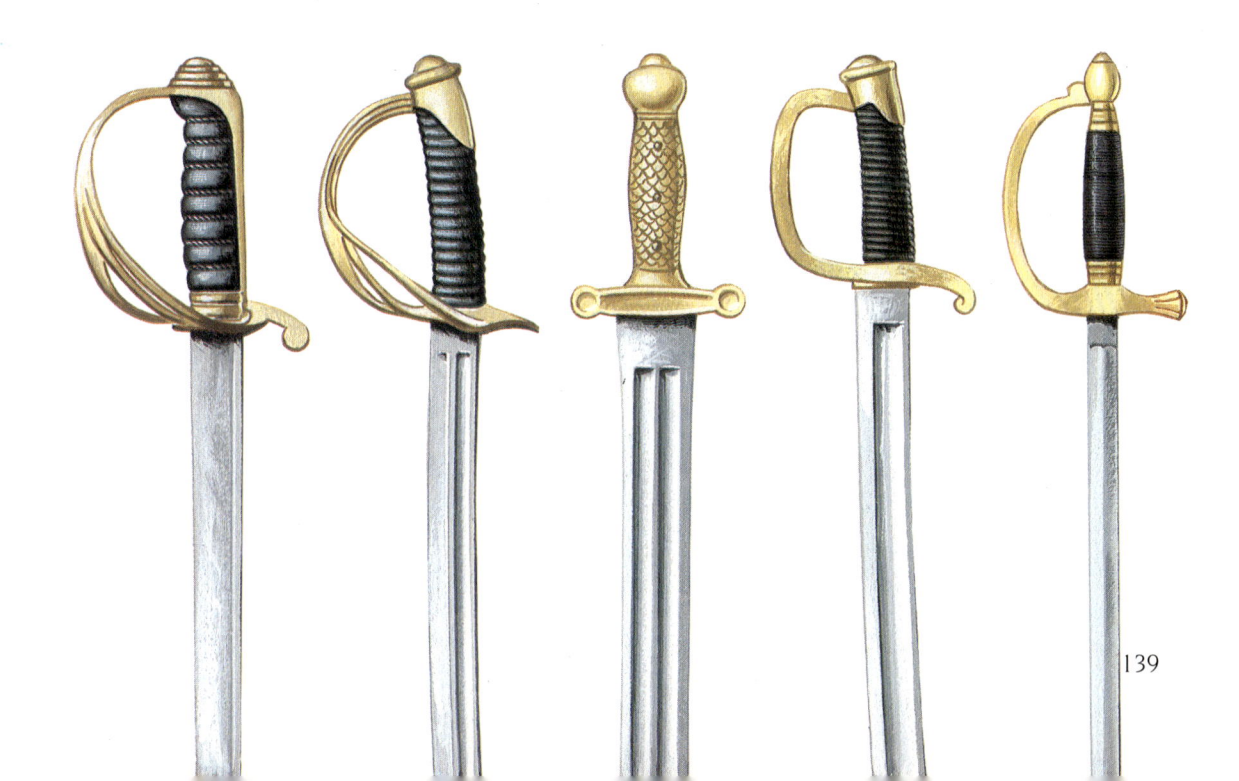

THE MILITARY HISTORY OF THE UNITED STATES

tionary War argued in favor of a central government with a moderately strong executive and the right to levy taxes directly on the people, to call out the militia, and, most important of all in purely military terms, to "raise armies and navies."

Tactical Conclusions Difficult to Reach

At a strictly military level it was more difficult to draw firm conclusions from the Revolutionary War. No completely new tactics were developed during the war. However, by the end of the war, a practice that had begun in the French and Indian Wars (1754-60) had become standard on both sides. European line formations, with men arranged in several ranks across the front, were used in conjunction with light infantry deployed forward of the main body as skirmishers. Ironically, the British adopted the American concept of skirmishers and fighting from behind cover wherever possible. The American army meanwhile tried to match the British discipline of fighting in ranks. Militia officers praised the rifle as a weapon that provided the accurate long-range fire. It had proved decisive in actions such as Saratoga and King's Mountain, both fought in hilly and wooded terrain. More sensible men pointed out that the rifle was slow to reload and also lacked a bayonet, which made it less useful than the smooth-bore musket for most military actions.

In the post-war assessment of the United States' future army requirements, some supported a large regular army. Others felt that most resources should be allocated to a militia army. As Washington saw, however, the problem did not lie with such a choice between a large regular army or large militia forces. Because of its geographical situation and political nature, the United States did not need or even want a large regular army. It needed a small professional army and comparatively large militia forces. The important thing, as Washington and others correctly saw, was that both forces should be organized and trained on similar lines to create a large and

Most of the firearms used by the Continental Army were imported. This German holster pistol, with a carved trigger tip and a carved stock is typical.

140

homogeneous national reserve. Such an organization would allow each state to raise and run its own militia force, but each of these "state armies" would be run according to standards decided at national level. The militia forces could be then called into effective national service in the event of war or any other national emergency. Washington and others wanted a limited form of what the French were soon to call "the nation in arms." This concept allowed political and economic freedom to be balanced by the obligation of all citizens to fight for the state when required.

In this can be seen the first step toward the "democratization of war." This ultimately led to the concepts of a national draft and, by extension, of total war waged at the national level.

Demobilization for the Continental Army

Even as the first military lessons of the Revolutionary War were being discussed in the Continental Congress and various military headquarters, the men of the Continental Army were growing restless. Through the winter of 1782-83, the army had become impatient with its treatment by the Congress. This impatience became clear when anonymous pamphlets began to enter circulation among the officers of the garrison at Newburgh. One pamphlet urged the officers to lay down their arms if peace was declared but their pay was not settled. Another argued that the officers should refuse to fight even if the war was not ended. Washington was all too aware that his officers and men had many real grievances. In a direct approach, he offered to fight their case with the Congress. Eventually, he won a full settlement of back pay for the men, and five years' full pay for the officers in place of half pay for life. With this thorny problem settled, men started to leave the Continental Army as early as June 1783. However, it was not until September 24, just four days after the Treaty of Paris had become effective, that the Congress ordered Washington to demobilize "such parts of the Federal Army now in Service as he shall deem proper and expedient." Washington decided to keep the force facing the British in New York, but demobilized the rest of the Continental Army. When the British finally pulled out of New York, the commander-in-chief ordered that only one infantry regiment and one artillery battalion (600 men) should be kept in service to protect the major depot at West Point and some other smaller depots.

The Hamilton Committee

The Congress was meanwhile beginning its definitive survey of the type of army the United States would be needing in the future. A committee, headed by Alexander Hamilton, was to study the facts and make recommendations. The Congress was already worried that the Newburgh situation showed the army's inclination toward coercion of the states. Some feared that this tendency might lead to a military dictatorship. The Congress therefore veered toward the establishment of a militia army. It felt that a "well-regulated and disciplined militia

Alexander Hamilton
For further references see pages 145, 146, 153, 154.

New York
For further references see pages 140, 146, *147*, 149, 185, 187, 228.

THE MILITARY HISTORY OF THE UNITED STATES

REVOLUTIONARY AND EARLY AMERICAN WARS

President George Washington reviews the Western Army at Fort Cumberland in about 1795.

U.S. Captain, 2nd. Sublegion of the Regular Army (1795)

Under Major General "Mad Anthony" Wayne, the regular army for the wars against the Indian tribes of the Northwest was reorganized into the Legion, which was then further divided into four Sublegions. Men of the Legion's infantry wore a blue coat with red facings, and a leather cap or ordinary round hat trimmed with a roach of bearskin, a cloth band, a cockade, and a feather. By an order of September 11, 1792, the men of the 1st Sublegion wore a cap with black hair and a white band and plume; those of the 2nd Sublegion a cap with white hair and a red band and plume; those of the 3rd Sublegion a cap with black hair and a yellow band and plume; and those of the 4th Sublegion a cap with white hair and a green band and plume. Company officers wore the same headgear as their men, while field officers wore the standard cocked hat with the appropriate sublegion feather. It should be noted, however, that this was the parade dress, worn with pipe-clayed belts, polished brass and, in the case of officers, powdered wigs. In the field, however, the men reverted to the more practical fringed hunting jacket.

REVOLUTIONARY AND EARLY AMERICAN WARS

One of the major difficulties faced by the fledgling United States at the end of the 18th century was consolidation and control of its northwestern frontier. The local Indian tribes and the Canadian-based British both had a vested interest in spoiling American ambitions. The disputed area was potentially rich, but presented many military problems. These problems were worse in winter, as this painting of a scouting party suggests.

sufficiently armed and accoutered" was militarily adequate, avoided the expense of a regular army, and simplified the argument between those wanting a strong central government and the adherents of the present situation of loosely federated states.

Not unnaturally, Hamilton's committee turned first to Washington, who pointed out the financial and political dangers of a large regular army. He urged the creation of a citizens' militia enrolling all manpower aged between 18 and 50 years, with a volunteer militia recruited as units and trained periodically for use under national rather than state control. Washington had also correctly analyzed the British use of seapower in the Revolutionary War. He advised setting aside available funds for "building and equipping a Navy without which, in case of War we could neither protect our Commerce, nor yield that assistance to each other which, on such an extent of seacoast, our mutual safety would require." Washington also felt that a small regular army of one artillery and four infantry regiments (2,630 men) would be an asset "to awe the Indians, protect our Trade, prevent the encroachment of our Neighbors of Canada and the Floridas, and guard us at least from surprises; also for security of our magazines."

Key Role for the Militia

The Hamilton committee also listened to advice from other officers and to Benjamin Lincoln, the Secretary of War. It recommended a scheme based on Washington's concept, but with a more capable militia component. The committee's advice was rejected by the Congress, largely on economic grounds, although constitutional problems and the rivalry of congressional factions also contributed. The Hamilton committee then reworked its recommendations. Eventually, it came up with a plan for a larger army that would cost the Congress less. The regimental officers would be paid at a lower rate than in the original scheme. Washington maintained that a larger army for less pay was not realistic, but he admitted that the need to provide for detached service along the frontiers and coasts demanded a larger army than

145

he had recommended. The Congress agreed with Washington on the impossibility of providing a larger army for less money. When the Hamilton committee's revised scheme was presented on October 23, the Congress refused to accept it. Matters rested there through the winter of 1783-84. Under the terms of the Articles of Confederation ratified in 1781, the "yes" vote of at least nine states was needed for the Congress to decide a number of important issues, including military affairs. During that winter, there were few times when the Congress had enough members present for a decision to be reached.

The debate about a permanent army was renewed in the spring of 1784, but it got bogged down in a dispute about state claims to the western territories. The army was then at a strength of one infantry regiment and one artillery battalion. Most of the men were provided by Massachusetts and New Hampshire, but they were unwilling to continue giving the men the additional pay they had been offered to enlist. The Congress said that it would take over responsibility for payment, but only if the New England states would vote for the permanent military establishment that was proposed. The New England representatives argued that the Congress had no mandate to maintain a standing army. At the same time, however, they were urging the Congress to use the existing army to occupy forts located in the western territories claimed by the New England states. This request met vigorous opposition from New York, which denied the New England claims to western territories (especially in the area of Oswego and Fort Niagara). New York refused to vote for a permanent military establishment unless the western forts were occupied with New York troops.

British Occupation of American Territory

The forts under claim were those controlling the Great Lakes and the upper

The northern frontier of the United States between 1783 and 1812.

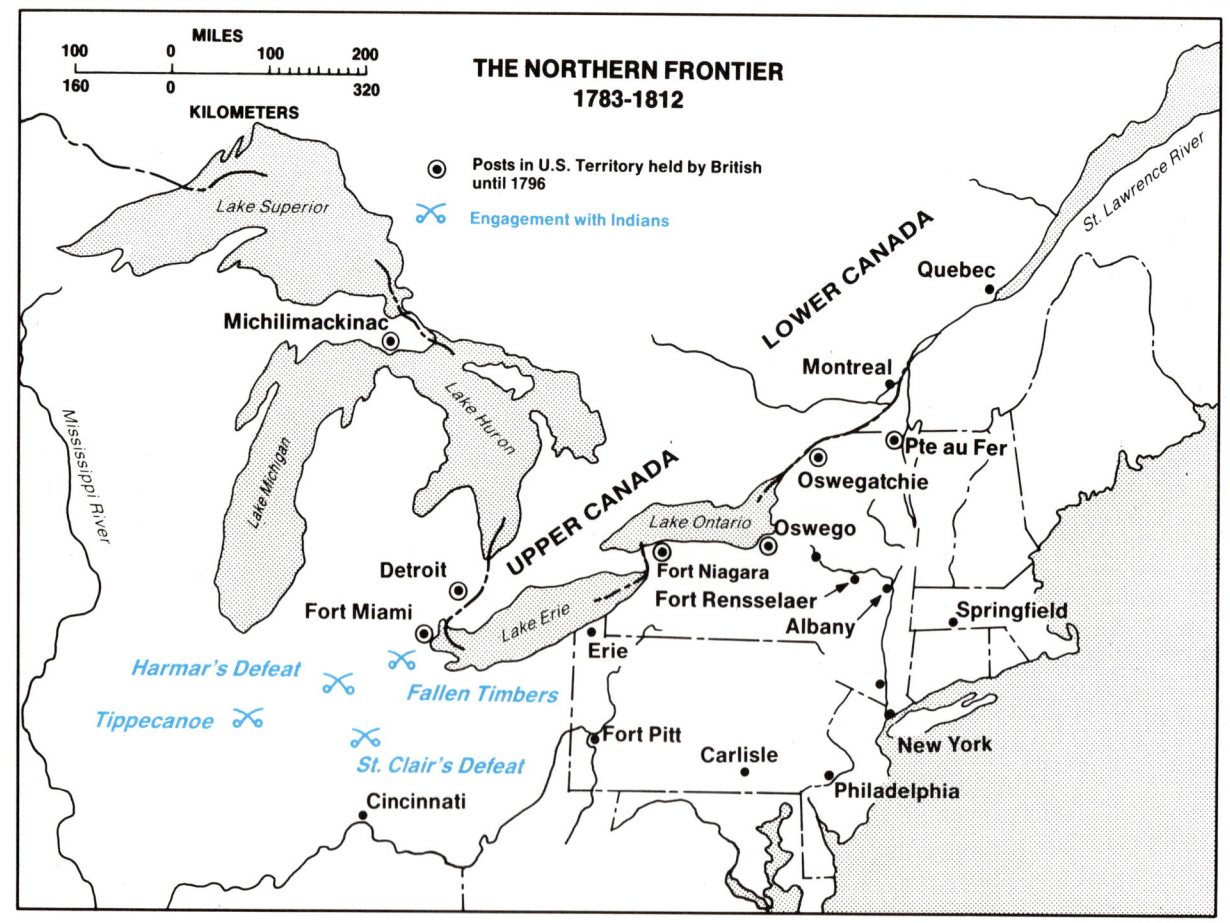

THE NORTHERN FRONTIER 1783-1812

◉ Posts in U.S. Territory held by British until 1796
⚔ Engagement with Indians

reaches of the St. Lawrence River. From east to west along the frontier between Canada and the United States, there were forts at Pointe au Fer at the northern end of Lake Champlain, Oswegatchie on the upper reaches of the St. Lawrence River, Oswego on the southern side of Lake Ontario, Fort Niagara on the northern side of the neck of land separating Lakes Ontario and Erie, Fort Miami at the western end of Lake Erie, Detroit on Lake St. Clair between Lakes Erie and Huron, and Michilimackinac on the southern side of the neck of land separating Lakes Michigan and Superior. All were in British hands at the end of the Revolutionary War, but were located in American territory as defined in the Treaty of Paris. The treaty provided for all of the forts to be handed over to the United States as rapidly as possible. The Congress agreed that a force should be available to occupy the forts as soon as the British left them, but could not agree how and by whom the troops were to be raised. A decision was needed urgently, because the Congress was negotiating a treaty with the resident Indian tribes. They understood that, as Washington had put it, a force "to awe the Indians" would be a useful negotiating asset. But New York was deadlocked with the New England states over the issue. It was June 1784 before the matter was resolved.

On the last two days of the Congressional session, a compromise was forced through. This measure ordered the disbandment of the existing infantry regiment and artillery battalion except for 80 artillerymen to guard the arsenals at West Point and Fort Pitt. Linked to the discharge of the existing force was an ar-

The Indian tribes were suspicious of American motives as the westward expansion gathered pace. Scenes such as this, with an Indian chief forbidding the passage of an American wagon train through his territory, inevitably led to clashes. These disputes became increasingly serious as the American government moved to protect its citizens.

THE MILITARY HISTORY OF THE UNITED STATES

rangement for the enlistment of a new force. Eight companies of one infantry regiment and two companies of artillery (800 men) would become the core of a new regular army. The Congress did not require the states to supply men, suggesting instead that the states provide them from their militia units. This sidestepped many of the objections of the New England states. By not imposing a quota on Massachusetts and New Hampshire, Congress met the objections of most of the other states.

The four states which were to provide troops were Pennsylvania (260 men), Connecticut (165 men), New York (165 men) and New Jersey (110 men). The commanding officer appointed for the new force was Lieutenant Colonel Josiah Harmar of Pennsylvania. By the end of September 1784, only New Jersey and Pennsylvania had supplied their quotas by enlisting volunteers from their militia units.

Payment for Loyalists Demanded From the United States

While the United States was struggling to establish the core of a regular army, the Congress learned that the British had little intention of leaving the forts named in the Treaty of Paris. Incensed by this treaty provision, fur trading companies with interests in upper Canada (the area that is now Ottawa) had joined forces with settlers to exert political pressure. The British government had with great secrecy instructed the governor-general of Canada not to evacuate the forts without direct instruction from London. When the matter came to light, the British government said that it was retaining the forts

Friction between the Indians and American settlers in the Northwest produced a crop of increasingly bloody episodes as raid was followed by counter-raid. Much heated "propaganda" emerged, such as this picture entitled "Massacre of the Christian Indians," claiming that "of the number cruelly murdered by the backwoodsmen of the upper Ohio, between fifty and sixty were women and children - some of them innocent babes."

148

REVOLUTIONARY AND EARLY AMERICAN WARS

The Indians proved themselves masters of the type of irregular warfare waged along the frontier, and this Indian war party is typical of the bands that launched many "hit and run" raids on the settlers who encroached ever more frequently on Indian lands.

because the United States had failed to implement another treaty provision. This involved the recovery of debts owed to loyalists, of whom at least 40,000 had moved into Canada after the end of the Revolutionary War.

In these circumstances, the New Jersey contingent of the new army was sent to Fort Stanwix on the upper reaches of the Mohawk River in New York to play its part in persuading the Iroquois to abandon their lands. Meanwhile, the Pennsylvania contingent was sent to Fort MacIntosh, 30 miles down the Ohio River from Fort Pitt, to play a similar role against the Delaware. Since 1660, this tribe had been drifting west from their original homes on the eastern seaboard after their defeat by the Dutch in the Esopus War. It was not until 1796 that the British finally handed over the seven frontier forts in question.

As the United States emerged from the turmoil of the Revolutionary War, it became increasingly clear that there were severe defects in the new nation's system of government. The most important were the central government's lack of an executive and a judiciary. As a result of the ratification of the Articles of Confederation, the Congress could manage to a certain extent in these two fields. Then the greatest stumbling block faced by the Congress as an instrument of central government was its lack of the legal right to levy taxes. This absence of any real central power worried many of the delegates to the Congress. They felt that the new nation did not have the strength to survive a possible civil war which they felt could break out as a result of constant bickering about the western territories. Another indication of trouble to come was rioting in Massachusetts, which started in August 1786 and continued during the winter of 1786-87. The riots were caused mainly by an economic depression, which had followed the postwar economic boom. It inflicted great hardship on back-country farmers, and mobs formed in the Massachusetts hills. They halted the judicial process completely by breaking up court meetings and harassing lawyers. In a more obviously threatening move, the mobs seemed to be heading toward the government arsenal at Springfield, Massachusetts.

Shays' Rebellion (1786-87)

As the situation worsened, the Congress acted on October 20, 1786. Several states were urged to contribute to a force of 1,340 men to serve for three years. This time, there was no delay by the New England states, but before the complete

THE MILITARY HISTORY OF THE UNITED STATES

Shay's Rebellion began in 1786. It was caused by unfair taxation and cruel evictions. Here is a sample eviction notice.

To the Constables of the Town of Pittsfield in the County of Berkshire, or either of them, greeting. Whereas it has been represented to us that Elisha Eggleston, his wife and family; John French, his wife and family; Calvin Dunham, his wife and family, - are likely to become burdensome and chargeable to the town if they continue their residence in it, these are therefore to authorize and require you forthwith to warn and notify the above-named persons that they, with their families, immediately depart and remove out of the town, and not to return again, without giving security to the town.

The Massachusetts government called out the militia to crush the rebellion. In their ranks were many Revolutionary War veterans. One of the Lancaster volunteers had served under Captain Daniel Shays during the Revolution. When the militia and volunteers mustered at Worcester, an observer described them:

They are as fine a body of men as were ever assembled, composed of the most respectable characters in the places where they were raised. A circumstance worth relating is: there are in this regiment fifty or sixty persons who have borne commissions, some of which to command regiments in the late continental army and militia, who do duty in the ranks and submit to the hardships attendant on a soldier's life in this inclement season, with a spirit of patriotism and cheerfulness which nothing but the cause they are engaged in could inspire.

In the winter of 1787, General Benjamin Lincoln sent soldiers on sleighs across the countryside to capture the rebels. Learning of success, he recommended that most of the prisoners receive lenient treatment:

To Major-General Paterson
Dear Sir: I congratulate you on our late success. I have no doubt but we shall have it in our power in a short time to disperse the people now in arms against the Government, and that if the Legislature in their present session shall act with decision and firmness we shall effectually crush the present Rebellion.

If among the insurgents there are any youth or simple men in years, who, from the want of the means of information or from the want of abilities to apply to right objects the information they do receive, such persons I think might be permitted to return to their several homes, after giving up their arms (such men ought not at present to hold them) & taking the oath of allegiance to the Commonwealth.

Those of another Class who have known better than they have acted & are now so convinced of their error, as that their liberation, under bond, may not be dangerous to the well affected, they I think might also be liberated on taking the oaths; There are another class, who, I think should be committed by a warrant from a Justice of the Peace being too inimical to be at large.

I am fully in sentiment with you, that you should not at present, attempt the arresting the most dangerous characters.

Shays has pushed himself into Pelham where he has the strongest ground. I hope however that we shall have it in our power soon to dislodge him: it would be too great a division of our force to detach at present; the earliest opportunity will be embraced for doing it.

You must I think be perfectly secure by keeping your men together as the Insurgents cannot now collect in force without your knowledge & may be taken in detachment.

You may assure all the privates in your division that if they sill surrender themselves, give up their arms & take the oath of allegiance to the State before some Justice of the Peace in your County that they will be recommended to pardon

I have the honor of being Dear Sir with real Esteem
Your obedt. Serv.

B. LINCOLN

Officer Ranks in the U.S. Army (1776-1800)

Ensign
Lieutenant
Captain
Major
Lieut. Colonel
Colonel
Brigadier General
Major General
Lieut. General

---

force could be raised, the local militia had handled the problem in Massachusetts. This event became known as Shays Rebellion.

Late in January 1787, a portion of the Massachusetts mob led by Daniel Shays attacked the Springfield Arsenal, but was driven back by Massachusetts militiamen. A few days later, a larger force of militiamen from the eastern part of the state arrived in the area and joined with local forces to put down the last remnants of the disorders.

By April 1786, the new force authorized by the Congress had grown by 550 men, whose pay was becoming an embarrassment to a Congress which no longer needed the force. The Congress thus ordered the states to stop recruiting and in fact discharge the men already enlisted, retaining only the two artillery companies required to provide a guard for West Point and Springfield Arsenal. The Massachusetts rebellion is therefore notable for having spurred the first growth in federal forces. It persuaded Americans in general that there was a good case for a stronger central government as the only body that could respond with adequate speed and firmness to any such emergency.

The 1787 Constitutional Convention

These concerns about national security and the nature of the army combined with worries about finance and commercial regulation. The result was a Constitutional Convention that met in the spring of 1787. The main focus of the Convention was the need for a central government with power to regulate military, financial, and commercial affairs. The Convention also concerned itself with how such power could be limited to prevent the central government from becoming too strong. The subject that caused the most concern to the Convention delegates was the military. A general fear about the dangers of a standing army combined with suspicion about the corruptibility, both moral and physical, of a strong central government. The delegates finally decided after much argument that it was necessary to sacrifice a little freedom for the United States to be safer in the purely military sense. It was decided accordingly that the central government should have considerable military power, but that this power should be checked and balanced by features built into the new Constitution.

The Constitution gave the central government power to raise and maintain an army without making demands on the states. To achieve this military objective, the central government was given the authority to levy taxes to provide the necessary resources. The creation of an entirely new executive branch allowed the day-to-day running of the government without constant reference to the states. However, the exclusive right to declare war, to raise armies, and to create a navy was reserved to the Congress, which also received the right to execute the Laws of the Union, suppress Insurrections and repel Invasions. At the same time, the power of Congress over the militia was limited. While Congress could undertake the organization, equipment, and discipline of the militia and also control "such Part of them as may be employed in the Service of the United States," the states were responsible for the appointment of officers and the training of the militia "according to the discipline prescribed by Congress."

Executive Power to the President

The most important new feature of the Constitution was the giving of all executive power to an elected president. From the military point of view, therefore, the Secretary of War was now responsible not to Congress but to the President, who was named in the Constitution as the Commander-in-Chief of the Army and Navy. In this capacity, the President's powers were very large, but limited "by their nature and by the principles of our institutions." The president could assume command of the forces in the field, but could also delegate this power. The president also became responsible for the

THE MILITARY HISTORY OF THE UNITED STATES

use and disposition of the armed forces during peace, and for their overall direction in war.

Perhaps inevitably, the first president was George Washington, who assumed office on April 30, 1789. Congress created the Department of War on August 7 of the same year. In the short term, this was an administrative modification that had little effect on military affairs. Major General Henry Knox remained in charge of the department just as he had headed the army in succession to Washington under the previous system of government. There was no navy as such, so there was no Department of the Navy, and the limited number of naval matters was handled by the Department of War. By now a brigadier general, Harmar was confirmed in his post along with all his officers, so the existing military establishment was taken into the new system in its entirety. At the time that the Department of War came into existence, the United States Army totaled about 800 officers and men. With the exception of the two artillery companies stationed at West Point and Springfield Arsenal, this force was deployed along the Ohio River in a line of forts created after 1785.

Henry Knox
For further references see pages 138, 153, 156, 157, 161.

Continued Supply Problems

The most important problem faced by the new army was the same one that had plagued the old army, namely supply. The military wisdom of the day said that a quartermaster department was necessary only in war. Therefore, in 1783, the quartermaster general and his staff had been among those discharged from the Con-

A lithograph of Fort Harmar in 1790 depicts this type of frontier post more idyllically than realistically. It suggests that rural Virginia has been transplanted neatly to the northwest.

tinental Army in favor of a system of civil supply organized by the Secretary of War and funded by the Board of Treasury. This meant that while the Treasury procured and paid for all military supplies, the Secretary of War was responsible for the storage and distribution of these supplies. With the exception of a short time when the Secretary of War was made responsible for food and clothing, the same system was adopted by the new federal government. The one major change was the establishment in 1792 of an Office of the Quartermaster General under civil control for the movement of supplies to frontier posts during the expeditions against the Indians. A more formal organization along the same lines came into being during 1794 with the establishment of the Office of Superintendent of Military Stores within the Department of War, and of the Office of the Purveyor of Public Supplies within the Treasury.

Despite the creation of these new offices, little changed at the practical level of buying and distributing supplies. Contracts were awarded to the lowest civilian bidder for the purchase and delivery of supplies to the men at the contracted military post. Each contractor was obliged to have enough food to feed the troops at all times, and to provide food for at least six months in advance to the more distant posts. Purchase, storage, and transportation of all other supplies were the tasks of a central depot in Philadelphia, where the Superintendent of Military Stores was responsible for issue to the troops as needed. The result of the system was indeed economy, but the food was generally poor and all supplies arrived late.

American Sources of Weapon Procurement

Weapons were supplied through a similar system. As early as 1783, Hamilton had said that the "public manufacture of arms, powder etc." would offer great advantages in terms of guaranteeing the United States independence from foreign deliveries. This sentiment was echoed ten years later by Knox, who told Congress that, while arms could be bought more cheaply in Europe, this was of little importance "compared with the solid advantages which would result from extending and perfecting the means upon which our safety may ultimately depend." Congress was partially convinced by this

A Kentucky pistol of the late 18th century. This flintlock weapon was as distinctive as the Kentucky long rifle. Made in about 1780 by Clark & Son, of London.

argument. The number of American arsenals and magazines was expanded for the storage and supply of more weapons and their ammunition, while national armories were established for the manufacture of weapons. The first national armory was established in 1794 at Springfield, Massachusetts, with a second at Harper's Ferry, Virginia, during the same year. Even so, it was many decades before the United States became independent of European arms supplies.

Control of the Militia Remains in State Hands

The basis on which Washington and Hamilton had argued for the creation of a small standing army was the coexistence of considerably larger militia forces that could boost the numbers of men available in emergencies and wars. The efficiency of these reserve forces would rest on their levels of equipment and training, but Washington and Hamilton were unsuccessful in their efforts to have the militia made subject to federal regulation. In May 1792, Congress passed the basic militia law, which demanded the enrollment of "every able-bodied white citizen" between the ages of 18 and 45 into state companies, battalions, regiments, brigades, and divisions; each militiaman was to be responsible for providing his own weapon, ammunition, and clothing. The result was not the federally controlled militia seen as essential by Washington and Hamilton, but the maintenance of the original militia concept of colonial days with control exercised by the individual states. The importance of the act did not lie in the creation of an effective militia, but in maintaining the American ideal of the citizen-soldier. More important by far in the provisions of the act was the creation of volunteer units to bolster the compulsory system. These volunteer units were formed as companies under elected officers. They trained regularly and formed the basis from which the National Guard was eventually created.

In general, the militia units were not well trained or well disciplined. This was no hindrance to simple military tasks such as defense in fixed fortifications, but made it very difficult to use the militia as an effective field force. The usefulness of the militia was further reduced by the limits imposed by law on militia tours of duty and the circumstances under which such units could be called into federal service. The militiaman could be called for service in no more than three months in any year, for example, and could not be ordered to serve outside the United States.

The Whiskey Rebellion (1794)

The first occasion on which the president had to call out the militia was the Whiskey Rebellion of 1794. In the western part of Pennsylvania, there had been considerable unrest and resistance to Congressional law since July 1794. Washington responded by sending in a major militia force under Major General Henry Lee. In the face of this armed strength, the unrest faded away without resistance during November of the same year. To this extent, the effort of the militia was completely successful, but Lee's "campaign" failed to provide any indication of the militia's capabilities in a real emergency, civil or military.

In the later 1780s and 1790s, the United States thus found it difficult to create an effective army and its supporting force of militia units. Under these circumstances, the military policy adopted by the United States sensibly took account of four basic factors. First, there was little real threat to the United States. Although Great Britain and Spain wished to prevent the new nation's expansion into their own territories, there was no British wish to reverse the result of the Revolutionary War. Second, the jealous maintenance of states' rights made the creation of a federal army very difficult and defeated all attempts at realistic federal influence on their militia units. Third, the federal government lacked the money to create any more than the framework of an army. Finally, Americans in general were extremely reluctant to serve in the army for more than the briefest time as either a regular or a volunteer. The results were a regular

---

Officer Ranks in the U.S. Navy (1800-1850)

Midshipman
Sailing Master
Lieutenant
Lieut. Commanding
Master Commandant
Captain
Rear Admiral
Vice Admiral

army that never reached its authorized strength and militia units that were not effective reserves for the regular army.

Trouble in the New Territories

There may have been no external threat to the United States, but in the new territory ceded by Great Britain in 1783, there was plenty of trouble. Settlers were moving into this vast area, larger by far than the original 13 colonies. Their numbers were swelled by ex-soldiers of the Continental Army, who were given grants of land. Both groups wanted government protection against the Indians as well as the establishment of a fair administration. Congress at first thought that a solution could be found in the creation of treaties with the various Indian tribes. But the treaties failed to cope with the problems caused by the large number of settlers and the speed with which they pushed west. The Indians fought back with bitter courage against the encroachment on their lands, aided by British weapons as well as the presence of the British to the north and west. The scale of the Indian effort is suggested by the death toll in 1787: in that year Indian raids resulted in the killing or seizing of about 1,500 settlers in the Kentucky territory alone.

Sporadic fighting went on along the entire new western frontier, but for a variety of reasons, the government refused to intervene in the southwestern region during the early years of the first presidential administration. The most telling of these reasons was the American treaty of 1790 with the Creeks, the most powerful of the Indian tribes in the southwest. They enjoyed the support of the Spanish in Louisiana, who wished to see no interruption in their profitable trade with the tribe. Direct intervention would have been difficult, because Georgia and South Carolina both made it clear

American problems with the Indians of the southern regions were not as acute as in the northwest. Nevertheless there was trouble, although it was sometimes nipped in the bud by the capture of local chiefs as shown in this illustration.

Army Unpopularity in the Northwest

The northwest was completely different. Here the main task of the army was protection of Indian treaty rights and the expulsion of squatters from public land. Necessary as these tasks were, they made the soldiers unpopular with the settlers and failed to provide the tiny numbers of troops with any realistic training for what was about to happen.

In 1786, the Ohio Company had been formed in Boston to buy from the American government a tract of land for settlement by New Englanders in what is now southeastern Ohio. In 1787, Congress enacted the Northwest Ordinance, a body of law to govern the western lands. Among its provisions were the right of any section of the territory to apply for statehood once its population had reached 60,000 persons, the setting aside of land in every township for the financing of local education, and the outlawing of slavery and involuntary servitude (debt bondage). An indication of the geographical scope of this western movement is provided by three events in one area of present-day Ohio. During April 1788 the first New England settlers began to arrive in the tract of 1,500,000 acres bought by the Ohio Company, traveling down the Ohio River in a clumsy riverboat to the point where the Ohio River is joined by the Muskingum River. Here they soon created the settlement that is present-day Marietta. Later in the same year, a flatboat loaded with New Jersey settlers passed Marietta and reached the mouth of the Little Miami River, where they established Losantiville near Fort Washington (now Cincinnati). In the same year, Virginia claimed a large tract along the Ohio River between the Great Miami and Scioto rivers as the Virginia Military District. It was parcelled out to Virginians who had fought in the Revolutionary War. These early movements soon became a flood of westward migration.

that they would object to the presence of federal forces in either state.

The Maumee War (1790-94)

The Indians were at first happy with their new neighbors, but soon realized that they were being squeezed out. Before long, the first fighting had broken out, and the settlers started to demand federal protection. Implicit in this demand was the threat that if the American government failed them, they would turn for aid to the British or Spanish, striking a severe blow to the unity of the new nation.

The government had not anticipated the problem and was slow to respond. In his first annual message to Congress, Washington demanded the defense of the frontier against the Indians. Congress responded by raising the authorized establishment of the regular army to 1,283 men. As Secretary of War, Knox realized that this force was completely incapable of undertaking what was being asked of it.

Major General Arthur St. Clair, painted by V. Ramage. St. Clair was governor of the Northwest Territory and, after Harmar's defeat in 1790 near the site of present-day Fort Wayne, Indiana, took command of the second expedition against the Maumee people. The Indians inflicted a devastating defeat on the Americans on the upper reaches of the Wabash River. At the time, St. Clair was suffering from asthma, rheumatism, and "colic."

> **Officer Ranks in the U.S. Marine Corps**
>
> Lieutenant
> Captain
> Major

He called in militia forces to bolster the regular army in their first task: punishing the Indians of the Maumee (or Miami) tribe for their raids against the settlers. Knox emphasized the planned expedition as a potent show of force to deter other Indian tribes from following the same route as the Maumee. Arthur St. Clair, local military commander as well as governor of the Northwest Territory, was appointed co-commander of the expedition with Harmar in June 1790. During the fall of the previous year, St. Clair had been authorized to call on the militias of Kentucky and Pennsylvania if needed, and he now demanded the assembly of 1,500 militiamen at Fort Washington to support Harmar.

Militia Support for the Regulars

As an officer with much experience of the militia's strengths and weaknesses in the Revolutionary War, Knox realized that while this reinforcement for Harmar might not amount to much in the conventional military sense, it offered advantages in fast-moving frontier warfare. Knox accordingly instructed Harmar to use the mounted militiamen as support for the regulars in a "rapid and decisive" expedition to seek out and destroy the Indian tribe and its food supplies. Remote from Knox's personal authority, Harmar and St. Clair instead devised a two-stage campaign completely lacking Knox's fast and decisive movement. Harmar planned a steady advance from Fort Washington north to the Maumee villages near the headwaters of the Wabash River. Under the command of Major John Hamtramck, a second force would advance 150 miles up the Wabash River from Fort Vincennes in present-day Indiana to destroy the Indian villages in this area before linking up with Harmar's force.

Harmar's Defeat

Not surprisingly, given the Indians' knowledge of the country and the American columns' ponderous and highly visible movement, the expedition was a major disaster. Hamtramck left Fort Vincennes on September 30 with the Virginia militia and 330 regulars. Eleven days later, the column had achieved little but the burning of a few villages, and the militiamen refused to move any farther up the Wabash River. Harmar departed from Fort Washington on the same day that Hamtramck left Fort Vincennes. For two weeks, this column of 320 regulars and 1,133 militiamen struggled through the wilderness before reaching the site of the main Maumee settlement near what is today Fort Wayne, Indiana. Harmar paused here, but then, instead of using his complete strength for a decisive attack, on three separate occasions between October 18 and 22, he sent forward detachments of 50 to 60 regulars and between 200 and 500 militiamen each. In each case, the regulars found themselves abandoned as the militiamen took off in search of Indians and booty. Two of these detachments suffered heavy losses in skirmishes with the elusive Indians, and Harmar then returned to Fort Washington after suffering the loss of 200 men. A great deal of criticism was leveled at Harmar, but a court of inquiry cleared the brigadier general on the grounds that he had been forced to use untrained troops and had been compelled to retreat because of the lateness of the season.

The lesson was there to be seen, but was blindly ignored when a second expedition was launched against the Maumee in 1791. The previous year's operations had convinced an unwilling Congress that the regular army was too small, and a second infantry regiment had been added to the authorized establishment. Congress also permitted Washington to enroll a corps of 2,000 men for six months, either from the militia or by enlisting volunteers into federal service. St. Clair was commissioned as a major general and placed in command of the expedition, but recruitment and the building up of supplies proceeded so slowly that it was September 17 before the expedition could depart. As it was, St. Clair could bring his force up to strength only by calling on the militia of neighboring states. The expedition used almost the entire infantry strength of the regular army, some 600 men, supported by 800 enlisted volunteers and 600 militiamen.

> **The Maumee**
> For further references see pages
> *156*, 158, 161, 162, *163*, 166.

> **Fort Washington**
> For further references see pages
> *146*, 156, 158, 162, *164*, *174*, 175.

> **Arthur St. Clair**
> For further references see pages
> *156*, 158, 161, 162, 166.

St. Clair's Defeat

The force moved off from Cincinnati, renamed from Fort Washington at St. Clair's instigation. By November 3, it had covered about 100 miles. On that night, St. Clair camped close to the waters of the Wabash River at a point close to what is today Fort Recovery, Ohio. The Maumee had noted the size of the expedition with alarm; but with considerable skill their chief, Little Turtle, had quickly created a confederation of several tribes. Some of the militiamen had already deserted, and, as the commander had neglected the elementary precaution of scouting the area, the rest of St. Clair's command was then taken completely by surprise when a force of Maumee, Shawnee, and Delaware Indians attacked just before dawn on November 4. Badly trained, poorly led by an officer suffering from rheumatism and asthma, and inadequately supplied, the Americans were decisively beaten. St. Clair escaped with less than half of his command, with 637 killed and another 263 wounded.

The defeat was a national scandal, and St. Clair resigned in disgrace. So great was the shock of St. Clair's defeat, moreover, that some Americans urged the government to abandon the war and instead take up the British suggestion of an Indian buffer state between the United States and the British possessions in North America. Washington was too

Above: St. Clair's defeat on November 4, 1791, was not the organized occasion suggested by this contemporary illustration, but a rout. The Indians fell on an American force taken completely by surprise; no scouts had been sent out.
Right: The Indian War of 1789-1794, showing the main locations and the sites of important engagements.

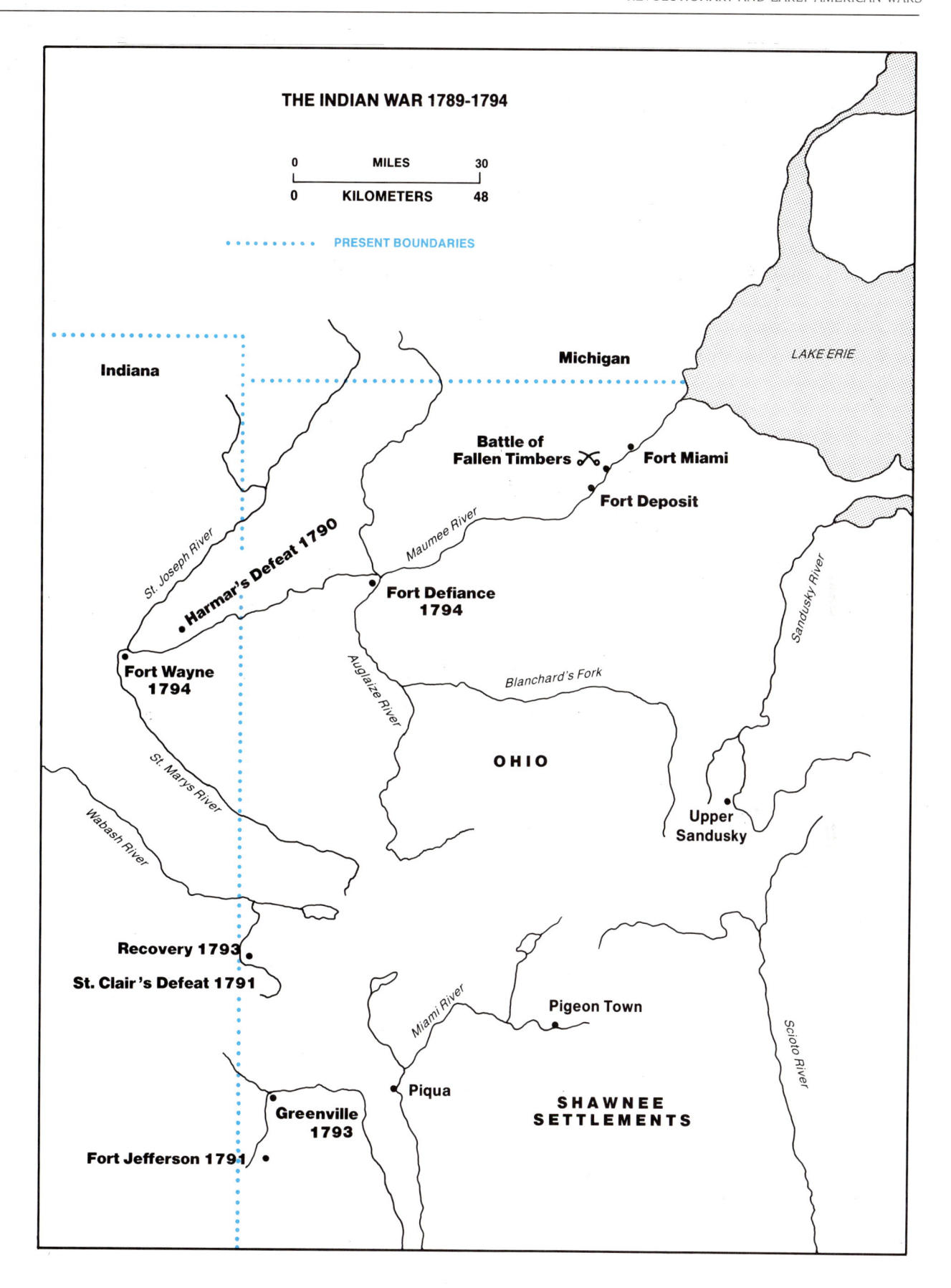

THE INDIAN WAR 1789-1794

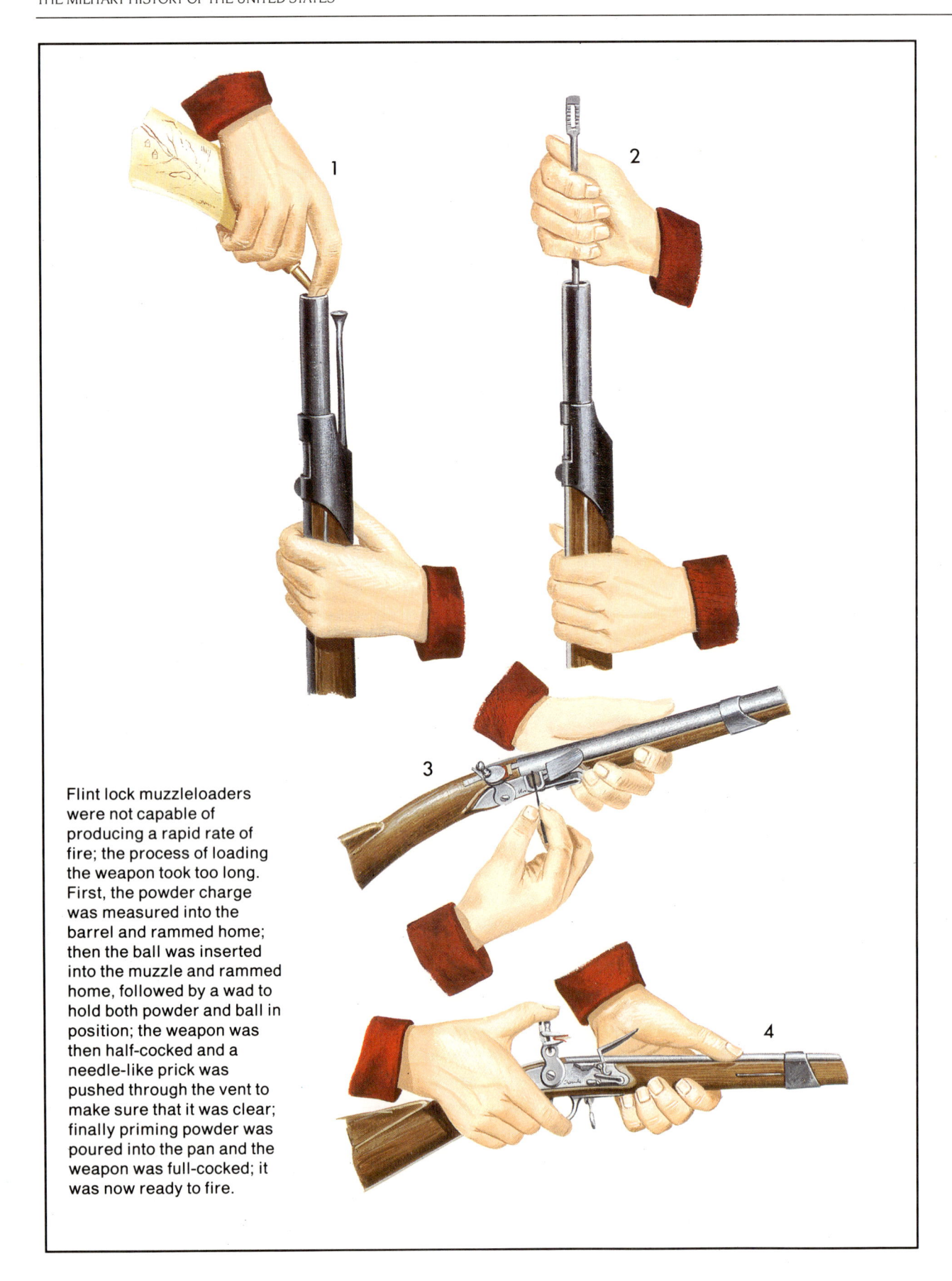

Flint lock muzzleloaders were not capable of producing a rapid rate of fire; the process of loading the weapon took too long. First, the powder charge was measured into the barrel and rammed home; then the ball was inserted into the muzzle and rammed home, followed by a wad to hold both powder and ball in position; the weapon was then half-cocked and a needle-like prick was pushed through the vent to make sure that it was clear; finally priming powder was poured into the pan and the weapon was full-cocked; it was now ready to fire.

REVOLUTIONARY AND EARLY AMERICAN WARS

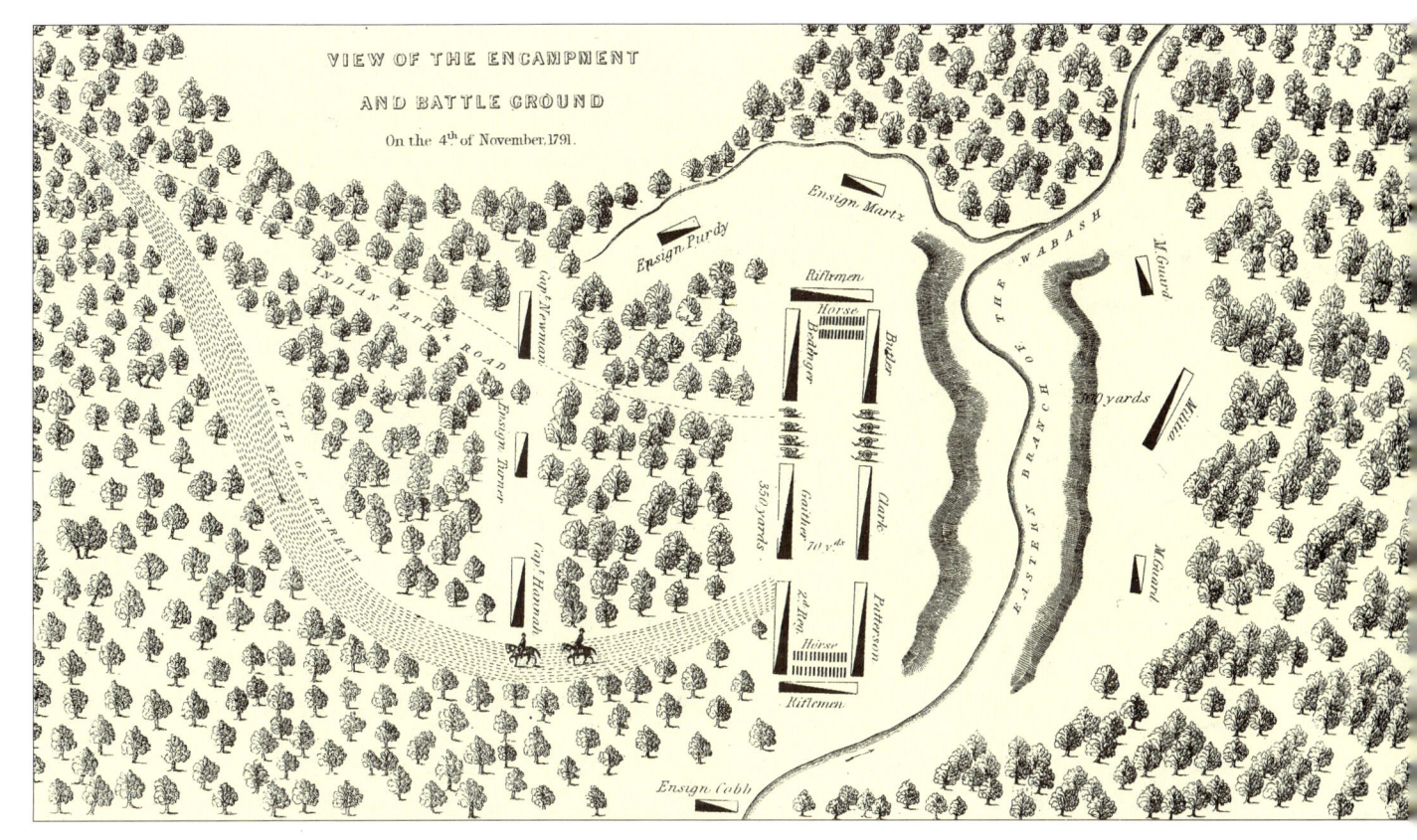

A contemporary illustration of the site of St. Clair's defeat on the upper Wabash River, and the disposition of the American forces at the time the Indians fell on them.

clever a political and military leader to be taken in by the superficial attractions of the concept. It would have antagonized the settlers and their supporters in several states and created a power vacuum that would inevitably have led to either or both powers being sucked in, possibly in conflict with each other. Washington therefore ordered the preparation of a third expedition against the Maumee, this time under the leadership of Major General Anthony Wayne. Recalled from retirement after having distinguished himself in the Revolutionary War, Wayne started training his command near Pittsburgh.

New Forces Raised

It was clear that extra forces would have to be found for the new campaign, and Congress effectively doubled the size of the regular army by authorizing three additional regiments, two of infantry and the third as a mixed infantry/light dragoon unit. Short-term enlistment had already shown its limitations, so Congress sought to avoid the problem by adding the new regiments to the army establishment to be "discharged as soon as the United States shall be at peace with the Indian tribes." At this time, Congress also agreed with Knox's suggestion that the army should be reorganized as a Legion. This name was extensively used in the period to mean a ground formation of the all-arms type. Infantry, cavalry, and artillery components under a single commander were expected to provide the capability for self-sufficient operations. The regular army was thus reorganized as four legions, each commanded by a brigadier general and consisting of two battalions of infantrymen, one battalion of riflemen, one troop of dragoons (cavalry that could fight on their horses or dismounted), and one company of artillery.

Wayne had acquired the nickname "Mad Anthony" in the Revolutionary War, and he was disliked in some circles for his self-centered nature. These characteristics were seldom in evidence as the commander prepared his offensive with a thorough program of training and an insistence that all supplies and equipment be adequate. Wayne demanded tight

161

discipline as he trained his command, and this paid handsome dividends when the carefully planned offensive was committed. In the spring of 1793, Wayne moved his force down the Ohio River to Cincinnati and tried to persuade the Indians to surrender. The offer was refused, and Wayne moved his force 80 miles north to Greenville on the river of the same name. There Wayne completed the preparation of his force during the summer, creating what was almost certainly the best trained force ever to be committed under the American flag. In July, Wayne was bolstered by the arrival of mounted militiamen, and in August, the 3,000-man force set off into the wilderness following St. Clair's route. In its methodical progress, Wayne's force built a series of forts and blockhouses along the line of communication. Despite the training and the commander's clear effort to secure his communications, desertion was still a problem. Morale began to fall before Wayne's command arrived near Fort Miami, recently built by the British on the site of what is now Toledo, Ohio. Here, on the site of present-day Defiance, the Americans caught up with the Maumee main body, which was gathered in a forest clearing created by a storm that had knocked down a number of trees.

The Battle of Fallen Timbers

The fighting on August 20 in the Battle of Fallen Timbers was brutally hard. Almost within range of the guns in the British fort, the Americans held their ground against a determined Indian attack under Little Turtle and, after one hour, counterattacked with the bayonet. The Indians were driven back and then out of the forest so that Wayne's cavalry reserve could launch a planned double encirclement. The result was a complete rout of the Indians at a cost of 33 American dead and another 100 wounded.

Despite the fact that his fort had been built illegally on American soil, the British commander protested about the American action. Wayne ignored the protest and remained in the area to destroy the Indian villages in the area and to burn the crops before returning to Cincinnati. The Battle of Fallen Timbers broke the spirit of the tribes in this region. In the Treaty of Greenville signed on August 3, 1795, the Indians made peace in an agreement that ceded all their lands in Ohio to the United States. The agreement was made more certain by news that reached them shortly before the treaty negotiations: the British were finally about to abandon their forts on American soil, making continued British support for the Indians improbable.

After the disasters that had befallen the expeditions of Harmar and St. Clair, much rested on the shoulders of Major General Anthony Wayne in the third expedition against the Indians of the northwest. This time,

REVOLUTIONARY AND EARLY AMERICAN WARS

the Americans prepared thoroughly and advanced methodically, and the Battle of Fallen Timbers was a major success that broke the will of the Maumee to resist the settlers any longer.

The Shawnee War (1811)

The suppression of the Maumee and their allies was good news for those waiting to move into the Northwest Territory, and settlers flooded into the region in larger numbers after the Treaty of Greenville. Ohio filled rapidly, which inevitably created pressure on the tribes further west as the flood of settlers showed no sign of ending. In their search for unoccupied farmland, the settlers pushed west past the limits of the territory ceded by the Maumee in the Treaty of Greenville, into the land of the Shawnees.

In the pattern established by the Maumee under Little Turtle, the Shawnee Chief Tecumseh and his brother, Shawnee Prophet, put together a confederation of Indian tribes throughout the Mississippi Valley to resist the settlers' encroachment into their lands. This alliance received active support from Anglo-Canadian fur interests, which viewed the "domestication" of the Shawnee lands with as much repugnance as the Indians themselves.

During 1800, Congress had divided the

163

THE MILITARY HISTORY OF THE UNITED STATES

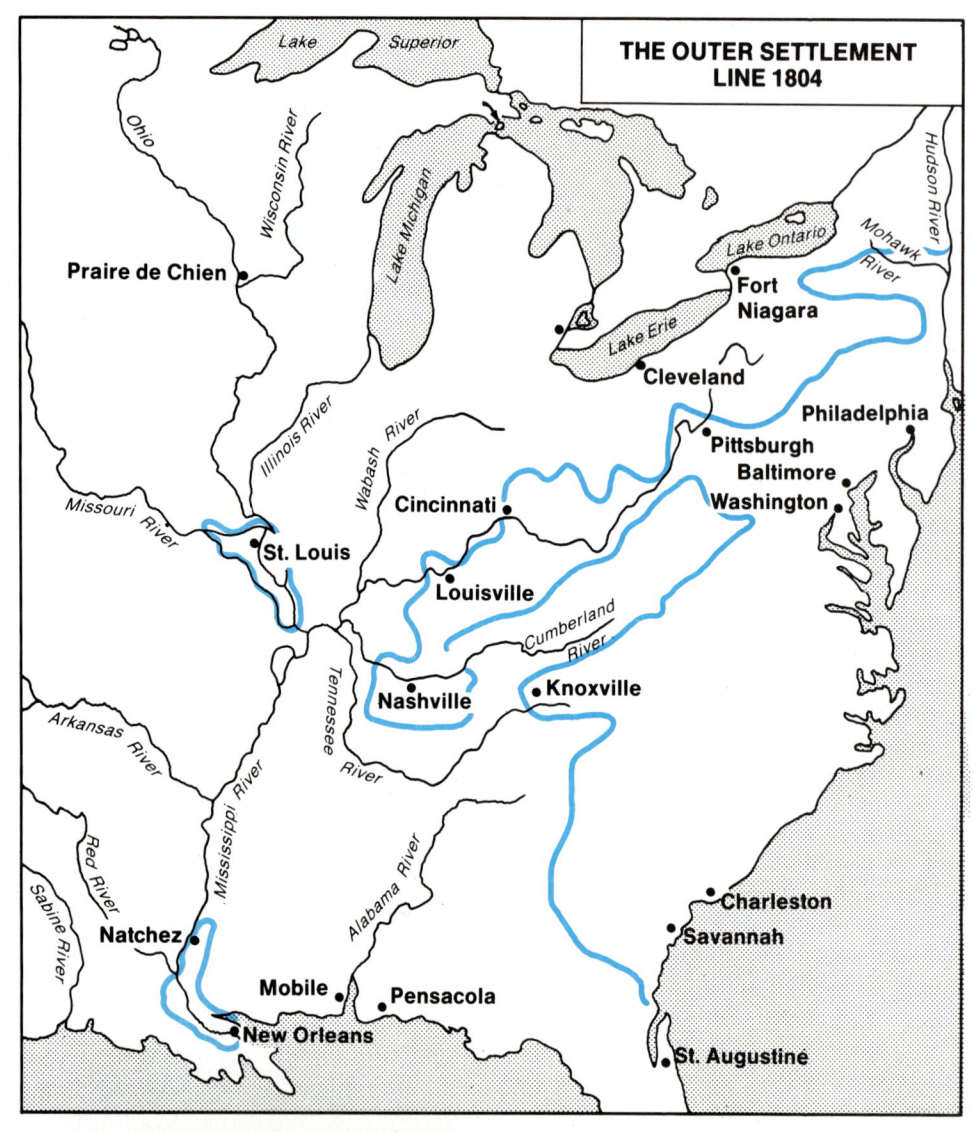

THE OUTER SETTLEMENT LINE 1804

This map of the outer limits of American expansion in 1804 shows how the opening of the Ohio and Cumberland rivers paved the way for development toward the junction of the Missouri and Mississippi rivers.

Right: Generally known as "The Prophet," Tenskwatawac was Tecumseh's brother and another notable Shawnee leader. This painting is by V. Inman.

Northwest Territory into two parts. The western section became the Indiana Territory, and the rest continued as the Northwest Territory. In 1811 the governor of the Indiana Territory was Brigadier General William Henry Harrison. He was urged by the settlers to pre-empt the Indian activities that were becoming inevitable as friction between the settlers and Indians became worse. Harrison agreed that a pre-emptive strike was necessary and devised an operation to defeat the Indians before they could organize any action against the settlers. The operation was approved by the Secretary of War, William Eustis, who added 300 regulars to Harrison's own force of 650 militia, which included a number of mounted riflemen.

Left: Chief Tecumseh of the Shawnee was one of the ablest Indian leaders faced by the Americans in this early phase of the United States' westward expansion.

William Harrison
For further references see pages 166, 172.

REVOLUTIONARY AND EARLY AMERICAN WARS

THE MILITARY HISTORY OF THE UNITED STATES

Women and Children
FALLING VICTIMS TO THE
INDIAN'S TOMAHAWK.

While many of our most populous cities have been visited by that dreadful disease, the Cholera, and to which thousands have fallen victims, the merciless Savages have been as fatally engaged in the work of death on the frontiers; where great numbers (including women and children) have fallen victims to the bloody tomahawk.

Left: An illustration of the period reveals how urban Americans were kept "informed" of conditions and events on the frontier.

Right: A major figure in the history of the northwestern expansion in this period was William Henry Harrison (1773-1841), seen here in an 1812 painting attributed to Rembrandt Peale. Harrison was the victor of the Battle of the Tippecanoe and then an important figure in the War of 1812.

The Battle of the Tippecanoe

Toward the end of September 1811, Harrison led his force north from Vincennes, built a fort on the edge of the Indian lands, and then pushed forward toward "Prophetstown," as the settlers dubbed the main Shawnee village on the Tippecanoe River about 150 miles north of Vincennes. The U.S. force halted on November 6 about a mile from the village on a piece of wooded high ground that commanded the marshy plain surrounding it on all sides. The troops camped in an irregular diamond pattern around the force's wagons. Harrison's situation was not unlike that which led to the defeat of St. Clair in the Maumee War, and it seemed for a time that his

The Shawnee
For further references see pages 163, 172, 179.

166

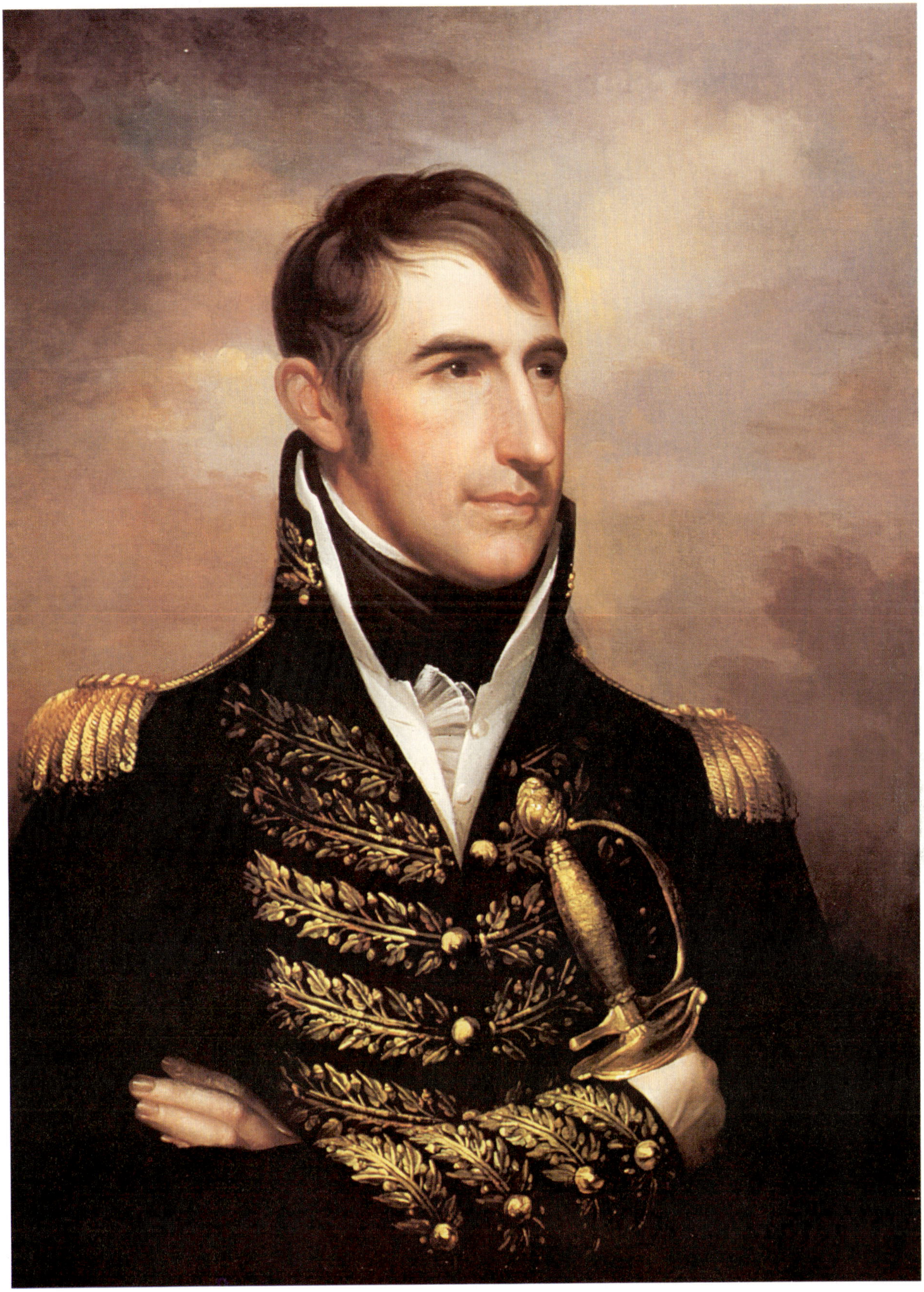

THE Military History OF THE UNITED STATES

Left: The vanguard of American expansion was provided by traders. The Indians initially welcomed the advantages of trade. When they realized that the traders were being followed by settlers, their attitude to the traders frequently altered, a situation encouraged by the British.
Below: The Battle of the Tippecanoe started with a Shawnee attack into the American camp, but the Americans then rallied and drove the Indians back until a virtual stalemate was reached.
Overleaf: The stalemate position in the Battle of the Tippecanoe was broken when mounted riflemen charged the Shawnee position and produced a decisive American victory.

U.S. Army, Light Artillery Regiment, Private (1808)

The Light Artillery Regiment was well equipped and very mobile, with all its men mounted on horses. It was therefore a very valuable support for the infantry, and its men considered themselves an elite force. There was also a militia light artillery company raised by the District of Columbia.

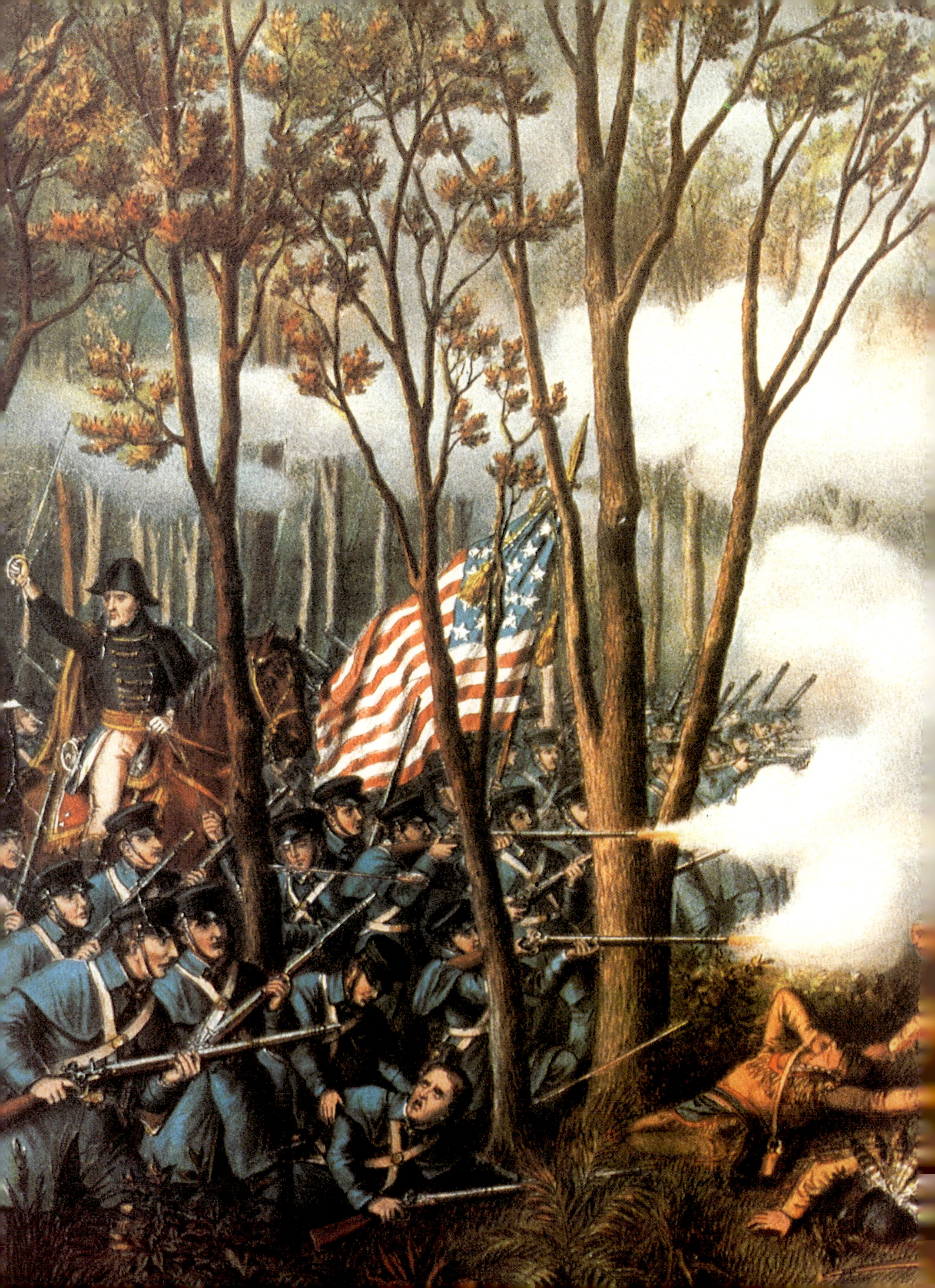

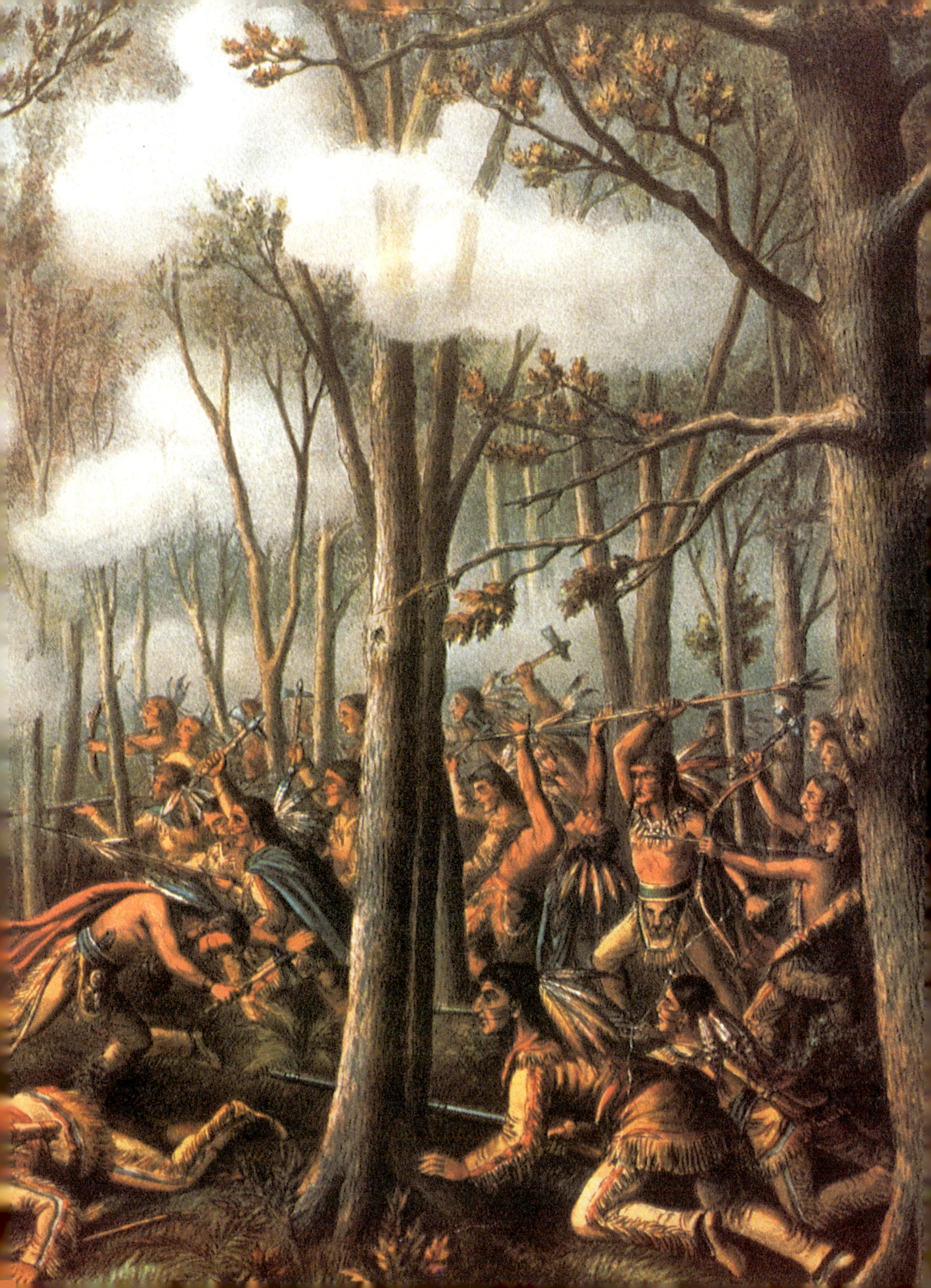

The original of this illustration of Brigadier General William H. Harrison at the Battle of the Tippecanoe carries the caption *"Upon one occasion, as he (General Harrison) was approaching an angle of the Line, against which the Indians were advancing with horrible yells, Lieutenant Emmerson seized the Bridle of his Horse, and earnestly entreated that he would not go there, but the Governor (of the Indian territory), putting spurs to his Horse, pushed on to the point of Attack, where the Enemy were received with firmness and driven back."* Such publicity was instrumental in Harrison's overwhelming success in the 1840 presidential election. Inaugurated in March 1841, Harrison then secured the two unfortunate distinctions of being the first president to die in office, and the president who served for the shortest time.

force would suffer a similar defeat. The Shawnee and their allies attacked just before dawn to start the Battle of the Tippecanoe. The first charge by about 700 men was pressed home with such determination and courage that the Indians penetrated right into the U.S. camp. Although Harrison's force had been taken by surprise, it rallied and then turned the tables on the Indians. The Indians were driven back from the camp, which provided the opportunity for the mounted riflemen to charge and sweep Tecumseh's men from the field.

In the Battle of the Tippecanoe, the U.S. troops suffered 39 dead and 151 wounded, of whom 29 later died. They counted 36 Indian bodies left on the battlefield, but the Indians almost certainly suffered considerably heavier losses, for they carried away a large number of their dead along with the wounded. Harrison then moved on to Prophetstown and burned it, in the short term breaking the power of Tecumseh and causing his tribal federation to dissolve. The problem of white encroachment into Indian lands was not solved, however, so further trouble was sure to follow. The American government realized this, but was faced with renewed war against the United Kingdom, as Great Britain had been renamed on January 1,

A participant in the Battle of the Tippecanoe, Robert McAlee, described the combat in a history he wrote five years later.

The night was dark and cloudy: the moon rose late, and after midnight there was a drizzling rain. Many of the men appeared to be much dissatisfied: they were anxious for battle, and the most ardent regretted that they would have to return without one. The army generally had no expectation of an attack; but those who had experience in Indian affairs suspected some treachery. Colonel Daveiss was heard to say, he had no doubt but that an attack would be made before morning.

It was the constant practice of governor Harrison to call up the troops an hour before day, and keep them under arms till it was light. After 4 o'clock in the morning, the governor, general Wells, colonel Owen, and colonel Daveiss had all risen, and the governor was going to issue his orders for raising the army; when the treacherous Indians had crept up so near the sentries, as to hear them challenge when relieved. They intended to rush upon the sentries and kill them before they could fire: but one of them discovered an Indian creeping towards him in the grass, and fired. This was immediately followed by the Indian yell, and a desperate charge upon the left flank. The guards in that quarter gave way, and abandoned their officer without making any resistance. Capt. Barton's company of regulars and capt. Keiger's company of mounted riflemen, forming the left angle of the rear line, received the first onset. The fire there was excessive; but the troops who had lain on their arms, were immediately prepared to receive, and gallantly resist the furious savage assailants. The manner of the attack was calculated to discourage and terrify the men; yet as soon as they could be formed and posted, they maintained their ground with desperate valor, though but very few of them had ever before been in battle. The fires in the camp were extinguished immediately, as the light they afforded was more serviceable to the Indians than to our men.

As soon as the governor could mount his horse, he proceeded towards the point of attack, and finding the line much weakened there, he ordered two companies from the centre of the rear line to march up and form across the angle in the rear of Barton's and Keiger's companies. General Wells immediately proceeded to the right of his command; and colonel Owen, who was with him, was proceeding directly to the point of attack, when he was shot on his horse near the lines, and thus bravely fell among the first victims of savage perfidy. A heavy fire now commenced all along the left flank, upon the whole of the front and right flank, and on a part of the rear line.

In passing through the camp, towards the left of the front line, the governor met with colonel Daveiss and the dragoons. The colonel informed him that the Indians, concealed behind some trees near the line, were annoying the troops very severely in that quarter; and he requested permission to dislodge them, which was granted. He immediately called on the first division of his cavalry to follow him, but the order was not distinctly heard, and but few of his men charged with him. They had not proceeded far out of the lines, when Daveiss was mortally wounded by several balls and fell. His men stood by him, and repulsed the savages several times, till they succeeded in carrying him into camp.

In the mean time the attack on Spencer's and Warwick's companies on the right, became very severe. Captain Spencer and his lieutenants were all killed, and captain Warwick was mortally wounded. The governor in passing towards that flank, found captain Robb's company near the centre of the camp. They had been driven from their post; or rather, had fallen back without orders. He sent them to the aid of captain Spencer, where they fought very bravely, having seventeen men killed during the battle. The battle was maintained on all sides with desperate valor. The Indians advanced and retreated by a rattling noise made with deer hoofs: they fought with enthusiasm, and seemed determined on victory or death.

As soon as day light appeared, General Wells took command of the corps formed on the left, and with the aid of some dragoons, made a successful charge on the enemy in that direction, driving them into an adjoining swamp through which the cavalry could not pursue them. At the same time Cook's and lieutenant Laribie's companies, with the aid of the riflemen and militia on the right flank, charged on the Indians and put them to flight in that quarter, which terminated the battle.

THE MILITARY HISTORY OF THE UNITED STATES

1801, by an Act of Union.

While the attention of the United States had been focused on the establishment of the new federal government headed by a president, and by the problems on its northwestern frontier, Europe had entered a period of great turmoil. The immediate cause was the French Revolution of 1789, which had led to a general European war. In 1793, Great Britain had joined a European alliance fighting revolutionary France. Immediately, British seapower was applied as its major instrument of strategy. This use of seapower included a blockade of France, and within a year, 300 American merchant ships had been seized. The problem was reduced in 1794 by the signing of Jay's Treaty. The U.S. accepted a British definition of contraband and in return received a firm commitment for the removal of British garrisons in forts on the American side of the frontier with Canada. The treaty played a major part in easing tension between the United States and Great Britain. On the other hand, it antagonized the French and caused distress among many Americans, who were alarmed by this reversal in American policy from its original pro-French and anti-British position.

The United States had a strong desire to remain neutral at a time when the rest of the western world was becoming increasingly polarized for or against France. The ensuing problems were still unresolved when Washington was succeeded as president in 1797 by John Adams. At this time, the authorized strength of the regular army was 3,300

Built in 1790, Fort Washington was one of the bases created in the United States' northwestern expansion. The location of this rural scene is now 3rd Street, east of Broadway, in Cincinnati, Ohio.

John Adams
For further references see pages 191, 221, 223.

men, and the all-arms "legionary" establishment that had been successful in frontier fighting was discarded in favor of a return to a traditional military establishment. The army therefore had four regiments of infantry, two companies of light dragoons, and a Corps of Artillerists and Engineers. The shifting nature of the frontier tasks faced by the army in 1796-97 is reflected by a redeployment of the main strength from the northwest to the southwest during these two years. In the northwest, there was a major force of one infantry regiment at Fort Washington, as well as five companies of infantry in Detroit and small garrisons in several frontier forts. In the southwest, nine companies of infantry, the complete dragoon force, and two companies of artillery were stationed. Elsewhere in the United States, small garrisons had been fortified by French experts in a number of ports along the frontier with Canada from the Great Lakes eastward, as well as in older forts such as Carlisle, Fort Pitt, and West Point.

Problems with France and Great Britain

During this period, the main trend of American foreign and military policy was influenced by the country's relations with France and Great Britain. On the larger world stage, therefore, the results were the Quasi-War with France (1798-1800) and the War of 1812 (1812-15). The military establishment evolved considerably during this period.

Soon after Thomas Jefferson became the third president in 1800, France bought a vast territory west of the Mississippi River called Louisiana from Spain. The sale was a blow to the American belief that any weakening of the European presence in North America would automatically lead to the absorption of ex-European possessions into the United States. It also represented a physical problem for the United States for a number of reasons. American policy on the western frontier had until this time been concerned mainly with pacification of the Indians, preventing separatist tendencies by the inhabitants of the western territories, and limiting any friction between American settlers and the Spanish. French ownership of Louisiana opened the possibility of a powerful neighbor to the west. It also led to a restriction on the American practice of sending goods down the Mississippi River for export via New Orleans. Just before the Spanish sold the Louisiana Territory, they cancelled this right, and the French rapidly halted American trade down the river. Another factor that worried the United States was the vast size of the territory, a huge area covering virtually the whole of the modern United States from the Mississippi River westward to the Rocky Mountains with the exception of Texas.

THE MILITARY HISTORY OF THE UNITED STATES

Thomas Jefferson, seen here in a 1788 painting by Trumbull, was the third president and the man responsible for the single largest expansion of the United States through the Louisiana Purchase of 1803. Despite this enormous growth in the United States' land area, Jefferson was also responsible for a reduction in military strength.

The Louisiana Purchase

In 1803, Jefferson offered to purchase Louisiana from the French. To the great surprise of knowledgeable Americans, Napoleon agreed to the sale, because he was faced with the prospect of renewed war in Europe. The Louisiana Purchase, as it is known, added 827,000 square miles to the area of the United States, nearly doubling the size of the nation. Formal possession of Louisiana was taken by the army on December 20, 1803, and small garrisons were soon established in New Orleans and a number of other ex-Spanish posts on the lower reaches of the Mississippi River. The first governor of the territory was Brigadier General James Wilkinson, who had weathered a number of reorganizations to become the army's senior officer.

Even before the Louisiana Purchase, Jefferson had persuaded Congress that an exploration of the continent west of the Mississippi would pay great dividends. The men selected for this extraordinarily important task were a couple of veterans from Wayne's operation in the Northwest Territory, Captain Meriwether Lewis and Lieutenant William Clark. With a party of

Thomas Jefferson
For further references see pages 175, *177*, 178, 179, 191, 202.

176

REVOLUTIONARY AND EARLY AMERICAN WARS

Right: Even before the Louisiana Purchase, Jefferson had persuaded Congress of the need for an exploration of the unknown lands west of the Mississippi River, and the acquisition of this vast new territory made the exploration that much more urgent. In May 1804, Jefferson selected his private secretary, Captain Meriwether Lewis, who had served under Wayne against the Indians in the northwest, as joint leader of the expedition.
Below: A contemporary map of the route of the Lewis and Clark expedition between 1804 and 1806.

177

THE MILITARY HISTORY OF THE UNITED STATES

27 men, Lewis and Clark departed from St. Louis in the spring of 1804, traveled up the Missouri River, crossed the Rocky Mountains, and moved down the Columbia River to reach the coast of the Pacific Ocean near present-day Astoria, Oregon, in November 1805. The expedition returned by a different route, exploring central Montana before marching down the Missouri River to reach St. Louis again in September 1806.

Exploration in the West

Another party sent out by Wilkinson was led by Captain Zebulon M. Pike. Again departing from St. Louis, this 1804 expedition explored the upper reaches of the Mississippi River, reaching a point level with Fort du Lac on the western side of Lake Superior before returning to St. Louis. Pike was sent out from St. Louis once more in 1807. This time, he went west to explore Colorado. Near what is now known as Pike's Peak on the border of the American territory, the 20-man expedition was intercepted by hostile Spaniards, who controlled the land to the west. They escorted the American group south to Santa Fe. The expedition was led by a very circuitous route into Mexico and finally back to American territory at Natchitoches very close to the Red River northwest of New Orleans.

Such incursions into Spanish territory seemed acceptable to most Americans, but they were strongly resented by the Spaniards. During Jefferson's second term of office, the border problem with the Spanish in the west and in the two Floridas became increasingly acute. In 1806, it was reported that Spanish regular troops had been deployed into eastern Texas to bolster the local militia units. Jefferson reacted by calling out the militia forces of the Orleans and Mississippi Territories and sending in about 1,000 regular troops. The report that had spurred this American response proved to be untrue; at no time did the Spanish forces in the area outnumber those of the

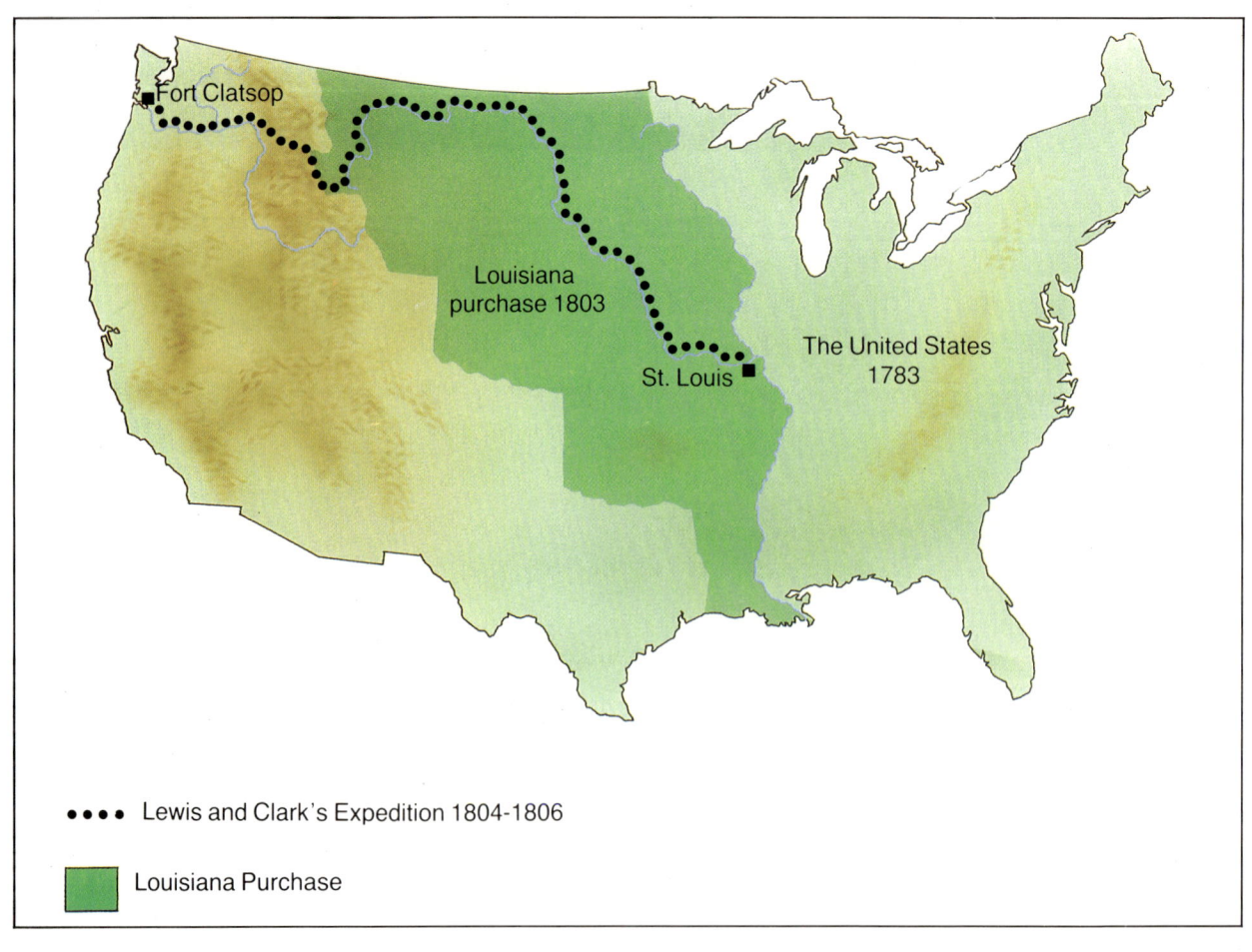

The Louisiana Purchase more than doubled the territorial area of the United States. It is worth noting that Lewis and Clark did more than survey a large portion of the new territory. They also pushed beyond it to reach the Pacific Ocean at the mouth of the Columbia River in what is now Oregon.

•••• Lewis and Clark's Expedition 1804-1806

▮ Louisiana Purchase

178

REVOLUTIONARY AND EARLY AMERICAN WARS

Americans. The tension of the period is reflected in a number of cavalry skirmishes fought along the Sabine River, but nothing more serious was allowed to happen. The two powers sensibly decided to establish a neutral zone between the Arroyo Hondo and the Sabine River, which became the national frontier up to 1812.

During this period, the political and economic attention of the United States turned increasingly toward Europe. The beginning of the second act of the war between the United Kingdom and France in 1803 was soon to develop into the vast war that ended only with the defeat of Napoleon at the Battle of Waterloo in 1815. The war was fought on an economic as well as military and naval basis, and this trade war involved the United States, which wished to continue its normal pattern of commerce with the fighting powers. This desire led ultimately to the War of 1812.

As the tensions grew, Jefferson finally persuaded Congress that a larger army was essential. In the last month of his administration, Jefferson sent 2,000 men of the regular army to join Wilkinson for the defense of "New Orleans and its dependencies" against the British invasion that was expected. It did not materialize, but the almost criminal maladministration of the army at this time meant that more than half of Wilkinson's army died in Louisiana. Disease and bad leadership played their part in this dismal tale, but the main burden of guilt must fall on corrupt and inefficient bureaucracy.

The Creek War (1813-14)

Just as Tecumseh and his Shawnees had found the arrival of the white settlers in their lands intolerable, so too the Creeks of the Mississippi Territory found themselves inevitably at loggerheads with American settlement and other influences. The Creeks took a leaf out of Tecumseh's book, and in July 1813 created an alliance with the British, who were at war with the United States at this time.

The Creeks lived in the area of the
Continued on page 196

The fur trade created in the territory explored by Lewis and Clark enabled John Jacob to become the richest man in America.

The Creeks
For further references see pages
155, 197, 206, 212, 214, 237, 243, *247*, 253.

THE BEGINNINGS OF THE U.S. MARINE CORPS

In traditional terms, the role of marines has been that of "shipboard soldiers," sailors with the discipline and weapon skills of the land soldier. Marines were organized in a sea-going corps whose detachments on each warship meant that the ship's officers could retain control of their seamen. They also manned some of the ship's guns and operated on the ship's fighting tops (platforms on the masts) to provide sniper fire into enemy ships in close-range sea battles. Marine detachments also provided a small but useful force that could be landed from ships for small-scale coastal operations.

The first Continental Marine recruits on the Philadelphia waterfront during November 1775. They were soldiers assigned to fight on ships, but not to sail them.

The First Records

The first surviving record of marines in American service dates from May 3, 1775, when Lieutenant James Watson is listed as a marine officer on the payroll of the *Enterprise*, which starts on this date. It is clear, therefore, that marines became a feature, although a small one at first, of the American military effort very early in the Revolutionary War. The word "Marines" was first used by the Continental Congress a few months later, when Major General George Washington of the Continental Army was ordered, on October 5, to secure two armed ships "on Continental risque and pay" and to provide "proper encouragement to the Marines and seamen" for service on these vessels.

Even though American colonial forces and the Continental Army had used marines since the spring of 1775, the birthday of the U.S. Marine Corps is officially November 10, 1775. On this date, the Continental Congress ordered that two battalions of marines should be raised and provided with adequate officers. The senior officer of these "Continental Marines" was Captain Samuel Nicholas, who is therefore reckoned to have been the first Commandant of the U.S. Marine Corps, although the title was not used until 1800. Nicholas received his captain's commission from President John Hancock of the Continental Congress a little more than two weeks later, on November 28. It was, in fact, the first commission issued for service in the Continental Navy and Continental Marines. With the aid of his junior officers, Nicholas set about raising the Continental Marines. By the end of 1775, there were five companies of Continental Marines. Assembled at the Willing and Morris Wharves in Philadelphia, they were allocated to guard duty for Continental warships and stores in Philadelphia. From January 1776, the Continental Marines were deployed on board seven ships of the Continental Navy, starting with the *Alfred*, Commodore Esek Hopkins's flagship.

The First Amphibious Assault

On February 17, 1776, ships of the Continental Navy sailed from Cape Henlopen, Delaware, under the command of Hopkins. Just two weeks later, they made rendezvous off Nassau harbor on the northern side of New Providence in the Bahama Islands, a British possession garrisoned only by small militia forces. The American force made no effort to surprise the British garrison, but when the alarm was raised on the island, the Americans decided to deal first with Fort Montagu, the weaker of the two British forts guarding the island. Just before midday on March 3, Nicholas led a force of 230 Continental Marines and 50 sailors in a landing about two miles east of the fort. This is considered the first amphibious assault by American marines. After his men assembled on the beach after disembarking from their longboats, Nicholas led them against the fort, which they captured in a fight as "bemused as it was bloodless." The U.S. force remained in the fort overnight. On the following day, it moved

REVOLUTIONARY AND EARLY AMERICAN WARS

Within a month of the Continental Marines' establishment, American marines sailed on the *Alfred*. Their task was to maintain order on the ship and, in battle, to man positions in the fighting tops. Here they could hurl grenades and fire down onto the deck of the enemy ship.

Samuel Nicholas
For further references see pages 182, 184, 185, 188.

THE MILITARY HISTORY OF THE UNITED STATES

Above: Accompanied by sailors of the Continental Navy, Continental Marines make the first amphibious landing in American history on New Providence in the Bahamas on March 3, 1776.

forward to occupy the rest of the island, taking Fort Nassau and capturing Montfort Browne, the island's governor. That night, the American landing force rested in Fort Nassau, and the fleet patrolled well to the east. This gave the British still at liberty the chance to deprive the Americans of their greatest prize: a sizable quantity of gunpowder was shipped out of the unguarded harbor to St. Augustine, Florida. Hopkins was very angry about the loss, and he stripped the town and the two forts of all their major weapons (about 100 cannon and mortars in all), some powder and ammunition, and a quantity of other military stores. The American force evacuated New Providence on March 17, well satisfied with this first foray by the Continental Marines.

The First Marine Casualties

As the invasion force sailed north, the Continental Marines suffered their first casualty. During the night of April 6, the American squadron met two British ships, HMS *Glasgow* and her tender. On the *Alfred*, the embarked company of Continental Marines was divided into two parties. One was commanded by Nicholas with Second Lieutenant John Fitzpatrick on the main deck, and the other by Nicholas's second-in-command, First Lieutenant Matthew Parke, on the quarterdeck. The first American ship engaged by the *Glasgow* was the *Cabot*. As she fell away under the weight of the British cannon fire, the *Glasgow* turned her attentions to the *Alfred*. In one of the

184

first exchanges of fire, Parke was killed by a musket ball, probably fired by a British marine in one of the *Glasgow*'s tops. Nicholas later wrote of Parke that "In him I have lost a worthy officer, sincere friend and companion, that was beloved by all the ship's company." As the fight continued, a shot from the *Glasgow* ripped away the *Alfred's* steering gear. The position for the American flagship was now very difficult, but when the other American ships arrived on the scene, the *Glasgow* made off toward Newport.

On September 5, 1776, a standardized uniform for the Continental Marines (and for the Continental Navy) was adopted by the Marine Committee of the Continental Congress.

The Battle of Lake Champlain

The next battle in which the Continental Marines were involved was defeat for the Americans, but nonetheless provided invaluable time for the American cause at a time of great danger. In the fall of 1776, the British decided to exploit the failure of the American effort against Canada. They planned an advance south up the Richelieu River to Lake Champlain with the objective of taking Saratoga and Albany, and then linking up with the British force in New York. Success would split the rebellious colonies, so that those in New England could be defeated without interference from the middle and southern colonies. The naval battle of Lake Champlain was fought off Valcour Island on October 11, 1776, and resulted in a defeat for the United States under Colonel Benedict Arnold. The survivors of the American squadron managed to slip past the British in the night, but on October 13, the British closed in on the American ships again. Arnold decided that further fighting would result only in useless loss of life and ordered the five remaining galleys to be beached.

Below: Continental Marines raise the American flag over Fort Nassau in the Bahamas on January 27, 1778. This was the first time that the "Stars and Stripes" had been hoisted over a foreign fortification.

Their Continental Marines waded ashore and provided covering fire as the sailors torched the beached vessels.

Changes in Organization

Further organizational change for the marines came on October 30 of the same year, when the Continental Congress resolved that the Continental Marines should have the same titles and ranks (lieutenant, captain, and major) as officers with similar tasks and responsibilities in the Continental Army. The same resolution covered details of how "commanders, officers, seamen, and marines in the continental navy" should be entitled to prizes they took, including privateers. Less favorable to the Continental Marines was an occurrence less than a month later. On November 24, Private Harry Hassen was court-martialed for desertion from the Continental Marines. In this earliest known instance of desertion from the Continental Marines, Hassen pleaded guilty and was sentenced to 50 lashes for desertion and 21 more for "quitting his guard" without being relieved.

The Battle of Princeton

The Continental Marines were also involved in the land war. After his success at Trenton on December 25, 1776, when the Hessian garrison had been completely routed, Washington crossed the Delaware River once more on December 30 and occupied this New Jersey town. Major General Lord Cornwallis, the British commander, responded with an advance from Princeton. Washington sidestepped this

The Continental Marines were involved as ordinary infantry in one of George Washington's most important victories, the Battle of Princeton on January 3, 1777. The American success here, coming hard on the heels of victory in the Battle of Trenton eight days earlier, fanned into flame the embers of a revolution that was dying late in 1776.

REVOLUTIONARY AND EARLY AMERICAN WARS

British attempt to bring him to battle. On January 3, 1777, he prepared to attack the British base at Princeton. As they got ready to attack, the Americans ran into the last of the British forces marching to reinforce Cornwallis. The British commander, Colonel Charles Mawhood, bombarded the Americans with cannon fire and then sent in a bayonet charge by the 17th Regiment of Foot. The American force under Brigadier General Charles Mercer were pushed back and had to be reinforced by Pennsylvania troops under Brigadier General John Cadwalader and Continental Marines under Nicholas. They, too, were pushed back at first, but Washington arrived and rallied the Americans. The British were defeated.

In 1777, the United States was faced with the loss of Philadelphia, the new national capital. Defensive positions on the Delaware River were built to check any British waterborne approach. The British instead chose an overland approach from Chesapeake Bay. On September 28, Washington realized that the river defenses were being outflanked. He ordered the garrison of Billingsport, on the New Jersey side of the Delaware, to be evacuated to Fort Mifflin, closer to Philadelphia. The land route was closed by the advancing British, so the 112-man garrison of Colonel William Bradford's command had to be taken out by water on October 2, 1777. The task was entrusted to guard boats manned by Continental Marines of the brig *Andrew Doria* under Lieutenants Dennis Leary and William Barney. The marines managed to get out all the men and most of the ammunition; a party remained on shore to spike the American guns and burn the fort. There was a brisk firefight at about midday as the last marines pulled out just as the British arrived.

The Taking of Fort Nassau

At this point, the Bahamas re-enter the history of the Continental Marines. The sloop *Providence*, commanded by Captain John Peck Rathbun, received news in Georgetown, South Carolina, that an old enemy was in Nassau harbor for repairs. It was the British brig *Mary*, which a few months earlier had engaged the *Providence* off New York and caused considerable damage, as well as killing the American ship's sailing master. According to the sloop's captain of marines, Captain John Trevett, "we ware...Determind to Take Fort Nassau and then we Could Have Command of the Town and Harber and take What we Pleased." The American sloop anchored off Hog Island just before midnight on January 27, 1778, and a party of 26 Continental Marines under Trevett was landed one mile west of Fort Nassau. The Americans approached silently, climbed into the fort, and captured the two-man garrison! At dawn, the American flag was raised over the fort, the first time that the "Stars and Stripes" had been hoisted above a foreign possession. The *Mary* and

187

two schooners were captured in the harbor, and a considerable quantity of supplies was seized on shore. On January 30, the captured vessels sailed out to meet the *Providence* for the return journey to New Bedford, Massachusetts.

A Volunteer Company

The Continental Marines also cast their net considerably farther afield in this period. Before the Revolutionary War's beginning, James Willing, a member of an important Philadelphia family, had built up a small trading empire based at Natchez on the lower reaches of the Mississippi River. In the fall of 1777, the influence of his brother was instrumental in securing permission for Willing to create a volunteer company of Continental Marines drawn from the garrison at Fort Pitt, Pennsylvania. This company was then to obtain and arm a large riverboat on the upper reaches of the Ohio River. As it traveled down the Ohio and Mississippi rivers, it would secure the aid (or force the neutrality) of settlers living on the rivers' eastern banks and then return to Fort Pitt with five boats carrying arms and dry goods. Willing and his 34 men departed from Fort Pitt on January 10, 1778, in the armed galley *Rattletrap*. They escaped past the British posts on the river and headed southwest, collecting more men and boats as they went. By the middle of February, Willing's flotilla of boats arrived just north of Natchez, at the plantation of Colonel Anthony Hutchins, a loyalist. By night, Hutchins, his slaves, and many of his possessions were seized and loaded on the *Rattletrap*. A few days later, the expedition reached Natchez, where more loyalists were seized. Then, once he had passed out of the Natchez district, Willing allowed his men far greater freedom of action. What could not be plundered was often burned as the expedition moved south to New Orleans. Here the expedition rested for a time and then launched a series of forays into the loyalist countryside. Willing finally returned to Pennsylvania by sea, while the men of his expedition, commanded by Lieutenant Robert George, headed up the western bank of the Mississippi River with the intention of joining Lieutenant Colonel George Rogers Clark in the Illinois Territory.

John Paul Jones and the *Ranger*

Thousands of miles away, Continental Marines also had their part to play in the activities of Captain John Paul Jones and the *Ranger*. Sailing from the French port of Brest in April 1778, Jones was determined to "end the barbarous ravages perpetuated by the British in America." He wanted to fall on a British coastal town, destroy all ships in its harbor, and seize an important person as a hostage against the release of

Below: Based on a painting by Alonzo Chappel, this engraving shows John Paul Jones, the most celebrated American naval commander of the Revolutionary War. After the Revolutionary War, Jones spent much time in France and then moved to Russia, where he secured a commission as rear admiral in the navy of Empress Catherine the Great. After falling foul of political machinations in Russia, Jones returned to France. He died of pneumonia in Paris during July 1792.

Americans held by the British. The town he selected was Whitehaven, one of the major ports in northwestern England. On April 22, the *Ranger* was too far from the port to attempt anything herself, but Jones, unwilling to lose the advantage of darkness, despatched two boats manned by 30 Continental Marine and seaman volunteers. One boat was commanded by Jones, and the other by a marine officer, Lieutenant Samuel Wallingford. The raid reached Whitehaven but achieved little; the same fate befell his descent onto St. Mary's Isle the next day. A day later, the *Ranger* fell in with a British frigate, HMS *Drake*. The British ship was beaten, but among the three American casualties was Wallingford, who was killed. Jones later commanded the frigate *Bonhomme Richard*, whose marines were volunteers from a French unit manned by Irish exiles, l'Infanterie Irlandaise, Regiment de Walsh-Serrant. A detachment of this regiment was serving on the *Bonhomme Richard* during the American ship's classic and ultimately successful single-ship action with the British frigate HMS *Serapis* off Flamborough Head on September 23, 1779.

The Assault at Penobscot

The Continental Marines had meanwhile been involved in the largest American amphibious operation of the Revolutionary War, the assault at Penobscot on July 28, 1779. The operation's origins lay with the creation in the spring of 1779 of a strong British outpost at the tip of the

The best known single-ship duel of the Revolutionary War was the September 1779 action between John Paul Jones's *Bonhomme Richard* and HMS *Serapis* off Flamborough Head or the east coast of England. Both ships were reduced to virtual wrecks before the *Serapis* struck her colors to the American ship; the *Bonhomme Richard* sank two days later.

BON HOMME RICHARD & SERAPIS

THE MILITARY HISTORY OF THE UNITED STATES

Bagaduce peninsula in Penobscot Bay, lying in the northern part of Massachusetts which is now Maine. Fort George was constructed and garrisoned by 700 men of the British 74th and 82nd Regiments of Foot under Brigadier General Francis McLean, military governor of Nova Scotia. The Americans decided to evict the British, and 3,000 militia troops assembled in Boston under Brigadier General Solomon Lovell. Meanwhile, Captain Dudley Saltonstall of the *Warren* coordinated a naval force of six Continental and Massachusetts state ships, bolstered by 13 privateers as escort for 20 troop transports. The American expedition sailed on July 19, 1779, and arrived in Penobscot Bay on July 26. Two days later, a force of 200 Continental Marines and 20 militiamen under Captain Walsh landed under the bluff on the peninsula's western approaches. With the marines to the fore, the American force took the bluff, but then failed to make much more progress. Two weeks later, a large British naval force appeared, and the American ships retreated up the Penobscot River. There the ships were burned, and the Americans retreated southwest through the wilderness of Maine. British losses included 13 killed, while those of the Americans amounted to 474 dead and many others wounded. Saltonstall was court-martialed and dismissed from the service.

The Continental Marines continued to find action, most notably on the ships of the Continental Navy. Typical is the action fought on May 29, 1781, between the frigate *Alliance*, under Captain John Barry, and two British sloops, HMS *Atalanta* and HMS *Trepassey*. The *Alliance* was returning from France and, between the Newfoundland Banks and the American coast, was engaged by the two smaller

The landing at the mouth of the Penobscot River on July 19, 1779, was the largest American amphibious operation of the Revolutionary War. The resulting operation was a complete disaster: it cost the Americans 474 lives, but the British lost only 13 dead.

ships on a virtually windless day. Visibility was soon reduced to zero by the cloud of gunpowder smoke that enveloped the scene, and the Continental Marine marksmen in the tops of the American frigate found it very difficult to find any targets. In mid-afternoon, the wind returned, and the *Alliance* devastated the *Trepassey* with a short-range broadside before meting out similar punishment to the *Atalanta*. Both British ships struck their colors.

On the other side of the United States, George Rogers Clark (now a brigadier general) was faced with the important but immensely difficult job of maintaining American control over the valley of the Ohio River. Particular emphasis was placed on command of the area between the mouths of the Miami River and Licking Creek, and Clark decided that an armed galley offered his limited manpower the best chance of achieving this task. Powered by 46 oars or - when the wind was favorable - the sails on two masts, the *Miami* had a 73-foot keel and was armed with eight cannon. The vessel was completed late in May 1782 and was manned by 110 men, including the gun crews provided by a company of Virginia State Marines under Captain Jacob Pyeatt. The vessel was effective in its planned role: the Shawnee Indians were so concerned that they abandoned a plan to raid Wheeling to concentrate their efforts on the invasion they thought was imminent. The vessel was sunk in September 1782, and the marines were transferred to the Illinois Regiment for the rest of the Revolutionary War.

The End of the Revolutionary War

News of the end of the Revolutionary War reached the *Alliance*, the last frigate of the Continental Navy on active service, on March 31, 1783, as she lay off Petuxet about five miles from Providence, Rhode Island. The ship was now marked for use as a cargo vessel, and the crew was paid off on April 1. Included in the total were 33 of the last 41 men remaining in the Continental Marines. The last man, Lieutenant Thomas Elwood, was discharged about six months later, and the seven-year history of the Continental Marines came to an end. It is thought that 131 officers held commissions in the Continental Marines, and that about another 2,000 men served as non-commissioned officers and enlisted men. Of this total, 49 had been killed in battle or died of their wounds, while another 70 had been wounded but recovered. This compares with 4,044 dead and 6,004 wounded in the army, and 342 dead and 114 wounded in the navy.

The need for marines was appreciated again in the Quasi-War with France. On July 11, 1798, President John Adams approved an act introduced to the Congress by Samuel Sewall, chairman of the House Naval Committee. The act provided for a Marine Corps of 33 officers and 848 "non-commissioned officers, musicians and privates," and Major William Ward Burrows was appointed the major commandant.

The Creation of the Marine Band

After the creation of the new Marine Corps, developments occurred quite rapidly. Some were small matters in themselves, but through custom and tradition, they enjoy greater significance. Typical was the creation on July 11, 1798, of the Marine Corps Band. Known as "The President's Own," it has the double distinction of being the oldest American military band and the only musical organization with the principal task of providing music for the president. The band played at the first New Year's Day reception at the president's new residence in Washington, D.C. Because of the limited space in the Oval Office, only six musicians could be used in this first important social event held in the president's official home. On July 4 of the same year, President Thomas Jefferson reviewed the Marine Corps, led by the Marine Corps Band, in the grounds of the White House. It was the first occasion on which a body of regular troops had been reviewed by the

THE MILITARY HISTORY OF THE UNITED STATES

The capture of the British brig *Reindeer* by the American sloop *Wasp* during the War of 1812 took only 29 minutes. In the action, the Marines on board the *Wasp* played a skillful and major part.

president in his role as commander-in-chief, at his official residence.

By this time, the Quasi-War with France had ended, but during this strange conflict, the new Marine Corps was blooded, principally in the detachments it provided for American warships. In the first half of 1800, the corps undertook its first amphibious operation, however, and thereby paved the way for the type of martial activity that was to become its main military task. Commodore Silas Talbot was cruising in the frigate *Constitution* north of the Spanish possession of Santo Domingo (now the Dominican Republic) on the eastern end of the island of Hispaniola. He learned that a French privateer was lying at Puerto Plata, protected by *Sandwich*, a British packet thought to have a valuable cargo on board. Talbot knew that the *Constitution* had too deep a draft for his scheme of cutting out the privateer, so he impressed the sloop *Sally*. This task was entrusted to Lieutenant Isaac Hull, whose sailors were reinforced by a detachment of the *Constitution's* marines under Captain Daniel Carmick. The *Sally* sailed into Puerto Plata during May 12 in broad daylight. The French privateer was protected not only by her own guns, but by a battery of Spanish artillery as well. Despite this fact, Hull took the *Sally* alongside the French ship and used his sailors to take her without losing a man. As this was being completed, Carmick and his marines landed, took the Spanish battery and spiked its guns, and then pulled back to the captured ship before the Spanish could send in reinforcements. In the absence of any wind, the Americans were forced to wait until the following morning to leave Puerto Plata with the *Sally* and their prize.

The War of 1812

The Marine Corps next saw land action on the shores of Tripoli later in the same decade. The corps was also involved in the War of 1812, losing a total of 45 men killed and 66 wounded. Most of the

Marine Corps activities were connected with the war at sea, but there was also a fascinating episode in the Marquesas Islands of the South Pacific. The frigate *Essex*, under Captain David Porter, was cruising in search of British whalers and other merchantmen. On May 30, 1813, one of the *Essex*'s prizes, the *Greenwich*, was entrusted to a Marine Corps officer, First Lieutenant John M. Gamble. He commanded the vessel in action against HMS *Seringapatam*, the first occasion on which a Marine Corps officer had commanded an American "naval" vessel in action. Toward the end of 1813, Porter concentrated his frigate and her prizes at the island of Nuku Hiva in the Marquesas. Intending to make a short cruise in the area, Porter left the prizes *Greenwich*, *Seringapatam*, and *Sir Andrew Hammond* under the command of Gamble. After building a small fort, he departed from the island during December, leaving a garrison of Gamble, one midshipman, and about 20 marines and sailors.

After the *Essex*'s departure, the is-

Lieutenant Stephen Decatur and his party of sailors and Marines board the captured *Philadelphia* in Tripoli harbor before burning the ship.

landers became hostile to the Americans. The local leader, Chief Gattenewa could not prevent a spate of thefts from the fort, and Gamble had to make a show of force before the islanders handed back the stolen goods and stopped creating problems. The situation lasted until May of the following year.

By this time, Gamble realized that Porter was not returning. During April, he ordered his force to start preparing the *Seringapatam* and *Sir Andrew Hammond* for the journey to Valparaiso, Chile the emergency rendezvous agreed with Porter. On May 7, however, the crew of the *Seringapatam* mutinied. Gamble was wounded, and the ship sailed from Nuku Hiva. Two days later, the islanders, realizing how weak the force now was, attacked the fort. The midshipman and three men were killed, and one of the marines was seriously wounded. This left Gamble with just three marines and three sailors for the *Sir Andrew Hammond*, and of the six men, only two were fully fit. The *Greenwich* was burned, and the *Sir Andrew Hammond* sailed on May 9. On the last day of the month, Gamble reached the Yahoo Islands and, securing a crew of islanders, sailed again on June 11. Only two days later, however, the American prize was captured by the British ship *Cherub*. Arriving in the Brazilian port of Rio de Janeiro, the British freed the Americans. The following year, Gamble managed to secure passage on a Swedish ship destined for Havre de Grace in France, but managed to transfer to an American ship, the *Oliver Ellsworth*, at sea. He finally reached New York in August 1815.

Marines at Puerto Rico

In 1824, the Marine Corps was involved in an extraordinary event. An American trading house on St. Thomas in the Virgin Islands had been robbed and the stolen goods shipped to the small port of Fajardo on Puerto Rico, then a Spanish possession. In October, news of these reached Lieutenant C.T. Platt of the *Beagle* who agreed to help recover the goods. Platt arrived in Fajardo on October 26 and, accompanied by Lieutenant Ritchie, called on the Spanish authorities. They promptly arrested the two officers as pirates, even though Platt produced his U.S. Navy commission. Finally, the Americans were allowed to return to the *Beagle*, and they departed. Soon though, the *Beagle* met the *John Adams*, whose Commodore John Porter decided that the Puerto Rican insult to the Americans must be punished.

The *John Adams* drew too much water to berth in Fajardo, so Porter embarked a party of his ship in boats and, escorted by

Commandants of the U.S. Marine Corps

Samuel Nicholas	1775 - 1781
William Ward Burrows	1798 - 1804
Franklin Wharton	1804 - 1818
Anthony Gale	1819 - 1820
Archibald Henderson	1820 - 1859
John Harns	1859 - 1864
Jacob Zeilin	1864 - 1876
Charles G. McCawley	1876 - 1891
Charles Heywood	1891 - 1903
George F. Elliott	1903 - 1910
William P. Biddle	1911 - 1914
George Barnett	1914 - 1920
John A. Lejeune	1920 - 1929
Wendell C. Neville	1929 - 1930
Ben H. Fuller	1930 - 1934
John H. Russell	1934 - 1936
Thomas Holcomb	1936 - 1943
Alexander A. Vandegrift	1944 - 1947
Clifton B. Cates	1948 - 1951
Lemuel C. Shepherd, Jr.	1952 - 1955
Randolph McC. Pate	1956 - 1959
David M. Shoup	1960 - 1963
Wallace M. Greene, Jr.	1964 - 1967
Leonard F. Chapman, Jr.	1968 - 1971
Robert E. Cushman, Jr.	1972 - 1975
Louis H. Wilson	1975 - 1979
Robert H. Barrow	1979 - 1983
Paul X. Kelly	1983 - 1987
Alfred M. Gray, Jr.	1987 -

the *Beagle* and the *Grampus*, entered Fajardo harbor. As the ships were about to anchor, it became clear that a shore battery was about to fire on them. A party of 14 marines under Lieutenant Thomas B. Barton, a passenger on the *Grampus*, was landed to spike the guns, which they did without difficulty. On November 14, Porter landed with about 200 marines and sailors, and sent forward a naval officer with a letter to the governor demanding apologies and restitution. These demands were met, and Porter's party returned to their ships. This was not the end of the matter, however, for the American authorities deemed that Porter had overstepped his authority. The naval officer was court-martialed, found guilty, and sentenced to a six-month suspension. Porter resigned, however, and later accepted a commission as commander-in-chief of the Mexican navy.

U.S. Marines Land in the Falkland Islands

In 1832, there was a marine landing in the Falkland Islands, at that time under Argentine control. In this period, the islands were the center of a considerable international trade in seals. In 1831, the American schooners *Breakwater*, *Harriet*, and *Superior* had been seized on the order of the islands' governor. Confusion about the sovereignty of the Falklands in the period is evident in President Andrew Jackson's annual report to Congress that year. He mentioned "a band acting, as they pretend, under the authority of the Government of Buenos Ayres" and suggested measures "for providing a force adequate to the complete protection of our fellow-citizens fishing and trading in those seas." Congress approved the president's plan, and the sloop *Lexington*, under Commander Silas Duncan, was ordered from Buenos Aires to handle the matter. The *Lexington* arrived in Berkeley Sound, East Falkland, on December 28, 1831, before sailing into the anchorage of St. Louis on January 1, 1832. Duncan sent ashore a party of two officers and 15 men (presumably marines) in a commandeered schooner. More marines and sailors followed in two boats later in the same morning. This was pressure enough to secure the release of the three arrested schooners. Virtually every American on the islands wanted to leave, and Duncan agreed to transport these refugees to Montevideo. Landing parties of marines patrolled the property of the Americans until the expedition set sail on January 22.

Early Landings

The early history of the Marine Corps is filled with such episodes. Landings were undertaken in 1832 on Sumatra; in 1833 in Argentina; in 1835 and 1836 in Peru; in 1838 and 1839 in Sumatra; in 1840 on the Fiji Islands; in 1841 on Drummonds Island and Samoa; in 1843 at points on the West African coast; in 1851 on Johanna Island; in 1852 in Argentina and Nicaragua; in 1853 in Japan, the Luchu (now Ryukyu) Islands, Nicaragua and Siam (now Thailand); in 1854 in China, Japan, the Luchu Islands, and Nicaragua; in 1855 in China, the Fiji Islands, and Nicaragua; in 1856 in China; in 1858 on the Fiji Islands and Uruguay; in 1859 in China; and in 1860 in Africa, Colombia, and Japan. All were small actions, usually in support of civil authorities or to rescue American citizens and interests, and frequently accomplished without bloodshed through a show of force.

It is also worth noting that on June 30, 1834, Congress passed a bill "For the Better Organization of the Marine Corps." The corps was established as part of the navy, its strength was increased, and its commandant, Archibald Henderson, was promoted to colonel. Henderson soon departed to fight in the Second Seminole War, leaving tacked on his door a note that read: "Have gone to Florida to fight Indians. Will be back when the war is over." Elements of the Marine Corps served in Florida until 1838, but in recognition of his services, Henderson was brevetted a brigadier general, the Marine Corps' first general officer, on January 27, 1836.

THE MILITARY HISTORY OF THE UNITED STATES

Born in March 1757 in Waxhaw Settlement, South Carolina, Andrew Jackson was a self-taught lawyer who saw the military as a way of publicizing his name and advancing his career. Jackson was also enthusiastic about the concept of a larger United States, and saw the opening of a southern theater during the War of 1812 as a heaven-sent opportunity for both the United States and himself.

Continued from page 179
Mississippi Territory that later became Alabama. In the summer of 1813, they took the offensive in a series of increasingly severe attacks that culminated in the overrunning of Fort Mims on August 30. The fort lay about 35 miles up the Alabama River from Mobile on the American side of the frontier with the western half of Spanish West Florida, which had recently been occupied by the Americans. Garrisoned by 550 militiamen, it had been swelled in population by the arrival of large numbers of civilians fleeing the rampaging Indians. More than half of those in the fort, numbering about 500, were massacred by the Indians.

At Natchez on the Mississippi River, a force of 2,000 Tennessee militiamen had been entrusted by the state to the command of Major General Andrew Jackson. He proposed an invasion of both Floridas as part of the War of 1812. The American government preferred a less ambitious scheme by regular forces under Wilkinson, and the Tennessee army was at Natchez awaiting return home. From this state militia, Jackson quickly created a volunteer force that advanced into

Andrew Jackson
For further references see pages
197, 199, 202, 210, 211, 212, 214, 219, 239, 252.

REVOLUTIONARY AND EARLY AMERICAN WARS

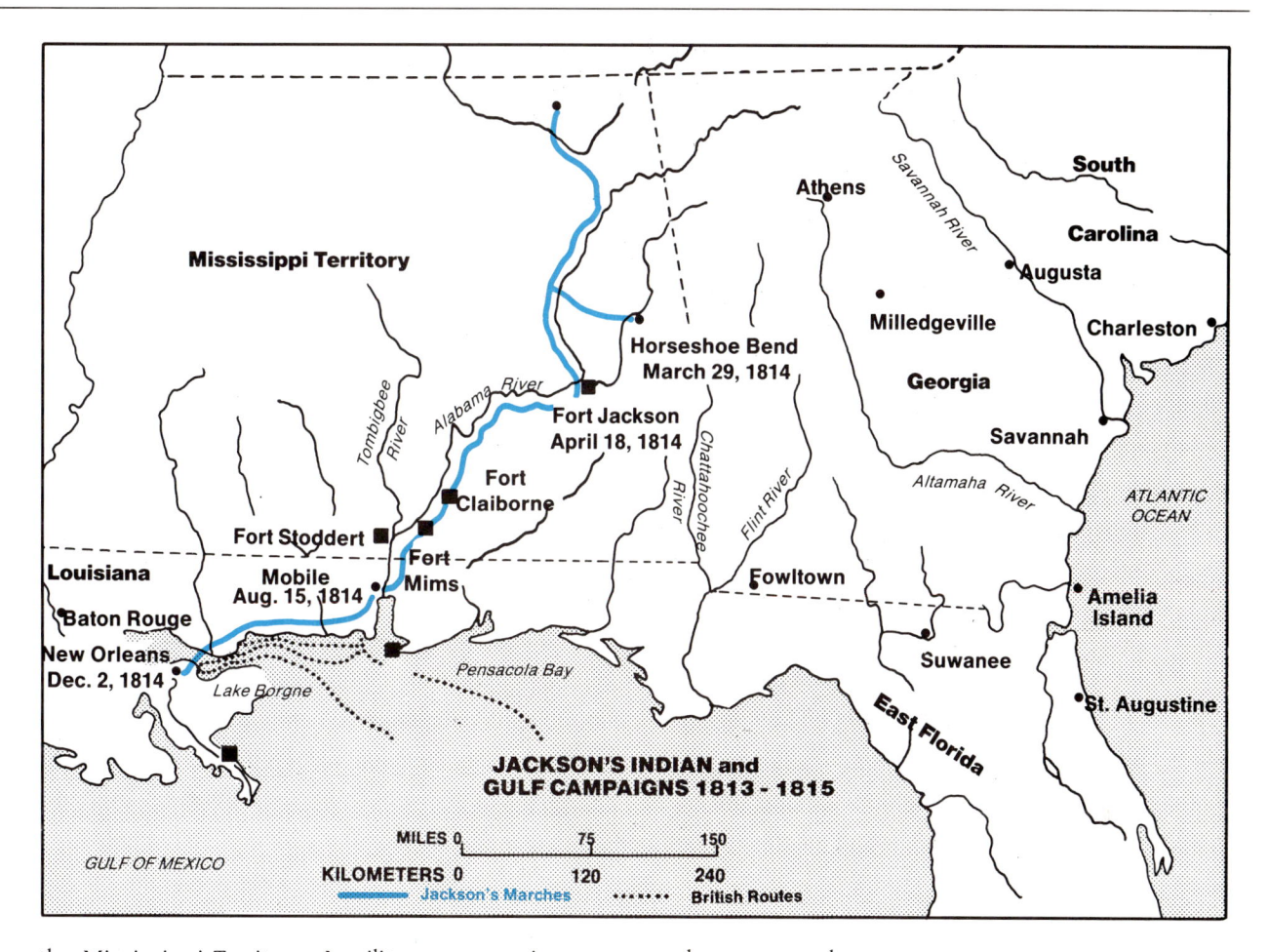

A map of Andrew Jackson's Indian and Gulf campaigns between 1813 and 1815.

the Mississippi Territory. A military commander notable for his enthusiasm rather than his concern with such essentials as adequate supplies and a safe line of communications, Jackson swept on so impetuously that he had soon moved beyond the limits of his minimal supply system and was forced to live off the land. Jackson's force nonetheless managed to inflict tactical reverses on the Creeks at Tallasahatchee on November 3 and at Talladega on November 9. The militia force was then itself defeated. As the men were already discouraged by their lack of supplies, Jackson decided to await supplies and reinforcements at Fort Strother on the upper reaches of the Coosa River. In this entrenched position, the increasingly mutinous Tennessee militia wintered, and only the arrival of an infantry regiment of the regular army in February 1814 made it possible for Jackson to restore order within his own command and plan further offensive action against the Indians. The Creeks meanwhile had recovered from their defeats of the previous year and now posed as great a threat as before.

The Battle of Horseshoe Bend

In March, Jackson felt that he was ready. He moved his command against the main Creek force of about 900 men, together with large numbers of women and children, gathered in the Horseshoe Bend area of the Tallapoosa River. Jackson's force was made up of about 2,000 militia and volunteers supported by just under 600 regulars, several hundred friendly Indians, and a few pieces of artillery. Jackson's force fell on the Creeks in the Battle of Horseshoe Bend on March 29. The main part was played by the regulars, who completely routed the Creek warriors with a firm bayonet charge. The rest of the force was launched in a ruthless pursuit of the Creeks as they fled toward Spanish territory, which only 100 warriors reached. American casualties were 201, and a few Creek noncombatants were

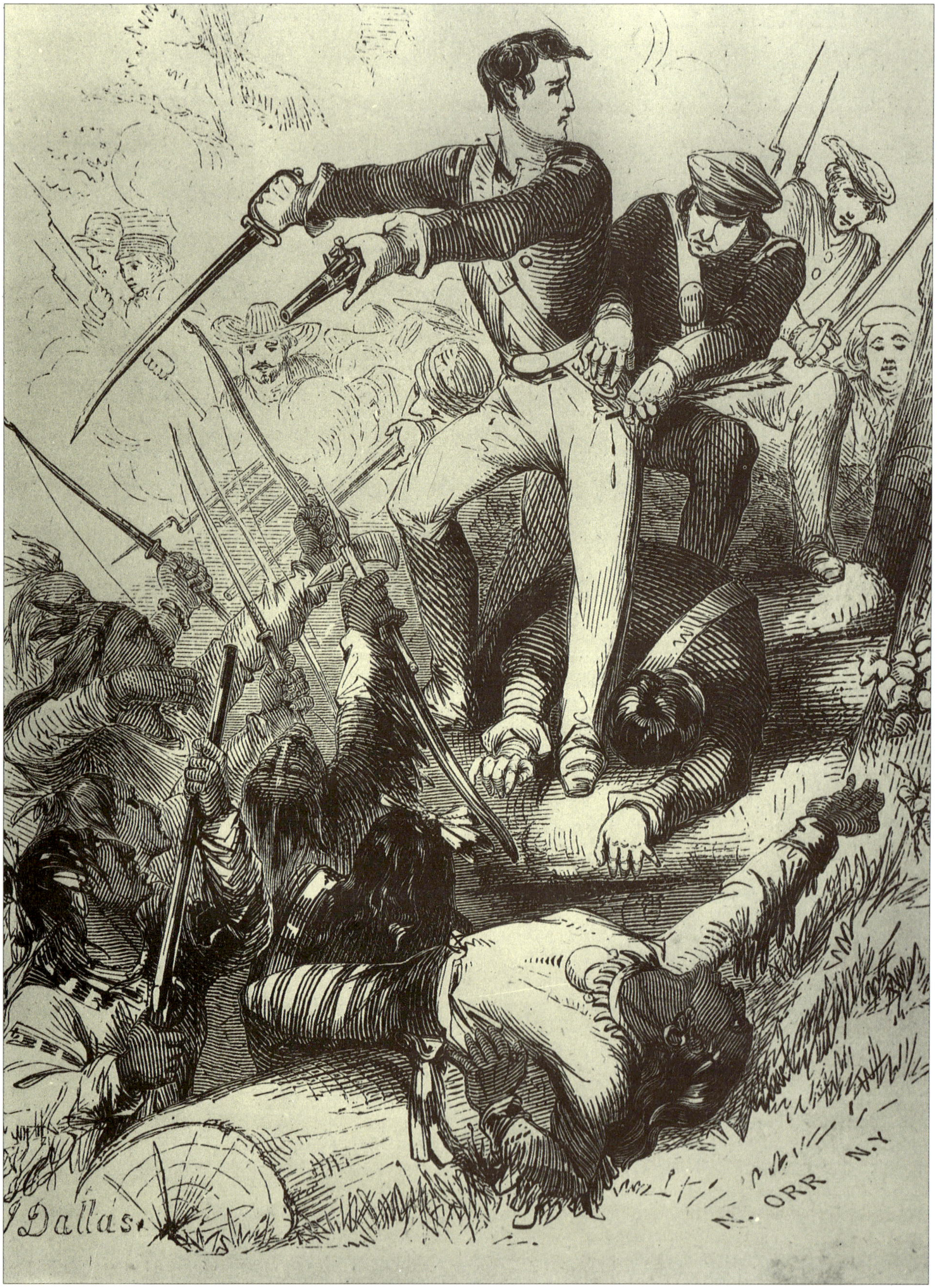
Dallas
N. ORR N.Y

REVOLUTIONARY AND EARLY AMERICAN WARS

also killed. Jackson himself said: "I lament that two or three women and children were killed by accident."

The war was ended by the Treaty of Fort Jackson on August 9, 1814. In overall terms, the Creek War had been of little significance, even within the context of the War of 1812. On May 22, Jackson had been rewarded for his success by a commission as major general in the regular army and was placed in command of the Gulf coast region.

The Treaty of Ghent

On February 13, 1815, news arrived in Washington, the new capital of the United States, that the War of 1812 had been ended by the Treaty of Ghent, signed on December 24, 1814. There followed a period in American military history often called "The Thirty Years' Peace." This period was certainly free of any type of warfare against foreign enemies, but it did

Left: Another man destined for greater things was Samuel Houston. At the time of the Creek War, young Houston was a second lieutenant. In the Battle of Horseshoe Bend he showed considerable courage when he was hit in the leg by an arrow.

Right: James Monroe, in a painting attributed to Herring. A protege of Thomas Jefferson, who taught him law and persuaded him to enter political life, Monroe was Secretary of State and then Secretary of War in the administration of President James Madison. Capitalizing on his considerable success in these two offices, Monroe won the 1816 presidential election and was inaugurated as the fifth president in March 1817.

199

U.S. Regular Army, Staff Officer (1810)

The military staffs of the period were very small by comparison with those of modern armies. Even so, the staff officer of the period had a distinctive uniform. In action, only the aide-de-camp (senior officer's assistant) was allowed to wear the crimson sash worn by all other army officers.

REVOLUTIONARY AND EARLY AMERICAN WARS

Throughout this period, there was continual skirmishing along the frontiers of the settled region. This striking image depicts an episode in the frontier fighting during 1812, when Daniel Boone and two companions were attacked by Indians, who killed and scalped John Stewart as the other two Americans escaped.

Washington
For further references see pages 191, 199, 202, 210, 232, 240, 243.

contain a number of frontier conflicts with various Indian tribes.

At the time, though, the prospect of sustained peace seemed unlikely. In Europe, it was generally assumed that the United Kingdom, having with its allies completely eliminated any armed threat from France, would soon turn its attentions to the re-conquest of the lost part of its American empire. This feeling was gloomily reported to the Secretary of State, James Monroe, by Brigadier General Winfield Scott, who was in Europe during the summer of 1815. Scott was impressed with the quality of the allied armies that had finally brought defeat to Napoleon, one of history's greatest captains. The American general was also devoting considerable effort to a tactical study of the Napoleonic Wars, and to collecting all current British and French studies on army organization and training. Professional soldiers in the United States argued about the tactical and operational implications of the Napoleonic Wars, and about whether there was still validity in the concept of total war as embodied in the phrase "the nation in arms." Intertwined with these thoughts about warfare as fought between the major European powers was consideration of the performance of the U.S. forces in the War of 1812. The consensus of professional soldiers was that the day of the militiaman was effectively over. All agreed that militia forces had undoubtedly contributed to American success in several battles, but the professionals were increasingly concerned about organizing an effective army and laying sensible plans when it was difficult to obtain from the states any accurate figures of how many militiamen they each possessed, and how each militia unit was armed, organized, disciplined, and trained.

Army Cut-backs

Almost immediately after the end of the War of 1812 had been announced publicly by President James Madison, Congress met to consider the future of the American army. The session was held at Blodgett's Hotel in Washington because the Capitol was in ruins after its destruction by the British in August 1814. This reminder of the nation's vulnerability clearly played its part in the decision of Congress to create a larger but more

201

efficient regular army that would form the major defense of the United States in collaboration with the state militias. The authorized strength was set at 10,000 men excluding the Corps of Engineers, a figure only about one-third of the army's peak strength in the War of 1812, but more than three times that of the 3,220-man establishment under Jefferson. Congress was determined that the army should be not only larger, but also considerably more efficient in terms of organization and leadership. The organization, created during the War of 1812, of nine military districts (headed mainly by elderly officers who had distinguished themselves in the Revolutionary War) was replaced by a more streamlined arrangement of two divisions. The Division of the North had four territorial departments and was headed by Major General Jacob Brown, while the Division of the South had five territorial departments and was headed by Major General Andrew Jackson. Both commanders had distinguished themselves in the War of 1812 and were expected to breathe new life into their commands.

At the head of this organization was a new Secretary of War, the first full-time holder of the office for more than 12 months. In August 1814, public opinion had reacted to a series of misfortunes, culminating in the British occupation of Washington, by forcing the resignation of John Armstrong. Over the next few months, Secretary of State Monroe had also acted as Secretary of War until the spring of 1815, when illness forced him to hand over the Department of War to Secretary of the Treasury Alexander Dallas. Then, President Madison appointed William H. Crawford, the U.S. Ambassador to France, as the new Secretary of War, and Crawford arrived back from Europe in August 1815 to take up his new position.

The new secretary had previously been a distinguished Senator and had refused the position of Secretary of War that had then been accepted by the unfortunate Armstrong. Despite his later assignment to France, Crawford had maintained a deep interest in the U.S. Army, particularly in the General Staff established by Congress in the spring of 1813.

It was not a general staff in the modern sense, covering the full spectrum of operational concerns, but an organization to oversee the army's "housekeeping functions." For this reason, therefore, the General staff controlled the Adjutant General's, Hospital, Inspector General's, Ordnance, Pay, Purchasing, Quartermaster's, and Topographical Departments, together with the Judge Advocates, the Chaplains, and the Military Academy. It also had authority over commanding generals of the nine military districts and their logistical staffs. Congress also decided that certain officers from this organization (most notably the Adjutant and Inspector General plus two assistants, the Commissary General of Ordnance plus three assistants, the Paymaster of the Army, and the Assistant Topographical Engineer) should be based in Washington to provide the Secretary of War with a small but professional staff in place of his previous "staff" of just a few clerks. As early as 1813, Crawford had urged from France that "For God's sake," it was essential to "endeavor to rid the army of old women and blockheads, at least on the general staff."

Crawford as Secretary of War

In fact, it was the reorganization in the spring of 1815 that finally removed those to whom Crawford rightly objected. Crawford urged Congress to maintain the General Staff as part of the peacetime establishment. The course of the War of 1812's early campaigns had convinced him of "the necessity of giving to the military establishment, in time of peace, the organization which it must have to render it efficient in a state of war." Crawford's understanding was extremely far-sighted. The only major modification wanted by the new Secretary of war was the addition of the Quartermaster General to those officers allocated permanently to the management staff in Washington, plus an increase in the size of the Corps of Engineers. Congress accepted Crawford's proposals on April 24, 1816, and only a few days later authorized the President to secure the
Continued on page 206

This map shows the military posts in the western United States in the period from 1815 to 1825, together with the boundary between the army's Eastern and Western Departments in 1821.

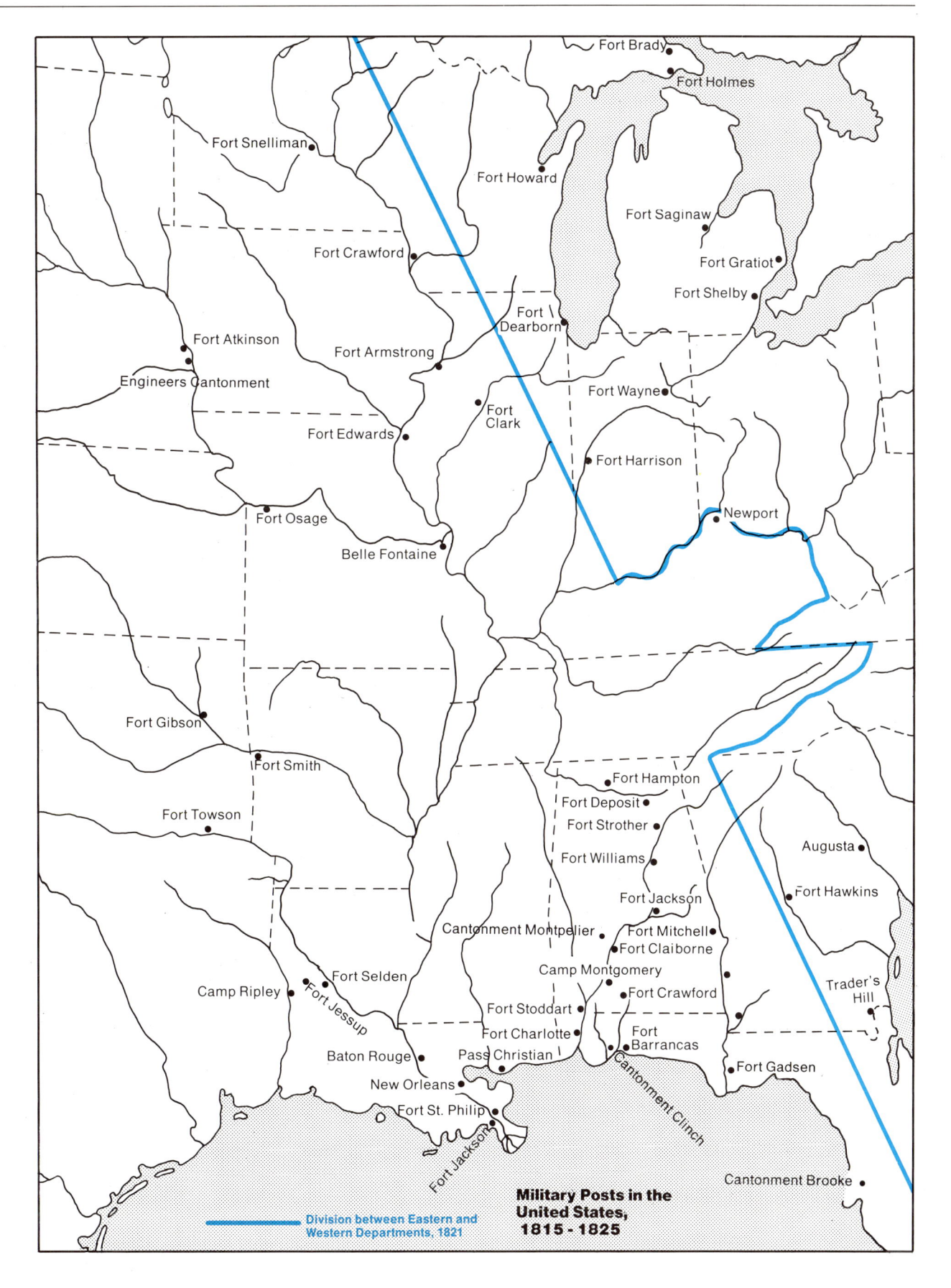

REVOLUTIONARY AND EARLY AMERICAN WARS

Military Posts in the United States, 1815-1825

— Division between Eastern and Western Departments, 1821

Early American Firearms

Very little is known of the firearms of the earliest colonists, though it is clear that they used the matchlock type of weapon. The match, a short length of hemp cord impregnated with saltpeter and other chemicals to make it burn steadily at between three and five inches an hour, was held in the screw-adjusted jaws of the lock's cocking piece. When the firer pulled the trigger, a spring turned the cocking piece so that the lighted tip of the match plunged down into a pan filled with priming powder, whose ignition flashed down a vent (the touchhole) into the barrel and set off the main charge of powder behind the bullet.

The Wheel Lock

The next development in weapon technology was the wheel lock, which offered a considerably higher chance of successful ignition. It worked on the same principal as the modern cigarette lighter: when the trigger mechanism was activated, a serrated steel wheel was spun by a coil spring that had to be wound with a special key. It struck a flint to produce a shower of sparks that ignited the powder in the priming pan. The wheel lock mechanism was expensive to make and difficult to maintain, so it never became common on the weapons of the American colonists.

Further development produced the snaphaunce, which was based on the tinder lock, an improved version of the matchlock. In the snaphaunce, the adjustable jaws of the cocking piece held a piece of pyrites. It was driven by the spring of the mechanism against a steel anvil beside the priming pan, creating the sparks needed to ignite the powder. The Massachusetts Bay Company imported snaphaunce weapons for its paid troops in 1628. The final development of this weapon was the flintlock, which was basically the snaphaunce with a lid over the priming pan to stop the powder from getting wet or blowing away. As the cocking piece descended, it struck the hinged cover and threw it back to expose the powder.

The Need for Firearms

From the beginning of the American colonies, the settlers had to hunt, and in due course they came increasingly into conflict with the Indian tribes of the eastern seaboard. They needed effective firearms, and although the records are scanty, it is inevitable that weapons were first imported, and facilities for maintenance and then manufacture were established in the colonies. The earliest settlers were British and so came from stock that was not notable for its interest or skill in the manufacture of firearms.

The arrival of German and Swiss settlers changed things. Many of the new settlers came from stock historically involved in the development and manufacture of firearms. The Germans settled mainly in Pennsylvania, and soon began to develop a truly American type of weapon. The heritage of the new gunsmiths was European, which emphasized heavy weapons with a large bore (internal diameter of the barrel). In Pennsylvania, the gunsmiths swiftly realized that modifications to this pattern were essential. Barrels up to 48 inches long were introduced for better combustion of the main powder charge, and as this also permitted the installation of the sights on a longer base, accuracy was improved to a very considerable degree. Despite the increased weight of the extended barrel, overall weight remained basically the same, gunsmiths re-designed the wooden stock (made mainly of American maple or walnut) to eliminate all sections that were not strictly necessary. Even so, the length of the stocks was gradually increased to protect much of the barrel, which might otherwise have been damaged in the thick forests.

American Gunsmiths

By 1700, small gunsmithing businesses were producing excellent and characteristically American weapons, and by 1732 men such as the Heinrich brothers and Peter Leman

REVOLUTIONARY AND EARLY AMERICAN WARS

"Trade from the Monongahela" by Gayle Hoskins reveals aspects of rifle manufacture, repair, and maintenance.

were producing weapons acknowledged to be as good as any in the world. The finest of these weapons were rifled types with sophisticated sights, capable of considerable accuracy over a long range. The early weapons had an average caliber of .54 inch and fired a ball weighing about half an ounce, but these figures were soon reduced in the interests of accuracy and range. Rate of fire, was improved considerably by a completely American revision to the art of loading the rifle. European loading meant that a slightly oversized bullet was started down the barrel by being hammered into the muzzle before being punched down onto the powder charge with the ramrod. The new American system used a slightly undersized bullet wrapped in linen or buckskin that had been soaked in tallow. This not only improved speed of loading, but also provided a better seal between the bullet and the barrel, reducing the loss of propellant gas when the rifle was fired and therefore improving range and accuracy.

These American weapons were made mainly in Pennsylvania but were called Kentucky rifles, because they were used mainly in the region then called Kentucky, lying between the Cumberlands and the Mississippi River. The Kentucky rifle's accuracy has been greatly exaggerated in stories over the years, but it was nevertheless the greatest precision firearm of its day.

The Demands of War

With the outbreak of the Revolutionary War in 1775, there was an urgent demand for military weapons, all flintlocks and mainly of the smoothbore musket type. Procurement resulted from the recommendation of the Committee of Safety, and flintlock weapons were made by more than 200 gunsmiths in Maryland, Massachusetts, Pennsylvania and Rhode Island. These weapons weighed about ten pounds each and had calibers ranging from .72 to .80 inch. French support for the American cause resulted in substantial deliveries of weapons and the Americans received large numbers of the Charleville musket, notably the Model 1763.

With the flintlock, the firearm had reached a plateau as a weapon using mechanical means for ignition. The next step was the adoption of chemical means in the percussion lock. In its first practical form, developed early in the 19th century, the percussion lock was a simple adaptation of the flintlock in which the cocking piece, now ending in a hammerhead, struck a cap filled with fulminate of mercury that exploded under the impact and sent a flash of flame down the touchhole to ignite the main powder charge. The major advantage of the system was greater reliability as neither rain or wind affected the cap.

The Percussion Principle

American military weapons were soon converted to the percussion principle. The most famous was the muzzle-loading Model 1841 rifle, otherwise known as the Yaeger (a corruption of the German *Jager*, or hunter), Harper's Ferry, or Mississippi Rifle. It was used in the Mexican War and remained in service right through the Civil War in both its original version and the improved Model 1855 with a Maynard Tape primer rather than individual percussion caps.

Over the same period, many Kentucky rifles were modified to pill lock configuration: the priming pan was replaced by an iron bowl and the cocking piece was revised into a hammer that would detonate the priming "pill" in the bowl. Further development turned the pill lock Kentucky rifle into the Plains rifle, which was better suited to the requirements of the plainsmen west of the Mississippi River. Produced by gunsmiths such as Hawkins and Dimick in St. Louis, Missouri, the Plains rifle weighed between six and ten pounds, and had calibers ranging between ·26 and ·40 inch. The barrels were generally between 26 and 38 inches long, though some weapons had longer barrels.

THE MILITARY HISTORY OF THE UNITED STATES

services of a "skillful assistant" within the Corps of Engineers. General Simon Bernard, who had served under Napoleon, was employed and became an important figure in the program of coastal fortification authorized by Congress in an effort to avoid a repeat of defeats suffered in such areas during the War of 1812.

Crawford was also responsible for expansion and academic improvement at the U.S. Military Academy at West Point. He could perhaps have moved on to a further improvement of the regular army, but in the fall of 1816, Crawford was asked to become Secretary of the Treasury so that Madison could bring Henry Clay into the cabinet as Secretary of War. However, Clay and several other men refused the appointment. George Graham, the Department of War's chief clerk, served as Acting Secretary of War for more than 12 months until John C. Calhoun became Secretary of War on December 8, 1817. By this time, the threat of renewed war with the United Kingdom had been recognized as imaginary, and Congressional interest in the army was waning. Army strength had declined to just 8,200 men, and Congress now proposed to cut back the authorized strength, dispose of the General Staff, and close the Military Academy. Calhoun was preparing to fight these proposals when the matter was again thrown into the spotlight by an outbreak of warfare with Indian tribes on the frontier between Georgia and the Spanish possession of East Florida.

The First Seminole War (1818)

After their defeat at the Battle of Horseshoe Bend, a group from the Creek nation had settled in Spanish Florida. These Lower Creeks, also known as the "Red Sticks" because they carried red-painted war clubs, moved into the swamplands and palmetto forests of Florida along with Seminole Indians and runaway slaves. Here they were left unmolested by the Spaniards, who effectively restricted themselves to the coastal towns of St. Augustine in the east, St. Marks in the center, and Pensacola in the west.

Operating from the Bahama Islands

As it appeared in 1813, Fort Meigs was typical of the frontier defenses of its period. However, it was built as protection against the British rather than the Indians. The fort lay on the southeastern side of the Maumee river in north western Ohio, and with Fort Stephenson it blocked the eastward advance along the southern side of Lake Erie.

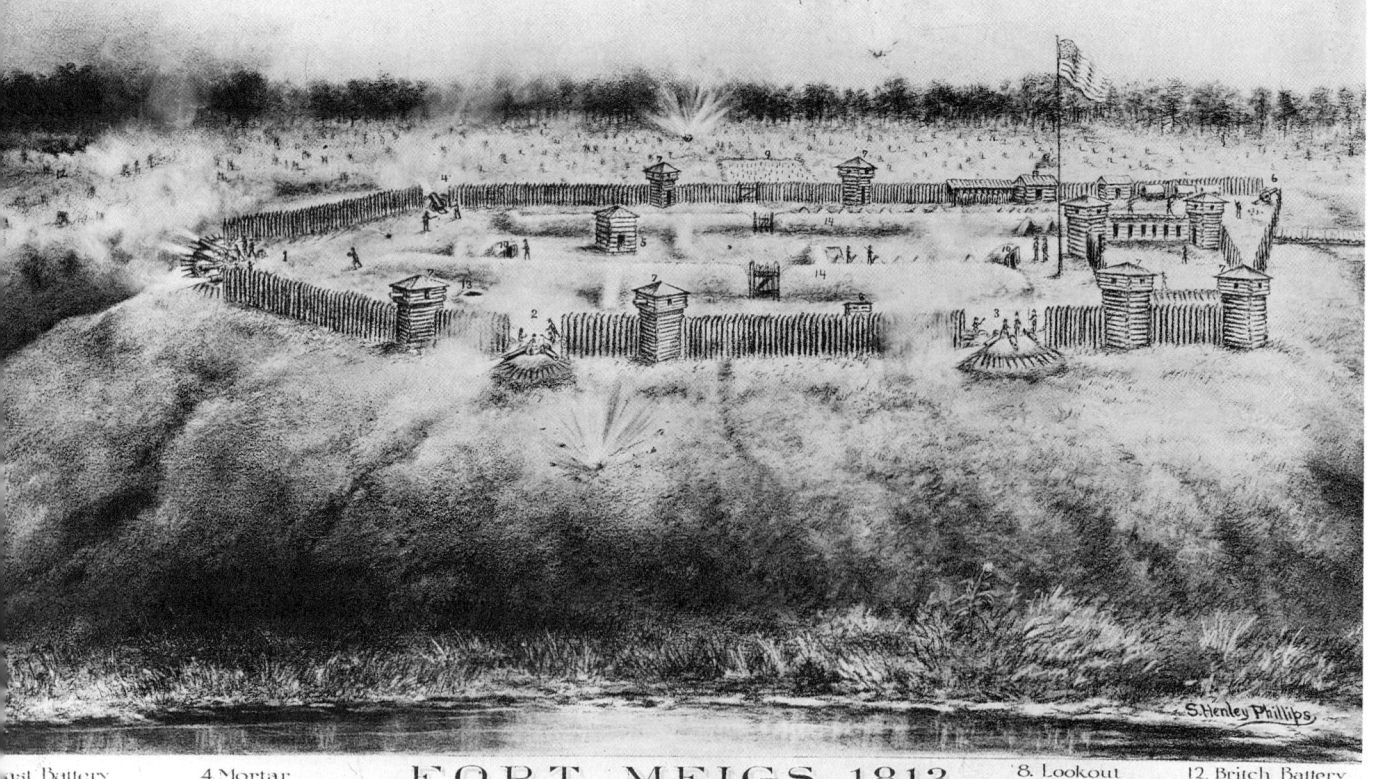

FORT MEIGS, 1813
Copyright 1913, by S.H. Phillips
PHOTO by C.L. LEWIS

ast Battery   4. Mortar   8. Lookout   12. Britch Battery
ajor Croghan's Battery 5. Meat House   9. Kentucky Blues Burial Ground
en. Cushing's Battery   6. West Battery 10. Magazines   13. Well
7. Block Houses   14. Traverse

U.S. Army, 1st Rifle Regiment (1814)

The men of the 1st Rifle Regiment wore green coats with facings of black, yellow collar lace, and yellow metal buttons. In the summer white linen leg wear was sported; but in winter, green woolen overalls were worn. The weapon was the Model 1803 rifle, and ammunition was stowed in a "belly" box, shot pouch and powder horn. The noncommissioned officers were similarly dressed but were distinguished by yellow worsted epaulets. In 1814, the 2nd, 3rd, and 4th Rifle Regiments were raised. There was a shortage of green woolen cloth available, so the new regiments were initially uniformed in green linen hunting smocks, soon replaced by gray uniforms.

THE MILITARY HISTORY OF THE UNITED STATES

east of Florida, two British adventurers intervened to cause trouble. Lieutenant Colonel Edward Nicholls had employed some of these Indians for an attack on Mobile in the summer of 1814 during the War of 1812. The attack had been unsuccessful. On departing for England in 1815, Nicholls left most of the weapons he had supplied for the expedition with the Indians. The other adventurer was a trader named Arbuthnot. These two persuasive Britons convinced the Indians of a complete lie. They told the tribes that the Treaty of Ghent, which ended the War of 1812, had restored to the Indians the land in southern Georgia which they had given up to the United States in the Treaty of Fort Jackson that ended the Creek War. The Indians therefore concluded that Americans were settling on land that was rightfully theirs.

A typical pattern of Indian warfare began to unfold as settlers were killed and their homesteads burned by parties

A piece of artillery equipment much used in North America was the British 6-pounder field gun, made up of a comparatively light metal ordnance on a simple two-wheeled carriage towed behind a two-wheel ammunition limber. At the top left of the illustration are three types of ammunition, namely canister (left), grapeshot (center) and round shot. Underneath the limber are the vent clearer (top) and the linstock, complete with slow match. Below the gun itself are (from top to bottom) the worm for extracting items lodged down the barrel, the rammer, the scoop, and the traversing spike.

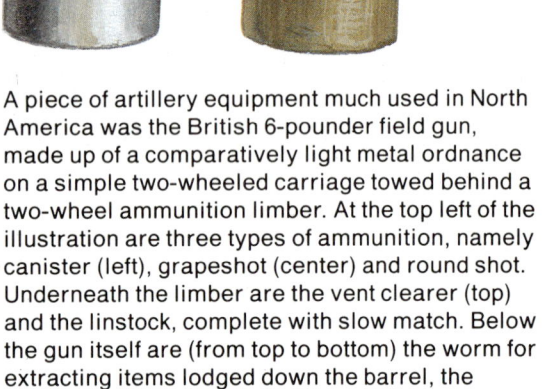

of irate Indians. The U.S. administration tried to control the situation, principally by reinforcing Fort Scott. This post was a log structure in the southwestern corner of Georgia where the Chattahoochee and Flint rivers combine to create the Apalachicola. This river runs through Florida to the Gulf of Mexico and, at that time, was the main route of supply to the fort from Mobile and New Orleans. In November 1817, the Indians attacked a keelboat making its way up the river to Fort Scott ahead of several supply boats, and killed or captured 34 of the 40 people on board, all soldiers or the wives of soldiers. At about the same time, a detachment of the regular army from Fort Scott attacked the Negro Fort (so called because it was garrisoned mainly by escaped slaves) on the Apalachicola River and destroyed it, thereby easing waterborne communication between Fort Scott and the coast. But with their main strength based in Spanish Florida, the

THE MILITARY HISTORY OF THE UNITED STATES

Indians were able to continue their campaign of raiding into American territory, massacring and pillaging white settlements and homesteads.

Jackson Ordered Into Action

Information about the attack on the keelboat reached Washington on December 26, 1817, and set off the First Seminole War. Secretary of War Calhoun ordered Andrew Jackson to move immediately from Nashville, Tennessee, and take personal command of Fort Scott, a garrison of 800 regular soldiers and about 1,000 Georgia militiamen. Jackson was authorized to call for more militiamen if he thought the situation warranted it. He had anticipated the nature of the trouble likely to break out in Florida and had already prepared his plans. Believing that the three-month service of the Georgia militiamen might expire by the time he reached Fort Scott, Jackson appealed for 1,000 west Tennessee volunteers for six-month service. He set off for Fort Scott with two companies of mounted militiamen, ordering the rest of his force to follow as rapidly as possible. Ahead of him, he sent an officer to Fort Hawkins in central Georgia with money to buy provisions in addition to those he had ordered from New Orleans. The supplies from New Orleans were to be moved by ship to Mobile and then farther along the coast before traveling up the Apalachicola to Fort Scott.

The sensational illustrations of eastern magazines helped to establish in urban minds the wild nature of the western frontier. This is entitled "The Sioux Massacre at Big Stone Lake, Minnesota."

REVOLUTIONARY AND EARLY AMERICAN WARS

The commander of the Division of the South reached Fort Hawkins on February 9, 1818, and found that the civilian contractor had failed to supply the food that had been promised. After sending an angry letter to Calhoun and managing to buy some pigs, peanuts, and corn locally, Jackson pressed on toward Fort Scott, where he arrived on March 9 and broke the Indians' siege of the fort. Here, he learned that the supply ships from Mobile had arrived at the mouth of the Apalachicola River. Jackson felt that the protection of these ships from Indian attack was vital to the success of his whole campaign, and on the following morning, he marched south down the eastern bank of the river with 400 regulars and the Georgia militiamen from Fort Scott. After six days of hard marching, the force arrived at the mouth of the Apalachicola, where there was no sign of the supply ships. Jackson decided to wait and ordered Lieutenant James Gadsen of the Corps of Engineers to build a fort for the storage of the supplies once they arrived.

The supply ships had been delayed by storms, and finally arrived on March 25. Jackson was now ready to unleash his campaign, which began on March 26 without any further delay. Jackson's plan was centered on the destruction of the Indians' main bases wherever they might be. His first objective was the Indian settlement on the Suwannee River about 150 miles to the east, where Chief Billy Bowlegs of the Seminoles was reported to be assembling a force of several thousand Indians and escaped slaves. Fort Gadsen was too far away from the Suwannee River to be a useful base, so Jackson decided to take St. Marks as a forward base. Jackson had about 1,200 men under his immediate command and, after ordering his supply ships to make for Apalachee Bay off St. Marks, moved into Spanish East Florida. The advance was delayed by the need to build canoes in

Magazine illustrations were produced to boost sales and were therefore made as lurid as possible. At the same time they may be regarded as an important part of the public information (or rather propaganda) campaigns of their periods. This "illustrates" the results of an Indian attack on the Motte family during the Seminole War.

John C. Calhoun
For further references see pages 206, 214, 215, 232. 233, 235.

THE MILITARY HISTORY OF THE UNITED STATES

which to cross the Ochlokonee River, and farther east by the need to root out resistance in several Indian villages, but St. Marks was taken on April 7. Here the Americans captured Arbuthnot, who was thrown into jail. Jackson's strength had already been increased by the arrival of some Tennessee volunteers as well as a sizeable party of friendly Upper Creeks, but the main body of Tennessee volunteers had inevitably been delayed by supply problems and joined the commander only on April 11. By this time, Jackson was pressing inland through the swamps to reach the main Indian settlement, the so-called Bowlegs' Town.

The Indians Escape

The Indians had been warned by Arbuthnot before his capture and had departed to safer havens. However, Jackson's men did capture a large quantity of corn and cattle with which to feed themselves. They also seized a third British adventurer from the Bahamas, Robert Armbrister, who had been drilling Bowleg's men and teaching them about firearms. Armbrister was sent back to St. Marks, where he and Arbuthnot were tried by a military court, convicted, and executed. Jackson released his Georgia militiamen and the Upper Creeks, and headed west with his regulars and the Tennessee volunteers. Resistance in Seminole and Lower Creek villages was being broken by a number of columns. At Fort Gadsen in early May, Jackson learned that Bowlegs was assembling a force at Pensacola in the extreme west of Spanish East Florida for a final effort against the American force. Jackson took Pensacola on May 24 before the Indians could build a formidable force. The Spanish governor fled to Fort Barrancas, but Jackson's artillery shelled the position and forced the surrender of the governor and his Spanish troops. In Pensacola, Jackson established an American garrison to match that in St. Marks, and toward the end of the month he departed for Nashville.

The First Seminole War had succeeded in its main objective, which was the

Another example of the same journalistic style is "American Frontier Life." Here, frontiersmen spring an ambush on Indians drawn into the light of a campfire by three dummies.

The Seminoles
For further references see pages
211, 214, 237, *239*, 240, *241*, *242*, *244*, 246, *247*, 249, 250.

212

U.S. Army, 6th Regiment, Private (1814)

In June 1812, the War of 1812 began, and a month later, the strength of the army stood at only 6,686 men out of an authorized establishment of 35,603. The regular establishment of the U.S. Army was soon expanded greatly, though the 37 new regiments nominally raised in 1812 and 1813 were at first no better than the state militia units beside which they served. Even though the new regiments were greatly below strength, it was impossible to supply the men with proper uniforms, and shortages of blue woolen cloth forced the Purveyor of Public Supplies to issue substitute uniforms of several different types. Gray, brown, and even olive drab cloth was used, and the facings were either omitted or simplified. This private of the 6th Regiment wears the regulation "coatee" above brown linen fatigue trousers. The leather cap is of the type adopted in 1813, with a flap that could be lowered to protect the neck; the cap decorations include a metal plate, a leather cockade with a brass eagle, a tasseled cord, and a felt pom-pom on the left, though the 6th Infantry (like the Volunteers and the Marine Corps) was permitted to wear a buck's tail in place of the pom-pom.

complete destruction of Lower Creek and Seminole military capability against American settlers in Georgia. But the whole campaign had also been extremely provocative. Jackson had led American forces into Spanish territory, attacked and captured Spanish forts, and executed two British citizens. Spain and the United Kingdom could have caused considerable international trouble for the United States, but preferred not to do so. Negotiations with Spain for the purchase of Florida were already under way and were finally completed by the signature of the Adams-Onis Treaty on February 19, 1819. In this treaty, the Spanish abandoned all claim to West Florida, which was already occupied by the United States, and ceded East Florida. The captured forts had been handed back to the Spanish late in 1818, but were now returned to American ownership. Other provisions of the Adams-Onis Treaty were a cancellation of all Spanish claims to the Pacific Northwest region, and the setting of the frontier between U.S. and Spanish territory from the mouth of the Sabine River in the Gulf of Mexico northwest to the Pacific Ocean.

Logistics Again Inadequate

As far as military operations in the First Seminole War were concerned, the U.S. could only be grateful that the opposition had been so poor. Throughout the campaign, Jackson had been forced to devote most of his energy to feeding and otherwise maintaining his force in the field. The supply system had failed completely. The fault was traced yet again to the continued use of civilian contractors, who invariably delivered quantities of rations below those contracted, and frequently delivered the supplies after the contracted date or to the wrong place. Calhoun appealed to Congress, and in April 1818, it was decided that in the future contractors would have to deliver rations in bulk at specified depots under a better system of transportation. The Congressional measure also guaranteed stricter army control of civilian contrac-

Not all American contacts with the Indians were bloody. This illustration shows Major Stephen H. Long listening to Indian grievances at a council of the Pawnee Indians in 1819-1820

Molds were the best way of making sure that each unit had the right caliber of bullet for its weapons. These molds could be of the single type (right) or any of several "gang" molds. With the mold closed, molten lead was poured into the open top. Once the lead had hardened, the mold was opened, and the ball(s) were extracted and cleaned, ready to use.

tors' supplies through a Subsistence Department of the type not seen since the Revolutionary War.

Secretary of War Calhoun was convinced that frontier security and operations would be better left to regular forces. He expressed this idea to a senior officer by writing that calling the militia into service was "harassing to them and exhausting to the treasury. Protection is the first object, and the second is protection by the regular force." But continued political fears about a large regular army combined with economic factors made Calhoun's notion impractical. Any regular army was now needed to protect northern, western, and southwestern land frontiers, as well as the coastal forts of the eastern and southern seaboards.

In 1820, Calhoun was instructed by Congress to comment on a plan to reduce the regular army to a strength of only 6,000 men. Calhoun replied that any reduction would be unwise, but that if

THE MILITARY HISTORY OF THE UNITED STATES

REVOLUTIONARY AND EARLY AMERICAN WARS

In September 1825, Governor Lewis Cass of Michigan and William Clark of Missouri were U.S. commissioners at the signing of a great treaty at Prairie du Chien on the upper reaches of the Mississippi River in Wisconsin. This painting was done on the spot by J.O. Lewis, and purports to show the occasion *"at which upwards of 50,000 Indian Warriors of the Chippeways, Sioux, Sacs & Foxes, Winnebagoes, Pottowattomies, Menomonies, Iowats and Ottowas tribes were present."*

THE MILITARY HISTORY OF THE UNITED STATES

reduction were essential, the best course would be to reduce the strength of each company by half, leaving in existence an organization that could be flushed out rapidly during an emergency to create a 19,000-man army. It was again a far-sighted concept - in effect, the origin of the later concept of the "expansible army" - but it was rejected by Congress. Instead, it was decided on March 2, 1821, that the strength of the army's standard companies would be reduced (in the case of the infantry company from 68 to 42); and that the current establishment of eight infantry regiments, one rifle regiment, one light artillery regiment, and the eight-battalion corps of artillery would be

Typical of a ship's armament is this light 6-pounder gun on a wheeled carriage, which here is seen without all the tackle for controlling the recoil and then running out the loaded weapon. Ordnance elevation was controlled by moving the quoin (wooden wedge) under the breech. Under the gun are (from top to bottom) a scoop, worm, rammer, swab, and traverse spike. Farther to the right are (top row, left to right) the priming powder horn, linstock in a water bucket, and round shot, and (bottom row, left to right) vent prick and knife, serge powder bag, and wad.

218

REVOLUTIONARY AND EARLY AMERICAN WARS

trimmed to seven infantry regiments and four artillery regiments. At the same time, the geographical organization of the army was altered from the existing Divisions of the North and of the South to an Eastern Department commanded by Brigadier General Winfield Scott and a Western Department commanded by Brigadier General Edmund P. Gaines.

Commanding General of the Army

The new establishment also allowed for only one major general. As Jackson had resigned from the army to become governor of Florida, this presented no challenge to the only other officer holding the rank, Major General Jacob Brown. To fill a

Continued on page 232

A weapon that was often mounted in boats and then in smaller warships was the carronade, a lightweight type based on a slide rather than a wheeled carriage. Designed to use only a small charge to fire a heavy ball over only a short range, the carronade was light, easy to make and therefore comparatively cheap.

THE BEGINNINGS OF THE U.S. NAVY

From the start of the Revolutionary War, there were "warships" in American service, although they were little more than armed merchantmen operating under the auspices of the colonial armed forces. The first naval action of the Revolutionary War is now considered to have been the capture, on June 12, 1775, of the British ship *Margaretta* by the *Unity*. After hearing of the events at Concord and Lexington, Jeremiah O'Brien and about 40 men seized guns, swords, axes, and pitchforks, boarded the *Unity* in Machias Bay, Maine, and then came up with the *Margaretta* at sea. After a fierce fight, the Americans captured the British ship.

On September 5, 1775, the schooner *Hannah* became the first regularly commissioned American warship. On the very day that she was commissioned, the *Hannah* sailed; two days later, she cap-

Born in Scituate, Rhode Island, during 1718, Commodore Esek Hopkins was the first commander-in-chief of the Continental Navy, and received his appointment on December 22, 1775. His brother was chairman of the Naval Committee of the Congress. Though instructed to operate against British ships in Chesapeake Bay, Hopkins used the excuse of a rendezvous (by six of his eight ships) off the Bahamas after his squadron had become separated to make a landing on New Providence. After his return Hopkins was censured by the Continental Congress, and in the following year, he was suspended from his command. A few months later Hopkins was formally dismissed.

tured a British ship. The *Hannah* was the first vessel of "Washington's Fleet," which soon numbered five other schooners and a brigantine.

The formal birthday of the U.S. Navy is officially October 13, 1775. On this date, the Continental Congress ordered two ships to be fitted out for use in the essential task of intercepting British supplies before they reached North America. The Congress had been much impressed with the success of "Washington's Fleet," and the first step toward the creation of a Continental Navy was entrusted to Silas Deane, Christopher Gadsen, and John Langdon. The first disciplinary framework for the new service was provided by the "Rules for the Regulation of the Navy of the United Colonies," prepared by John Adams and issued on November 28, 1775. (The name "The United States" was not adopted until September 6, 1776.)

The First Union Flag to Fly From an American Warship

On December 3, 1775, Lieutenant John Paul Jones hoisted the Grand Union flag (13 American stripes with the Union flag in the field) on his ship, the *Alfred*, the first occasion on which a flag had been unfurled on an American warship. Ten days later, the Continental Congress ordered the building of 13 warships for the Continental Navy. Only seven of them were completed, and all were lost in the Revolutionary War. The ships ordered were all frigates: five of 32 guns each, five of 28 guns each, and three of 24 guns each. The order also stipulated where the ships were to be built, to spread the work among the 13 colonies. Further progress in the establishment of the Continental Navy was made on December 22 of the same year, when Esek Hopkins was appointed commander-in-chief, making him the Continental Navy's equivalent of Major General George Washington in the Continental Army. (Only two years later, however, Hopkins was court-martialed for failure to obey orders and dismissed from the service.) In the short term, the Continental Navy had at its disposal four ships, which were soon joined by four converted merchantmen.

On January 5, 1776, this first fleet of the Continental Navy received its sailing orders: Hopkins was instructed to drive British raiders from Chesapeake Bay as well as the coasts of the Carolinas and Virginia. The American commander sailed from the Delaware River on February 17 with eight ships. After losing contact with two ships in foul weather, Hopkins made for the Bahama Islands, where the navy and marine raid on New Providence was undertaken. Returning from the Bahamas, Captain Abraham Whipple's 24-gun armed merchantman *Columbus* captured a British schooner, the *Hawk*, off Block Island, Rhode Island, the first action with a British warship in the Revolutionary War. The *Columbus* captured a total of five British ships before being run aground and burned in 1778.

A typical recruiting poster of the period urges men to come forward as crew of John Paul Jones's sloop *Ranger*, which was about to depart on a raiding voyage in English waters.

THE MILITARY HISTORY OF THE UNITED STATES

On September 5, 1776, the first standard uniform was adopted by the Marine Committee of the Continental Congress: naval officers were to have green coats with white facings, round cuffs with buttons, slashed sleeves and pockets, a silver epaulet on the right shoulder, turned-back shirt collars, buttons matching the facings, vest and breeches edged in green, black gaiters, and garters.

On November 13, 1776, John Paul Jones, captaining the brig *Providence*, took the transport *Mellish*, which was carrying 10,000 winter uniforms for British forces fighting in the Revolutionary War. This clothing was a godsend to the Continental land forces. Later, as he was escorting eight prizes to port, Jones fell in with the frigate H.M.S. *Milford*, which he persuaded to chase his American warship, thereby leaving the prizes free to enter an American port. Jones later evaded the British frigate and returned safely to harbor. It was also Jones who unfurled the first "Stars and Stripes" on a Continental warship, at Portsmouth, New Hampshire, on July 4, 1777.

The Capture of the *Lexington*

The first American warship to be captured overseas was the *Lexington* (originally the *Wild Duck*) on September 20, 1777. Encountering the cutter *Alert* off Ushant, France, the *Lexington* fought bravely until she had fired off all her powder and then, with her rigging shot to pieces, surrendered. A greater blow happened on March 7, 1778, when the frigate *Randolph* took on the British 64-gun ship H.M.S. *Yarmouth*. The American ship was apparently on the point of victory, but blew up for unknown reasons (perhaps a spark in the powder magazine) with the loss of 300 men. It was the worst disaster to befall an American warship until Pearl Harbor in December 1941.

On May 4, 1880, the Continental Congress authorized the first navy seal. It was in effect designed by Governor Morris and Richard Henry Lee, members of the committee charged with producing for the use of the Board of Admiralty, forerunner of the Department of the Navy, which was itself established in 1798.

The Last Naval Action of the Revolutionary War

The final naval action of the Revolutionary War was the inconclusive battle fought on March 10, 1783, between the 36-gun frigate *Alliance* and H.M.S. *Sybil*, the latter with H.M.S. *Alarm* and H.M.S. *Tobago* in company. News of the war's end had not reached the ships, and the *Alliance* badly damaged the *Sybil* with a single broadside. The British ship then hauled off to join her companions, which did not take part in the action. The losses of the Continental Navy in the Revolutionary War totaled 342 dead and 114 wounded.

Top: The first ship commanded by Captain John Barry in the Continental Navy was the brigantine *Wild Duck*, bought into the navy and renamed *Lexington*. Like John Paul Jones, Barry had been born in Ireland and was second only to Jones in the fame of his actions in the Revolutionary War. **Above:** The "Stars and Stripes" is hoisted for the first time on an American warship, John Paul Jones's *Lexington*, on July 4, 1777.

The Continental Navy effectively ceased to exist on June 2, 1785, when the service's last ship, the *Alliance*, was sold for merchant service. It was nine years before another U.S. navy started to come into existence. However, on August 4, 1790, Congress authorized the creation of the Revenue Cutter Service. This later became the U.S. Coast Gaurd, so the date of the Revenue Cutter Service's creation is generally recognized as the birthday of the Coast Guard.

By the middle of the 1790s, the activities of Barbary Coast pirates off North Africa were becoming a major thorn in the side of American merchant ships trading in the Mediterranean. On January 2, 1794, Congress resolved to create a United States navy to deal with these Algerine corsairs. Opponents of the plan were both numerous and influential. They pointed out that such a service would be very expensive, aristocratic in its overall nature, detrimental to democratic ideals, and officered by glory-hunters whose efforts could drag the country into unwanted overseas wars.

The Birth of the U.S. Navy

March 27, 1794, is generally regarded as the birthday of the U.S. Navy, for on that day the Congress ordered the building of nine frigates, six of them of 44 guns each and the other three of 36 guns each. The order was accompanied by the condition that the building program would be cancelled if peace with the Algerine corsairs was secured.

The order for these new ships was awarded on June 28, 1794, to Joshua Humphreys, a major shipbuilder of Philadelphia. Humphreys was appointed master builder at a salary of $2,000 per year, and the ships included such legendary vessels as the *Constellation*, *Constitution*, and *United States*. However, on March 2, 1796, Congress ratified a treaty with the Bey of Algiers. In addition to halting the construction of the ships, the treaty gave $1 million to the bey in ransom and tribute.

The navy survived this blow, however, and on February 22, 1796, President George Washington conferred the first U.S. U.S. Navy commission on Captain John Barry, a merchant who had commanded the brig *Lexington* in March 1776 when she captured the British tender *Edward* in the Continental Navy's first successful sea action. Barry's first command was the *United States*, which had been designed by Humphreys and Captain Thomas Truxtun, launched on May 10, 1797, and remained in service until 1864.

The Quasi-War With France

The fortunes of the navy began to climb once more with the "outbreak" of the Quasi-War with France. The first evidence of this improvement was the establishment on April 30, 1798, of the Department of the Navy under a Secretary of the Navy. Only a few days later, Congress authorized President John Adams to build or buy ten ships, "galleys or otherwise," for the defense of the United States, and also permitted the captains of armed public vessels to raid French merchant shipping. The first Secretary of the Navy was Benjamin Stoddert, who was appointed on May 18, 1798. In the next two years, Stoddert increased the Navy's strength to more than 50 vessels, including many allocated to the West Indies, where piracy was a major problem.

The Quasi-War with France was fought on an undeclared basis, and one of its high points was the capture, on July 7, 1798, of the French privateer *La Croyable* off Great Egg Harbor in the Delaware Capes region by the *Delaware* under the command of Captain Stephen Decatur, Sr. This event led to the first award of prize money by the U.S. Navy. The first warship-versus-warship success claimed by the U.S. Navy followed on February 9, 1799, when the *Constellation* captured the French frigate *L'Insurgente* in the Caribbean: raked by a devastating broadside that killed 29 men, the French frigate surrendered.

The navy also entered the shipbuilding market when it bought the 60-acre

THE MILITARY HISTORY OF THE UNITED STATES

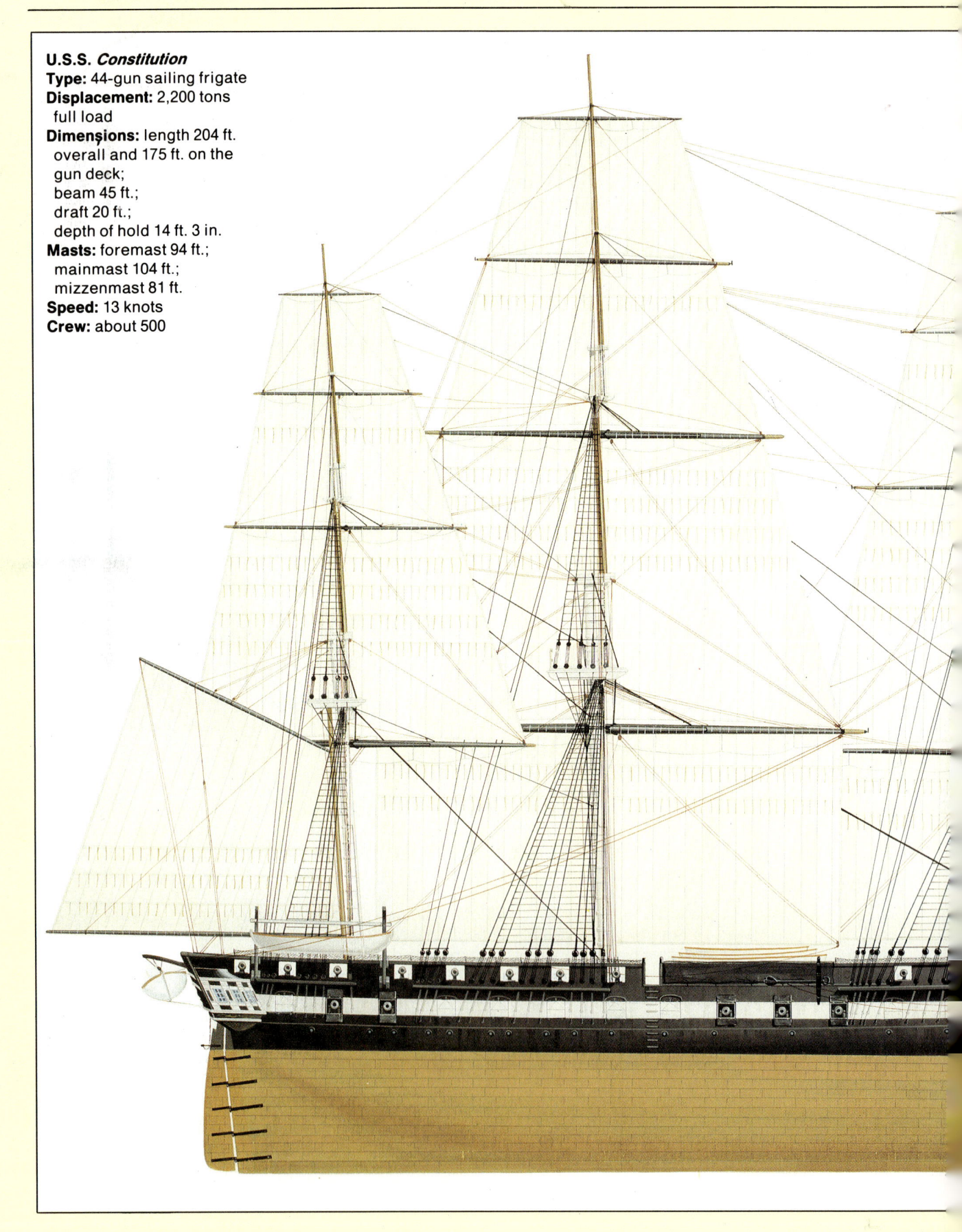

U.S.S. *Constitution*
Type: 44-gun sailing frigate
Displacement: 2,200 tons full load
Dimensions: length 204 ft. overall and 175 ft. on the gun deck;
beam 45 ft.;
draft 20 ft.;
depth of hold 14 ft. 3 in.
Masts: foremast 94 ft.;
mainmast 104 ft.;
mizzenmast 81 ft.
Speed: 13 knots
Crew: about 500

The first ships of the U.S. Navy, authorized by Congress in March 1794, are often known as the "six original frigates." They were the *United States*, *Constitution*, *President*, *Chesapeake*, *Constellation* and *Congress*. Their dimensions were fixed by three of the captains (John Barry, Richard Dale and Thomas Truxtun) commissioned by President George Washington to command them. The most famous of these celebrated ships is the *Constitution*, which was built at Hartt's Shipyard in Boston, Massachusetts; launched on October 21, 1797; and commissioned on an unknown date in 1798. The ship first put to sea on July 22, 1798, during the Quasi-War with France, and then served as Commodore Edward Preble's flagship in the Mediterranean during the Tripolitanian War. However, it was during the War of 1812 that the *Constitution* achieved her undying fame as Captain Isaac Hull's "Old Ironsides" during her action with the *Guerriere*. Under Captain William Bainbridge, the *Constitution* captured the *Java*, another British frigate, off Brazil on December 29, 1812. On February 20, 1815, under the command of Captain Charles Stewart, the ship fought a four-hour battle and captured two smaller British ships, the 32-gun *Cyane* and the 20-gun *Levant*. In 1828, the *Constitution* was condemned as unseaworthy and recommended for breaking up. The poem "Old Ironsides" by Oliver Wendell Holmes raised such public enthusiasm for the ship, however, that she was preserved. The ship has been rebuilt several times and restored as much as possible to her original configuration. Between 1917 and 1925, the ship was known as the *Old Constitution*, allowing allocation of her original name to a battle-cruiser that was never completed.

The *Constitution*'s last major reconstruction took place between 1927 and 1931, after which the ship toured some 90 American ports and received 4,500,000 visitors. Since 1934, the *Constitution* has been moored at the Boston Naval Shipyard and is the oldest commissioned warship still afloat. Twice each year, the ship is taken out into Boston Harbor and "turned around" so that her masts do not warp from the effects of the wind and sun.

THE MILITARY HISTORY OF THE UNITED STATES

yard of Mr. and Mrs. William Dennet in Portsmouth, New Hampshire, for $5,500 on June 12, 1800. The yard had already built warships; it later became the Portsmouth Navy Yard.

The best known single event contributing to the outbreak of the War of 1812 occured on June 22, 1807, when the frigate HMS *Leopard* fired at the *Chesapeake* off Norfolk, Virginia, killing three and wounding 18 of the American frigate's crew before impressing other of her men. War was declared by Congress on June 18, 1812. Sixteen ships were faced by a Royal Navy that had 1,048 vessels in commission, though very large numbers of these British ships were committed in other parts of the world, especially in the Napoleonic War with France. Navy losses in the War of 1812 amounted to 265 killed and 439 wounded.

New Technology

The period was also notable for the development of new technology, exemplified by the launch, on October 29, 1814 of the first steam warship, generally known as the *Fulton*, but more formally designated *Demologos (Fulton 1)*. This pioneering ship driven by a centerwheel paddle, was planned with an armament of 30 32-pounder cannon and two 100-pounder Columbia guns for her harbor-defense role. The War of 1812 ended before the ship was completed, and she was finally fitted out as a receiving vessel. Designed by Robert Fulton, the ship came to an unfortunate end, at Brooklyn Navy Yard on June 4, 1829, when her magazine blew up, totally destroying the vessel and killing 30 men, as well as injuring many more.

The battle between the American ship *Planter* and a French privateer during the Quasi-War with France. This undeclared war was very popular in the navy because all ranks received prize money from the sale of captured ships. During the conflicts, the fighting strength of the navy reached 45 ships.

Above right: In the early days of the U.S. Navy, American ships generally won single-ship duels because of their superior gunnery.

REVOLUTIONARY AND EARLY AMERICAN WARS

Below: A classic engagement of the War of 1812 was the victory of the 44-gun *Constitution*, under Captain Isaac Hull, over the 48-gun *Guerriere* on August 19, 1812. The *Constitution* was the third of the "six original frigates" ordered in 1794 and was built with spikes and copper bolts supplied by Paul Revere. The ship was nicknamed "Old Ironsides" by her sailors because the shot from the *Guerriere* failed to pierce her sides.

227

The United States was a pioneer of steam propulsion for ships. The world's first commercial steam vessel was Robert Fulton's *Clermont*, which steamed up the Hudson River from New York to Albany during 1807 (above), and in 1814 the navy bought its first steam warship.

On March 3, 1819, Congress passed legislation that materially affected the navy. First, rules about the naming of warships specified that ships of the line were to be named after states, frigates after rivers, and sloops after cities. Second, a stepped-up war against pirates who were capturing hundreds of American ships every year was authorized. The worst area for piracy was the Caribbean, and the new law gave permission for the navy to escort merchant convoys and to recapture ships seized by pirates. Third, the president was authorized to use the navy to suppress the West African slave trade.

The navy's second steamship, and the first to serve as a warship, was the *Sea Gull*. The shallow-draft ship had been bought in December 1822, and on February 14, 1823, was commissioned under Lieutenant William H. Watson as a shallow-draft warship capable of operating against pirates along the Cuban coast.

The Navy Expands

In 1825, Congress authorized the construction of a class of ten sloops. On September 3, 1826, one of them, the 700-ton *Vincennes* of 16 guns, left New York under the command of Commander William B. Finch. It became the first American naval vessel to circumnavigate the world before returning to New York on June 8, 1830. Just under six months later, on December 6, 1830, the navy established a Depot of Charts and Instruments under Lieutenant Fontain Maury. This important scientific adjunct of the navy became the US Naval and Hydrographic Office in 1854 and the U.S. Naval Oceanographic Office in 1862.

The first official controls for the dress of enlisted naval personnel were issued on February 1, 1841, and this "Regulation for the Uniform and Dress of the Navy of the United States" ended the practice of men being able to decorate their "frocks"

REVOLUTIONARY AND EARLY AMERICAN WARS

Captain, U.S. Navy (1862)

This captain of the Union navy is seen in typical undress uniform for the 1862 period, complete with straw hat of the type worn in southern waters. At this time, the world's navies were beginning to accept the implications of steam power for warships, and in the relatively unpompous U.S. navies there was no hinderance to the appearance of officers in uniforms of a practical, rather than ceremonial nature.

229

THE MILITARY HISTORY OF THE UNITED STATES

A hero of the U.S. Navy's early period was Captain Stephen Decatur, who secured great fame for his success against the Barbary corsairs and also against the British. He was killed in a duel during 1820.

Sailors from the *Constitution* board and take the French privateer *Sandwich* in the West Indies during May 1800.

230

REVOLUTIONARY AND EARLY AMERICAN WARS

The *United States* was launched on May 10, 1797, as the first of the U.S. Navy's "six original frigates." She is seen here as she appeared when she was commissioned later in the same year under the command of Captain John Barry, who had overseen the ship's construction. Her hulk was seized by the Confederacy at Norfolk Navy Yard in 1861 and used as a receiving ship (moored training vessel), but was burned when the Confederates evacuated Norfolk in 1862.

as they wished. It also established the device of a spread eagle on the stock of a foul anchor as the insignia of petty officers.

Mutiny

The navy's only mutiny occurred on December 1, 1842, on board the training brig *Somers*. The three persons involved, Midshipman Philip Spencer (son of the Secretary of War) and two enlisted men, were court-martialed for conspiracy to mutiny, found guilty, and hanged on the orders of their captain, Alexander S. McKenzie, who was later court-martialed and acquitted.

The End of Flogging

The Naval School, now the United States Naval Academy, was founded at Annapolis, Maryland, on October 10, 1845, with Commander Franklin Buchanan as its superintendent. The school's initial complement was seven staff and 56 students. Five years later, on September 28, 1850, Congress moved toward the abolition of flogging as a naval punishment. The navy said that it would be "utterly impractical to have an efficient Navy without this form of practice," but on July 17, 1862, flogging was finally banned, even though sailors had petitioned Congress not to end the practice. Between this date and the beginning of the Civil War, the most notable event in naval history, apart from small-scale operations mainly in the Pacific, was the decision announced on November 1, 1860, to convert seven sail-powered warships into steam-driven ships at a cost of $3,064,000.

THE MILITARY HISTORY OF THE UNITED STATES

Continued from page 219

gap in the chain of command that had become evident in the War of 1812, Brown was brought to Washington in a position between the Department of War and the army that later became known as Commanding General of the Army. This appointment was held by Brown until his death in 1828. Major General Alexander Macomb then held the position until his death in 1841, when he was replaced by Major General Winfield Scott. In 1847, Scott was promoted to brevet lieutenant general, and as the first lieutenant general since Washington, he remained Commanding General of the Army until he retired in 1861.

Calhoun's Great Importance

It is difficult to overestimate the importance of Secretary of War Calhoun in American military affairs. The vision and energy of this important official were very great and allowed responsible officers to use their administrative skills to maximum extent. Scott began working on the difficult problem of infantry tactics in 1815, and he eventually issued a new manual of infantry tactics for the army and militia. In 1821, the same officer prepared a new set of army regulations that detailed to the smallest item how the lives of the men were to be ordered. In 1822, the army began opening recruiting posts in larger cities to recruit for the army in general instead of recruiting for specific regiments as it had previously done. Regimental recruitment was allowed to continue, but in its first three years, the General Recruiting Service enlisted nearly 70 percent more men than the regimental recruiting offices. At Calhoun's instigation, an improved medical service was established under Joseph Lovell, the first commissioned Surgeon General.

A contemporary illustration of Fort Mellon on Lake Monroe in East Florida emphasizes the unusual aspect of this location. What it cannot even begin to suggest, however, are the nature and extent of the region's endemic diseases. They caused far more American casualties in the Florida campaigns than Indian weapons.

REVOLUTIONARY AND EARLY AMERICAN WARS

Swivel guns were used where more fire power than a musket, but less than a heavy cannon was required. Often mounted in boats or along bulwarks, they could fire devastating ball or grapeshot into other boats or at infantry on beaches. Some were fitted into the fighting tops of ships to fire down onto the decks of others about to attempt boarding. The swivel gun shown bottom right was designed to fire a large explosive (fuzed) ball against a target.

Lovell was instrumental in improving the soldier's diet, and in his search for a link between climate and disease, he created the basis of the world's first national weather reporting service.

As early as 1818, Calhoun had been able to put into effect the army's first complete artillery system involving all three branches of the service, namely field artillery, siege and garrison artillery, and coastal artillery. This amalgamation resulted from the deliberations of a board of artillery and ordnance officers appointed by Calhoun. Field artillery was based in general on a twin-trail carriage devised by a late 18th-century French artillery pioneer, Jean Baptiste de Gribeauval, though in 1839, Secretary of War Joel R. Poinsett approved a revised type of stock-trail carriage with a single trail of solid wood. It had been introduced by the British but perfected by the French, and offered both superior interchangeability of parts and greater simplicity than the 1818 type of carriage.

These organizational, administrative, and technical improvements were matched by a major program to better the nation's coastal defenses. By 1826, 26 ports between the Penobscot River in Maine and the mouth of the Mississippi River in Louisiana had been fortified with 31 works, generally grass-covered earthworks backed by stone or masonry walls. By 1843, the program had been stretched to cover 35 to 40 ports, with 69 large fortifications built or under construction containing heavy artillery in the form of 24- and 32-pounder guns as well as 8-inch howitzers to match the heavier firepower of contemporary warships.

Westward Expansion

Throughout this period, the westward expansion of the United States seemed relentless as settlers searched for new land. The army moved in front of the settlers, and the 30 years after 1815 saw the army in constant service as the pioneer of westward expansion. Soldiers surveyed, built forts, and constructed roads. Army posts in Iowa, Nebraska, and Kansas marked the western edge of American endeavor, and outside its forts, the army set up the blacksmith forges and lumber and corn-grinding mills that were a powerful focus for civilian settlement. Typical of these army posts, by geographical location from north to south, were Forts Armstrong, Snelling, and Atkinson built on the upper reaches

233

U.S. Military Academy, Cadet (1825)

The U.S. Military Academy was founded in 1802 at West Point, New York. By 1825, it was well established and developing into a far-sighted educational and training establishment for some 250 cadets under the overall command of Sylvanus Thayer. The uniform of the cadets, adopted in 1815 or 1816, was of gray cloth in honor of the gray-clad regulars who had beaten the British at the Battle of Chippewa in July 1814. White cross belts were worn for infantry drill, while a black waist belt and straight sword were normal for other occasions. The cadets used a shorter musket than the standard for line infantry, and other uniform and equipment items were modified to suit the cadets.

of the Mississippi River in 1819, 1822, and 1840 respectively, Fort Leavenworth built on the Missouri River in 1827, Fort Scott built between the Missouri and Arkansas rivers in 1842, Forts Smith and Gibson built on the Arkansas River in 1817 and 1824 respectively, Forts Towson and Washita built on the Red River in 1824 and 1842 respectively, and Fort Jesup built on the Sabine River in 1822. The main base for the supply and reinforcement of the more northern forts was the Jefferson Barracks, erected in St. Louis in 1826.

In addition to opening up new frontier regions for settlement, these army forts were also the launching points for expeditions deeper into the west. From Fort Leavenworth, for example, army expeditions surveyed the Santa Fe and Oregon Trails that opened the way to the southwest and northwest respectively. Another celebrated expedition was that of Captain Benjamin L. E. Bonneville, who during the 1830s took four years leave of absence from the 7th Infantry Regiment for an exploration of the Pacific coast.

This first phase of expansion into the midwest was undertaken mainly by infantrymen. Where possible, they were transported in steamboats, and then when the terrain permitted by mule- or ox-drawn wagons, but ultimately they covered the worst terrain on foot. Then the army discovered that the Plains Indians were mounted, and in 1832, the army organized a battalion of mounted rangers, expanded during 1833 into the 1st Dragoon Regiment, the first cavalry in the regular army since 1815.

In 1831, the army received as its political head Lewis Cass, previously governor of Michigan and eventually the first Secretary of War since Calhoun to serve over a long period. Like Calhoun, Cass had barely settled into office before he was faced with an Indian war.

The Black Hawk War (1832)

In 1824, the Erie Canal had been opened,

Painted from life in 1833 by J.O. Lewis, this impressive man was the chief of the Sac Indians. Known to the Americans as Black Hawk, his formal title was Mac-Cut-I-Mish-E-Ca-Cu-Cac.

Major General Zachary Taylor, seen here in a painting attributed to Lambdin, had a long military career that culminated in the Mexican War of 1846-1848. His success produced a wave of public enthusiasm that catapulted him into the White House as the twelfth president. In the Black Hawk War, Taylor was a colonel and victor in the decisive Battle of Bad Axe River.

encouraging a flood of immigration into Illinois. By 1831 this flood had reached the lands of the Fox and Sac tribes in western Illinois, pushing the Indians west across the Mississippi River into the prairies. Not unnaturally, the Indians were very unhappy with this situation, and under Chief Black Hawk, a group of Sac Indians crossed the Mississippi River in the spring of 1831 in a raid that burned the homesteads of many settlers. This Sac band was sometimes called the "British Band" because it had served with the British in the War of 1812. Its activities in 1831 prompted a major response from the Department of the West. Gaines moved against the Sacs with a large force of regulars and volunteers, but Black Hawk merely retired back across the Mississippi River and left Gaines' force with no military objective.

In the following year, Black Hawk decided that the time had come for a bolder move. In April 1832; he again crossed the Mississippi River, intending to re-occupy the ancestral Sac lands. In addition to 500 warriors, he brought with him 1,500 women and children. Cass decided that only a major show of force would settle the incipient Indian problem of the area. Accordingly, he instructed Colonel Henry Atkinson to move up the Mississippi River from Jefferson Barracks in St. Louis with the 6th Infantry Regiment and ordered General Scott to move about 1,000 more infantry and some artillery from the east coast. He reckoned that this combined force would be more than

PROPHET. BLACK HAWK. SON.

Chief Black Hawk and his two sons. It is estimated that between 850 and 1,400 Sacs died in the Battle of Bad Axe River or drowned after being hounded into the local marshes after the battle. Black Hawk tried to surrender, but his plea was ignored by the Americans, who were still smarting from a trick played on them by Black Hawk in an earlier engagement, the Battle of Wisconsin Heights. The battle has since become known as the Bad Axe Massacre, and in 1990 the state legislature of Wisconsin issued a proclamation of apology to the Sac and Fox nations.

adequate to defeat Black Hawk, and also to instill in the tribes of the area a fear of American military strength. To supplement these regular forces, the governor of Illinois Mississippi called out a major part of his militia, most of them mounted.

The Battle of Bad Axe River

The Illinois militia had an early and inconclusive encounter with the Sacs, and most of the militia then returned home. Atkinson had meanwhile been moving north with about 500 regulars and about 900 volunteers, as many as he had been able to muster. Advancing with great difficulty through swampland, Atkinson's force caught up with the Indians on August 2 in the area of southern Wisconsin where the Bad Axe River flows into the Mississippi. The main infantry force was commanded by Colonel Zachary Taylor and decisively beat the Indians, who were also decimated by canister shot from a 6-pounder field gun mounted on a steamboat.

Scott's force from the east coast only arrived five days later, but would in any event have been next to useless. Cholera had broken out on the transports ferrying the force across the Great Lakes: one-third of Scott's men had died of the disease or been left as invalids, while many of the others had desrted. The rest could not be brought into contact with Atkinson's men for fear of contagion.

The Second Seminole War (1835-42)

Even as the Black Hawk War was taking place, fresh trouble was brewing among the Creeks and Seminoles of Georgia, Florida, and Alabama. Early in 1832, Cass instructed the Indian commissioner in Florida to negotiate a treaty with the Indians, which was ratified in 1834. In the

Left: Determined to remain in their ancestral lands after returning across the Mississippi River, Black Hawk brought 500 warriors, together with 1,500 women and children who were a great tactical burden on the Indian chief at the time of the Battle of Bad Axe River.

Below: The decisive factor in the Battle of Bad Axe River was the steam vessel *Warrior* with a 6-pounder field gun mounted on her bow and firing canister. This consists of a mass of musket balls that spread out into a lethal cloud as their container breaks up as it leaves the gun muzzle.

REVOLUTIONARY AND EARLY AMERICAN WARS

Painted by the great George Catlin, Osceola was a half breed who led the Seminoles in their protracted effort in the Second Seminole War to avoid forcible removal to the west from southern Georgia and northern Florida. After their defeat, the surviving Seminoles were shipped to New Orleans and then moved into Arkansas and Oklahoma.

Texas
For further references see pages 175, 178, 248, 252, 253, *254, 255, 256,* 257, 258, 259, 260.

treaty, the Indians agreed to move from Florida to Arkansas by January 1, 1836, but long before this date, it became clear that many Seminoles were not prepared to move peaceably. There were several outbreaks of minor violence organized by a half-breed named Osceola, and the army decided that reinforcement of its Florida forces was needed. By December 1835, the army had 536 men in Florida, organized as two companies of infantry and nine companies of artillery under Brevet Brigadier General Duncan L. Clinch. The two main garrisons were Fort Brooke on Tampa Bay and Fort King about 100 miles to the northeast.

The decisive moment arrived on December 28, 1835. A party of 60 men under Osceola murdered the agent in charge of the Indian move as he took a walk outside Fort King. Another group of Indians attacked a party of 110 regulars under the command of Brevet Major Francis L. Dade as they were marching toward Fort King from Fort Brooke. The force was moving slowly through the Wahoo Swamp of the Withlacoochee River because they had with them an ox-drawn 6-pounder field gun; only two soldiers escaped alive (but badly wounded) from the "Dade Massacre."

Such outrages could not go unavenged and unpunished, and so the Second Seminole War began. The massacre had taken place just west of the line separating the Departments of the East and the West, and therefore fell theoretically into General Gaines' area of responsibility. But Secretary of War Cass and President Andrew Jackson agreed that command should be given to General Scott. Gaines, currently on a tour of inspection in New Orleans, was ordered to the southwestern frontier to assume command of troops in Louisiana, into Texas where trouble was brewing between American immigrants and Mexico, which had declared itself independent of Spain in February 1821.

Scott departed from Washington on January 21, 1836. In South Carolina and Georgia, he ordered supplies and arranged for the state militias to be called into service. He also established a supply base in Savannah, Georgia, and arrived at his new headquarters in St. Augustine, on the opposite side of the Florida peninsula from the scene of operations, on February 22. Supply and other logistical difficulties, including the movement of troops across the difficult and largely unexplored interior of Florida, delayed the start of the American campaign until April 5. Scott's plan was to undertake a three-pronged offensive designed to trap the Indians close to Tampa, but by the time he was ready, the Indians had disappeared into the swamps of the Everglades. To add to Scott's problems, hot weather had arrived, and his militia forces were ready to return home as they had completed their three-month period of active service. This first stage of the war was accurately summarized by a South Carolina militia officer: "Two months were consumed in preparations and effecting nothing, and the third in marching to Tampa and back again."

Differences Between the First and Second Seminole Wars

It is worth noting at this stage that, while Scott's initial experience in the Second Seminole War mirrored those of Jackson in the First Seminole War to a marked degree, there were two major differences. First, Scott's supply problem was based on difficulties of transportation rather than lack of the supplies themselves. Jackson had been unable to secure even basic provisions, while Scott found that the Commissary General of Subsistence had allocated adequate supplies in the depots, but that they could not be brought up to the forward troops for lack of transportation, roads, and maps. Second, Scott's plans were thrown awry by the intrusion of Gaines who, instead of confining his attention to the

> **Mexico**
> For further references see pages
> 178, 243, 248, 252, 253, *254, 255, 256,* 257, 258, 259, 260, 262, 263.

REVOLUTIONARY AND EARLY AMERICAN WARS

An Indian chief, Emachitochustern, tried to avoid a second war. He wrote:

"I don't like to make any trouble or to have any quarrel with white people, but if they will trespass on my lands and rights, I must defend myself the best way I can."

He sent a letter on behalf of ten Seminole villages describing the Seminole's plight.

To the Commanding Officer at Fort Hawkins.
DEAR SIR:
"Since the last war, after you sent us word that we must quit the war, our red people have come over on this side. The white people have carried all the red people's cattle off. Bernard's son was here, and I asked him what to do about it – he told me to go to the head white man and complain. I did so, and there was no head white man, and there was no law in the case. The whites first began to steal from us, and there's nothing said about that, but great complaints about what the Indians do. It is now three years since white people killed three Indians; and since, they have killed three more; and since, one more. The white people killed our red people first – the Indians took satisfaction. There are three men that the red people have not taken satisfaction for yet. There is nothing said about what white people do – but all that the Indians do is brought up. The cattle that we are accused of taking, were cattle that the white people took from us – our young men went out and brought them back with the same marks and brands."

Far left: Brigadier General Zachary Taylor used bloodhounds to track down the Seminoles. Even though it was not effective, the practice caused considerable anger (especially in the middle and northern states) and was soon ended.

Below: Osceola was captured in November 1837 after he had been lured to a parley with American officers. The Seminole leader was imprisoned in Fort Moultrie, near Charleston, South Carolina, and died in the following year. The attending physician was Dr. Weedon, who then removed and preserved Osceola's head.

Rawson Clarke was one of three survivors from the Seminole attack on Major Dade's command, which took place in December 1835. Dade's column comprised 112 soldiers.

"It was 8 o'clock. Suddenly I heard a rifle shot in the direction of the advanced guard, and this was immediately followed by a musket shot from that quarter. Captain Fraser had rode by me a moment before in that direction. I never saw him afterwards. I had not time to think of the meaning of these shots, before a volley, as if from a thousand rifles, was poured in upon us from the front, and all along our left flank. I looked around me, and it seemed as if I was the only one left standing in the right wing. Neither could I, until several other vollies had been fired at us, see an enemy - and when I did, I could only see their heads and arms peering out from the long grass, far and near and from behind the pine trees. The first fire of the Indians was the most destructive, seemingly killing or disabling half our men.

We promptly threw ourselves behind trees, and opened a sharp fire of musketry. I, for one, never fired without seeing my man, that is, his head and shoulders ... the Indians chiefly fired lying or squatting in the grass. Lt. Bassinger fired five or six rounds of cannister from the cannon. This appeared to frighten the Indians, and they retreated. We immediately began to fell trees, and erect a little triangular breastwork. Some of us went forward to gather the cartridge boxes from the dead, and to assist the wounded. I had seen Major Dade fall to the ground by the first volley. Whilst gathering the cartridges, I saw Lt. Mudge sitting his back reclining against a tree ... his head fallen, and evidently dying. I spoke to him, but he did not answer.

We had barely raised our breastwork knee high, when we saw the Indians advancing in great numbers over the hill to our left. They came on boldly till within a long musket shot, when they spread themselves from tree to tree to surround us.

"Our men were by degrees all cut down. We had maintained a steady fight from 8 until 2 P.M. or thereabouts, and allowing three quarters of an hour interval between the first and second attack, had been pretty busily engaged for more than 5 hours. Lieut. B. was the only officer left alive, and he severely wounded. He told me as the Indians approached to lay down and feign myself dead. I looked through the logs, and saw the savages approaching in great numbers. A heavy made Indian, of middle stature, painted down to the waist, seemed to be the Chief. He made them a speech, frequently pointing to the breastwork. At length they charged into the work; there was none to offer resistance, and they did not seem to suspect the wounded being alive - offering no indignity, but stepping about carefully, quietly stripping off our accoutrements, and carrying away our arms. They then retired in a body in the direction from whence they came.

"Immediately upon their retreat, forty or fifty negroes on horseback galloped up and alighted, tied their beasts, and commenced with horrid shouts and yells the butchery of the wounded, together with an indiscrimate plunder, stripping the bodies of the dead of clothing, watches and money, and splitting open the heads of all who showed the least sign of life, with their axes and knives, and accompanying their bloody work with obscene and taunting derisions and with frequent cries of "what have you got to sell."

"Lieut. B. hearing the negroes butchering the wounded at length sprang up, and asked them to spare his life. They met him with the blows of their axes, and their fiendish laughter. Having been wounded in five different places myself, I was pretty well covered with blood, and two scratches that I had received on my head, gave to me the appearance of having been shot through the brain, for the negroes, after catching me up by the heels, threw me down saying "d....n him, he's dead enough!" They then stripped me of my clothes, shoes and hat, and left me."

In 1835 Frances and Almina Hall were captured by Indians. Their abduction caused considerable consternation all over the country for a while, but they eventually managed to escape.

Louisiana frontier with Mexico as ordered, arrived in Tampa Bay by sea with a large force of Louisiana militiamen. Gaines fed his men the supplies intended for Scott's command and then, after an inconclusive action against the Indians, returned to New Orleans during March. To add insult to injury, Gaines reported the action as a victory and thereby caused a reduction in the flow of supplies to Scott, who was now thought to be involved in a simple mopping-up operation after Gaines' "victory."

In St. Augustine, Scott began planning a new offensive under adverse conditions: for he had severely antagonized his volunteers and also the settlers of Florida with a suggestion of cowardice in an official request for 3,000 "good troops (not volunteers)." Florida settlers happily burned an effigy of Scott, and many cheered at the end of May when Scott was transferred to Georgia to suppress a Creek uprising that had started in eastern Alabama, but then threatened Georgia and Florida. In Georgia, Scott fell foul of the local commander, Brevet Major General Thomas S. Jesup, who had put down the Indian uprising in a decisive manner before Scott could complete and put into action his own, more complex, plan of campaign. Jesup felt that Scott had been too slow to plan and to act, and informed Washington of the fact in no uncertain terms.

The upshot of the matter was an order for Scott to return to Washington, where he faced a court of inquiry. Scott was cleared by the court of any blame for the failure of the first Florida campaign, but was not returned to command in Florida. Instead, the general was employed on a number of sensitive diplomatic missions, in which he proved remarkably successful. Typical of these missions were the "Caroline Incident," the Arrowstook "War," and the Cherokee problem. The first was caused by the seizure on December 29, 1837, of the steamboat *Caroline* on the Niagara River by Canadian militia inside the United States. In the strict sense of the word, the Canadians had "invaded" the United States, and troops were concentrated along the border. Scott's diplomatic skills were used to good effect, however, and the possibility of war between the United States and the United Kingdom was removed. Then, in February 1838, the Arrowstook "War" occurred, when a dispute between Maine and New Brunswick about the incursion of Canadian loggers into American territory again threatened war. Scott's intervention eased tensions again, and the problem was removed by the Webster-Ashburton

Treaty of 1842, which settled the disputed frontier in this region between the United States and Canada. Scott's diplomacy was also instrumental in persuading 15,000 Cherokees to vacate Georgia and move peacefully to the west.

Meanwhile, the Second Seminole War continued in Florida. Jesup commanded from late 1836 until he was replaced in May 1838 by Brevet Brigadier General Zachary Taylor. Taylor was in turn relieved at his own request and replaced by Brevet Brigadier General Walker K. Armistead until May 1841, when the forceful Colonel William J. Worth was given the command by an exasperated Department of War.

The Battle of Lake Okeechobee

The sole decisive action of the war was the Battle of Lake Okeechobee, fought on December 25, 1837. About 1,000 Americans, consisting of about 500 regulars and 500 volunteers under Taylor's command, moved against the main Seminole position through the swamps. In the last two miles of the advance, Taylor arranged his force as two lines, with the volunteers in the first line. The volunteers broke against the Seminole defense, just as Taylor had reckoned. The American regulars were then able to smash forward against an Indian force already disorganized by the attack of the volunteers and sweep all before them. The Seminoles lost about half their effective strength, while the American losses were 26 killed and 112 wounded. Organized Seminole resistance was broken by the battle, but the will to resist was not seriously dented, and the war dragged on for almost six more years.

The war was fought on a desultory basis, with the Indians fighting a guerrilla campaign and the American side responding with a mixture of armed strength and attempted negotiation. Jesup was neither able to drive the Indians from the swamps nor to persuade them to leave Florida. The tactic devised by Taylor was the division of the Indians' area into small districts that were then sealed off individually and searched with the aid of bloodhounds. This search-and-destroy system might have worked in the long run, but the use of the dogs attracted severe criticism from all

This lithograph was published during 1837 in Charleston, South Carolina. The fury of this attack on an American fort is an indication of the general feeling in the south against the Seminoles.

U.S. Army, 7th Infantry, First Sergeant (1835)

For many years, the 7th Infantry was the garrison of Fort Gibson, on the Arkansas River in what is now Oklahoma. The fort was created by the regiment in 1824, when the commanding officer was Colonel Matthew Arbuckle. The soldier illustrated is a first sergeant, as indicated by his epaulets and sash; that he had served for more than ten years is shown by the chevrons on his sleeve. He wears an undress jacket (replaced on parade by a dark blue tailcoat). The cloth fatigue cap is fitted with a "poke" (visor).

quarters of American public opinion. The Department of War ordered Taylor to cease hostilities and try again to secure a negotiated settlement, but the only result was a sharp increase in Indian raids. Armistead also believed in negotiation, but he, too, failed to make any significant impact on the course of the war.

It was Worth who brought matters to an end. Previous commanders had not campaigned during the summer months for fear of fevers and dysentery. This respite had consistently allowed the Indians to plant, raise, and gather a harvest that maintained them through the following winter's campaigning season. Worth decided that the best way to defeat the Seminoles was to destroy their ability to sustain themselves. Throughout the summer of 1841, U.S. forces remained in the field, or rather the swamplands, with the intention of harassing the Indians and engaging all that they could trap, but more important, destroying their crops and their villages. The results fully justified Worth's reasoning, for increasing numbers of Indians emerged from the swamps into captivity and movement to the west. The Second Seminole War was declared officially ended in August 1842. In all, about 3,800 Seminoles were moved west over the "Trail of Tears," but the Second Seminole War had cost the army 1,600 dead, including a large number who had succumbed to disease. The war had involved a total of 10,000 regulars and 30,000 volunteers, and the strain imposed on the army was so great that, in July 1838, its authorized strength was increased from about 7,000 to 12,500 men.

Indian warriors attack Fort Mackenzie in the period 1840-1843.

REVOLUTIONARY AND EARLY AMERICAN WARS

Right: The removal of the southern Indian tribes toward Oklahoma resulted mainly from the political influence of white planters who wanted their lands, and the route of the displaced Indians became known as the "Trail of Tears." The tribes involved included the Cherokee, Chickasaw, Choctaw, Creek, and Seminole. The task of eviction and escort fell to the army, and this painting by Robert Lindneux emphasizes that the Indians were allowed to take relatively little with them, often leaving behind prosperous farms.
Below right: Another celebrated Seminole leader was Mito Chlucco, or "The Long Warrior."

Riverine Experience

The war was clearly not the type for which the army had been intended, trained, and equipped. As a result, the army acquired important experience in fighting a sustained war against irregular forces, and equally important, it improved its transportation system. River crossings were made easier by the adoption of a light pontoon wagon designed by the Quartermaster General's Department with a lining of rubberized fabric to make it waterproof and therefore buoyant. At the instigation of Jesup, the Corps of Artificers, disbanded after the War of 1812, was revived, and the corps' mechanics and skilled workmen soon became vital in the all-important task of keeping wagons and boats serviceable. The Second Seminole War also taught the army much about the usefulness and nature of water transportation. Until then, the army had hired civilian steamboats when necessary, but now turned increasingly toward the creation of its own fleet, which proved far more efficient and ultimately cheaper.

Army Exploration Teams in the West

Throughout this period, but on the other side of the United States, the army had been sending out expeditions toward the western coast of North America. During the 1820s and 1830s, the smallest of these expeditions had been concerned mainly with exploration, while larger efforts were undertaken with the aim of protecting trade caravans and contacting and establishing friendly relations with the Indian tribes of the Great Plains. In the 1840s, the emphasis shifted rapidly toward protection and support of the settlers who were sweeping into the newly opened west. This new wave of settlement spurred further exploration; typical were the two expeditions headed by 2nd Lieutenant John C. Fremont of the Corps of Topographical Engineers. The 1842 party explored and mapped the area

247

around the upper reaches of the Platte River to ease the task of settlers pushing northwest along the Oregon Trail. The 1843 party pushed across the Rocky Mountains to explore much of northern California. Reports from such expeditions also help to give an indication of how rapidly the wave of expansion was growing. The 1842 Fremont expedition, for example, reported seeing settlers totaling 64 men and 16 or 17 parties. Just three years later, Colonel Stephen W. Kearny and five companies of the 1st Dragoon Regiment traveled along the Oregon Trail for the protection of settlers, and reported 850 men and about 475 parties grouped into wagon trains with thousands of cattle.

However, the majority of settlers were not heading west into northern California, but were moving southwest toward Texas, then in northeastern Mexico. After an early experiment under the Spanish regime, Texas was formally opened to American immigration in 1823. It is estimated that in the period 1825-30 about 15,000 American citizens and several thousand slaves poured into the region in response to the Mexican government's offer of land grants and the promise of a fair legal system. Matters did not develop as the American immigrants, who soon came to call themselves Texans, had hoped. The American community in Texas grew away from the Mexican community as the Texans tried to create an American way of life for themselves. The Mexicans became increasingly worried that Texas was becoming too Americanized and sought to impose full Mexican control. At the same time, the Mexican garrisons in Texas were strengthened. The Texans saw both these factors as evidence of political repression, and this feeling was strengthened when a ban on further American immigration was imposed in April 1830. Immigration continued without much difficulty, however, and by 1835 there were about 28,000 Americans in Texas.

American dealings with the Indians were not all as unhappy as those with the southern tribes. This illustration shows "Camp Comanche," a trading establishment based on a wagon train, in 1844.

The Seminole Wars featured booby traps and ambushes, a type of combat much like that which a later American army experienced in Vietnam. An artillerist, Randolf Ridgely, provided the latest Indian news in a letter to a relative dated 4 March, 1840.

We have a little Indian news lately. Capt. Rains 7th. Infantry placed a shell on an Indian trail and covered it with a shirt. An Indian came and removed the shirt when the shell exploded and wounded him severely. Capt. R. then put 4 shells in a blanket and placed them on another trail. The Indians discovered and resolved to catch him in his own trap. So they collected their warriors to the number of 85 or 90 surrounded the spot; they then by means of a cord exploded the shell - down goes Capt. R. with a Sergt. Corpl. and 16 men - on coming to the place he found an old "Koon" dead - whilst he was kicking or turning the Koon over with his foot the Indians rose up and fired. The men behaved very handsomely, at once formed and extended. The Chief of the party was twice seen to step out and fire at the Sergt. who was very active in forming his men. The third time he struck the Sergt. when he (the sergt.) turned and rushed at the Indian until he got to pretty close quarters, he then fired and killed the rascal. When their chief fell the Indians fell back and slackened their fire considerably - in the mean time Capt. Rains had been shot down. The Sergt. seeing the effect produced on the enemy charged them boldly then rapidly retreated and thus succeeded in getting clear with Capt. R. and other wounded men. We had two killed, Capt. R. and 4 others wounded; the former mortally being shot through the lungs. They were separated at the commencement and could not join the party on account of the Indians being between them lay concealed - one says he counted 91 and the other says 93 Indians. The Indians lost their chief Halie-Tuskinuger and three others. The chief was in at Tampa last summer and boasted he could in two days bring into the field 80 warriors. As he had 4 or 5 days to collect them it is thought they are very little if any over rated. I heard Major McClintock and Capt. Gainor speak of this man two months ago; both agreed they considered him the most cunning, smart, hostile Indian they had yet seen in Florida.

Capt. Holmes also got on a trail of Indians and after following it for two days, he thought they were doging him and accordingly made a Sergt. and a few men conceal themselves, he had passed but a short time when two Indians came up with their rifles, the party killed one and captured the other. Holmes continued on, and captured 14 ponies. This is all the Indian news. It is thought by many Genl. Armistead will be in command, he is expecting orders daily as Macomb told him he would certainly have command he is now in St Augustine as also Col. Walback, Major Payne - and others being on a Court for trial of Capt. Howe - but the Court decided as the specification embraced man slaughter they would not try him. I write in the utmost haste as it is sun down and the boat leaves St. Augustine at Sun rise. Best regards to Drs. Baldwin, Tallifers, McLaughlin, Murray, Winder, Lese. I have had the tallest kind of fun in town lately

Your friend
RANDOLPH RIDGELY W.A. Carter Esq. Key Biscayne.

I believe the Regt. will go out this summer."

Major George McCall describes the pursuit of the Seminoles through the Big Cypress Swamp. The chase began on December 14, 1841.

The next morning I took forty men of my company for an exploring party. I steered south, and after wading about two miles, came in sight of a live oak hummock, for this I steered, and soon saw signs of Indians.

    Through many parts of the Cypress here, there grows in the water a long grass, which, when pressed down by a person in passing, does not rise again, and thus leaves a very plain trail. I followed this trail for some miles, when it led me to a small wet prairie. Here the party had separated for the purpose of leaving no trail on ground comparatively dry; but the guide soon found and pointed out to me the foot-prints of six men and one woman who had walked here abreast and about three yards apart. After some time I came to another and larger prairie, alternately dry and wet, having on the east in the distance a large live-oak hummock, on the south a formidable cypress, and on the west strips of pine woods. Here we pressed hot upon the trail, and the guide expressed his belief that the Prophet could not be many miles off, judging from the appearance of the country. But we had not gone far before the guide discovered that they had been playing a deep game, which is managed in this way: - When they wish to conceal their abode, their approach to it is never direct, and perhaps often leading you by a plain trail past it; the foremost of the party will, by making a high, long step over the top of the grass to the right or left, light upon the toe only, and step by step carefully arranging the grass thus disturbed, make his escape; his absence will scarcely be observed upon the trail, and the one who succeeds him as leader, pursues the route for some hundred yards, then he makes his escape in like manner; and so on, till but one is left, and he also continues the direct course, till deep water, a thicket, a rock, or something of the kind, affords him also an opportunity to escape, and the most skilful in this accomplishment brings up the rear.

    This game was successfully played in this case, the last one being a man with a very large foot (for an Indian). He led us to deep pond, where among the rocks he gave the slip to all pursuers. We searched around the pond, but could not discover a trace of where he had left it.

    It is thought, however, the Indians are somewhere down there still; and as we expect a supply of rations to-morrow, we shall set out with as much as we can properly carry, and penetrate, if possible, to the end of the land.

But the Army continued its relentless chase.

The Indians having been driven from the south and east, had (some of them) sought refuge in the scrubs and hummocks around *Is-tok-po-ga Lake*, and thither we marches. We were now, however, entering a country in which horses could be used, and from that time I had one at my command. But the idea of *catching* Indians even here was looked upon as perfectly ridiculous. They have become wilder and more vigilant than the beasts of the forest, and show more caution and sagacity in moving and concealing their wives and children than does the wild deer towards her fawn. A wiser and more humane policy was adopted; the troops were marched to the vicinity of the district known to be their abode, and then some friendly Indians were induced by *heavy* bribes to venture forward to endeavor by persuasion and large promises to induce them to come in; at the same time to assure them that the troops would continue the chase to the very last, in case of refusal.

    The hour was propitious; they were found much harassed and broken down in spirit and in body. The women, who throughout the war have displayed more than Spartan heroism, now wept and implored their husbands to yield to the entreaties of the envoys. Three days and sleepless nights were passed in combating the resolution never to leave Florida. But the ladies at length (as is always the case) prevailed, and Assinoah, the chief, consented to come in.

U.S. Army, New England Guards, Color-Bearer (1840)

Quite separate from the regular army and the common militia were the units of chartered State Volunteers. In name, these units were part of the militia organization; but in practice they were independent (and indeed almost private) units that formed a distinct part of the social system of most eastern cities. The man illustrated is a member of the celebrated New England Guards, located in Boston, Massachusetts. The blue uniform and tall shako complete with heavy brass plate and cock's feathers are typical of Volunteer style of the period, and the standard bears the arms of the State of Massachusetts.

The Texas Revolution (1835-36)

In June 1832, some Texans fought a brief skirmish with Mexican troops at Velasco. This encounter persuaded most Texans that something had to be done about the situation, and a convention was held at San Felipe. The convention prepared a formal request for Texan autonomy within Mexico, which would involve an administrative separation of Texas from the province of Coahuila and increased representation by Texans in the Mexican congress. The leader of the Texas faction demanding greater autonomy for Texas within Mexico was Steven Austin, whose father had emigrated from Missouri in 1811. A smaller faction, which wanted complete independence, was growing all the time. In December 1832, Sam Houston crossed the Red River into Texas, and soon became a leader in the independence party. Houston was an extremely colorful character, an ex-general of the militia, a governor of Tennessee, a friend of Andrew Jackson, an experienced sol-

"Sam" Houston, the architect of Texas independence, ultimately guaranteed that independence with his victory over the Mexicans in the Battle of San Jacinto.

Right: Frontier operations demanded considerable flexibility in uniform and equipment. In general terms, those units which displayed the greatest flexibility enjoyed the highest success. These are weapons typical of frontier warfare, including a fighting axe, a European dagger, and two fighting knives.

Steven Austin
For further references see pages 253, 255, 256.

Sam Houston
For further references see pages 199, 256, 257, 258, 260, 261, 262, 263.

REVOLUTIONARY AND EARLY AMERICAN WARS

dier who had been wounded twice in the Creek wars, and an adopted Cherokee.

In April 1833, the Texans held a second convention to demand greater self-government, and as a result, Austin was thrown into jail. Dislike of the dictatorial regime headed by General Antonio Lopez de Santa Anna was growing throughout Mexico during this period. During the first half of the 1830s, there were rebellions in eight Mexican states. Santa Anna crushed an uprising in Zacatecas during April 1835, and he sent General Martin Perfecto de Cos, his brother-in-law, to deal with the rebellion in Coahuila. In June 1835, the Texans learned from Mexican dispatches that civil rights were about to be suspended in Texas, and that Santa Anna was planning to tackle the Texans personally. This produced a further increase in strength for what had now become the Texas "war party." One of the leaders of this faction was William Barret Travers, a hothead who had previously been a lawyer in South Carolina. At his instigation, the garrison

> **Santa Anna**
> For further references see pages
> *254*, 255, *256*, 257, 258, 259, 260, 262, 263.

253

THE WAR OF TEXAS REVOLUTION

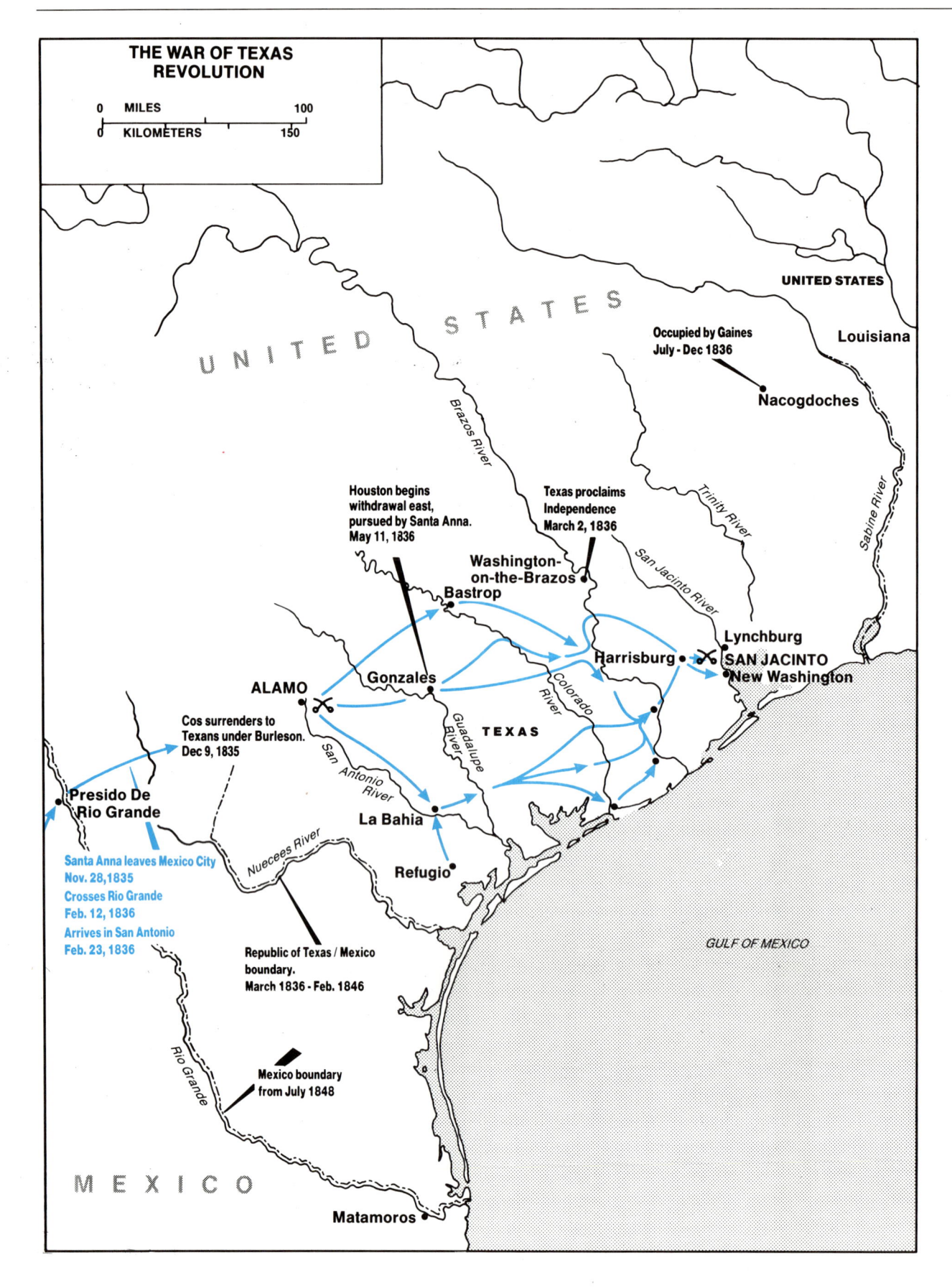

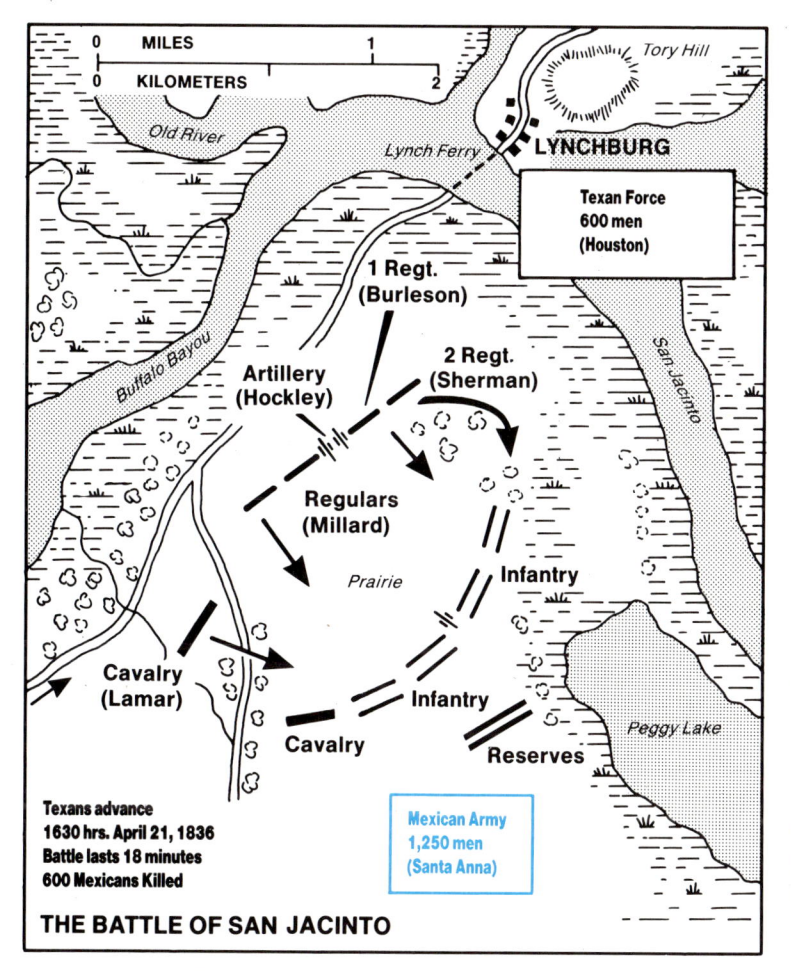

REVOLUTIONARY AND EARLY AMERICAN WARS

was ejected from the Mexican customs post at Anahuac. Even as Cos began to move Mexican forces into Texas, most Texans still wanted peace. However, this feeling was swayed toward war when a much-changed Austin was released from jail and declared both that Santa Anna was a "base, unprincipled bloody monster" and that "War is our only recourse. No halfway measures, but war in full."

The result was open rebellion. In October 1835, a detachment of Mexican troops was sent to recover a virtually useless cannon which had been lent to the citizens of Gonzales in 1831 to frighten the Indians. The Texans hung a banner underneath the cannon, with the legend "Come and Take It." On October 2, the Texas Revolution started when a force of Texans fired on the Mexican detachment, killing one man and putting the rest to flight.

In San Antonio, there was a Mexican strength of 1,400 under Cos. The quality of the force was low, for Santa Anna had sent to Texas what were in effect penal regiments manned almost entirely by criminals. About 500 Texans had gathered at Gonzales. Most were undisciplined farmers, but there were enough

Far left: The War of Texas Revolution.
Above left: The Battle of San Jacinto.
Left: The Siege of the Alamo.
Below: The Alamo.

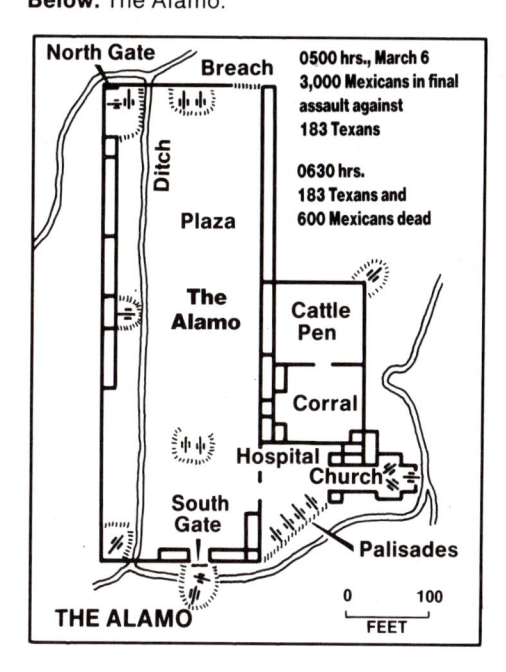

255

frontiersmen with rifles to give the Texas force some military capability. Austin was elected commander, despite his lack of military skills, and given the authority to prevent the men from coming and going as they pleased. A local command was voted to Houston, who then headed for the Texas convention at San Felipe.

"Democracy" Runs Riot

The Texas "army" now told Austin that it wanted to attack San Antonio, and the democratically elected commander was forced to agree, even though strength had fallen to only 300. On October 27 at Concepcion Mission, about two miles south of San Antonio, a Mexican detachment was severely handled by a much smaller party of Texans, led by James Bowie, the celebrated knife duelist and landowner. The Texans lost just one man killed, but the Mexicans lost 67 dead and about the same number wounded by the Texans' long-range but accurate rifle fire. Despite Bowie's success, the Texans were in no position to attack San Antonio and therefore laid siege to the town.

The Texas convention opened on November 3. All agreed that the Texans' war against Santa Anna's dictatorship had to be continued. While some argued in favor of the cause of independence, others wanted to fight in the name of the Mexican federal state. Houston was a supporter of the latter idea, which was adopted by the convention with the suggestion that Texas offer to help any other Mexican state wishing to throw off Santa Anna's shackles. Austin was sent to the United States to seek help, and command of the army passed to Edward Burleson.

There was considerable, although not total, public support in the United States for the Texans. Weapons and other supplies began to flood across the frontier into Texas, and volunteer companies were organized, most of them in the south. The United States decided not to participate, and strict instructions were issued to General Gaines to maintain a neutral zone along the Sabine River. Part of this order covered Gaines' responsibility in preventing Indian raids from American territory into Mexico, but Gaines understood this as meaning that there should be no conflict of American and Mexican interests. He therefore sent the 7th Infantry Regiment and part of the 1st Dragoon Regiment to Nacogdoches in July 1836, withdrawing them from this illegal excursion into Mexico only in December.

In Texas, the dividing line between the factions for and against independence from Mexico was becoming more defined, and so too was that between the Tejanos, inhabitants of Mexican descent. Meanwhile, the "siege" of San Antonio was progressing in an extraordinary way, for the democracy of the Texan "army" meant that all decisions were reached only by a majority vote of the officers, and the men came and went as they pleased. With the approach of winter, the volunteers began to depart in larger numbers, and a majority vote of the officers overruled Burleson and decided to break off the siege.

Despite the strength of the Mexican defense of San Antonio, with the garrison holding well-prepared positions, the volunteers from the United States had other ideas. Led by Ben Milam, a Kentuckian who had fought for Mexican inde-

General Antonio Lopez de Santa Anna proved unequal to the task of maintaining a Mexican grasp on Texas during the Texas Revolution. Despite his defeat in the Battle of San Jacinto, he harbored the belief that he would be able to reverse the decision of the war.

REVOLUTIONARY AND EARLY AMERICAN WARS

pendence and only recently escaped from the Mexican jail into which he had been thrown for his republican notions, 300 Texans and volunteers stormed into San Antonio on December 5. With two companies of American volunteers, the New Orleans Grays, in the lead, the Texans took San Antonio in four days of hand-to-hand fighting. Milam was killed by a sharpshooter, but Cos offered to surrender on December 9. Burleson accepted the offer and sent the Mexicans home with enough weapons to fight off Indian attack.

With such a victory under their belts, the Texans thought that the war was all but over and departed for home in large numbers. Houston was convinced that this was not the case, but his appeal for the men to remain under arms went unheeded. Texas strength was then reduced further by an unfathomable decision of some Texans to take Matamoros at the mouth of the Rio Grande. Those who departed toward Matamoros offered the reason that they would link up with the local anti-Santa Anna faction and start a Mexican war

The boat carronade was one of several types produced to give light vessels a devastating punch in short-range engagements. Such weapons were usually mounted in the bow of a boat: if it was mounted as a broadside gun, its recoil could have damaged the boat's structure or, under certain circumstances, even overturned it.

257

to overthrow Santa Anna. Houston was strongly against the expedition, which was nonetheless approved by the convention in San Felipe and dispatched under James Fannin, whose initial move was to secure a base at La Bahia. The Texas head of state, Governor Henry Smith, agreed with Houston and dismissed the council until March 1, 1836, when it was to reassemble at Washington-on-the-Brazos. The council responded by dismissing Smith as "vulgar and depraved." Houston argued with the men of the Matamoros expedition that the defense of Texas was more important, and by the time the expedition left La Bahia under Colonel Frank Johnson, it numbered just 70 men, who were massacred when they tried to execute the ill-conceived scheme.

The Undermanned Alamo

This division left just 104 men under Colonel James C. Neill to hold the Alamo, a fort improvised out of a mission station just east of San Antonio. The defenses were put in order by Green Jameson, and 18 of the cannon abandoned by the Mexicans were remounted and placed on earthwork ramparts inside and outside the 12-foot wall surrounding the compound.

Meanwhile, Santa Anna had been putting the finishing touches on his plan to keep Texas as part of Mexico. Early in 1836, Santa Anna's Army of Operations in Texas had about 6,000 men, a figure that had increased to about 7,500 by mid-April. Houston correctly saw that a pitched battle against this force of regulars and militia, regardless of its failings in equipment and discipline, would result in a defeat for the Texans. He therefore planned to concentrate and train his forces while fighting a guerrilla war that would cost Mexican lives and overtax their lines of communication. Only when the Mexican force had dwindled in numbers and capability would the Texan commander consider a formal battle. As part of this overall plan, Houston detached Bowie with 30 men to destroy the fortifications of the Alamo and bring out the garrison.

Arriving at the Alamo, Houston found

This watercolor by Shegogue, painted in 1831, reveals David Crockett the congressman, rather than Davy Crockett, the backwoodsman and hero of the Alamo.

that Neill's strength was down to 80 men. The others had returned home for lack of pay and supplies. Bowie and Neill then decided to hold the Alamo because they lacked the means to evacuate the cannons, and the remaining men were prepared to hold this fort on Santa Anna's inevitable northward march against Texas. Houston was again appalled, for first Fannin and now Neill and Bowie had disobeyed his orders. He tried to resign, but Governor Brown instead gave him leave until March 1. Houston departed on a mission to guarantee the neutrality of the Cherokees.

On February 1, Santa Anna left Saltillo at the head of his army, which was made up of two infantry brigades, one cavalry brigade, some artillery, and a crack engineer corps. At the Rio Grande, he planned to link up with a force already there under General Joaquin Sesma, while a small detachment under General Jose Urrea headed for Matamoros. Almost immediately, the deficiencies of the

Mexican supply system became clear. The march toward Texas became a feat of endurance as the starving men and animals moved through the dust of the lower areas and the snows of the mountains. The men were already on half rations when the army was hit by cholera, which swept through the already weakened ranks and killed many men.

The situation at the Alamo was improving slightly at this time. Bowie had used his contacts with the local population to get supplies, and as the defenses were put in order, a trickle of reinforcements arrived in response to Bowie's claim that "We cannot be driven from the post of honor." On February 3, Lieutenant Colonel William B. Travis appeared with 30 men, and five days later, "Colonel" David Crockett arrived with his Tennessee Company of Mounted Volunteers. Already famous as an Indian fighter, ex-Congressman, and storyteller, "Davy" Crockett announced that he had come with his small company "to aid you all that I can in your noble cause." By February 10, the garrison of the Alamo numbered 142 men, and Neill went on leave after giving command to Travis. This appointment did not meet with the approval of most of the volunteers, but as Bowie was in poor health and in any event was generally absent on drunken rampages in San Antonio, the decision was probably right. On February 14, Travis and Bowie settled the matter by agreeing to a joint command.

The Siege of the Alamo Begins

Just two days later, Santa Anna crossed the Rio Grande after linking up with Sesma's force at Presidio de Rio Grande. Final preparations were being completed in the Alamo with the creation of a hospital, the chopping of horseshoes into grapeshot, and the finding of accommodations for the families of several

The siege of the Alamo ended on March 6, 1836, when the Mexican forces launched their final assault on the vastly outgunned Texas position and its outnumbered garrison.

volunteers. Travis sent out requests for reinforcement, most of them aimed at Fannin, who was now settled in "Fort Defiance" at La Bahia.

Santa Anna's army arrived in San Antonio on February 23, about one month earlier than the Texans had anticipated. The men of the Alamo's garrison in San Antonio quickly pulled east across the San Antonio River and reached the Alamo, which now contained about 25 women and children in addition to about 150 men. Travis had time to send out a batch of appeals for reinforcement, again to Fannin and another to Gonzales, about 70 miles away, which was at the time the nearest point from which help could have been expected. Santa Anna set about besieging the Texas garrison with no delay. He even hoisted on the belfry of the church in San Antonio a red flag signifying that no quarter would be given.

Within a day, the Alamo was firmly under Mexican siege, and on February 24, Santa Anna's artillery opened up a bombardment of the fort. On the same day, Bowie's poor health finally caught up with him, and he took to his bed, leaving Travis in sole command. Another message was sent out by Travis: "..our flag still waves proudly from the walls - I shall never surrender or retreat. Then, I call on you in the name of Liberty, of patriotism & everything dear to the American character, to come to our aid...if this call is neglected, I am determined to sustain myself as long as possible & die like a soldier who never forgets what is due to his honor & that of his country - Victory or Death."

The next day, the Tennessee volunteers raided and burned the shacks south of the Alamo used by the Mexicans as advanced positions for the concealment of sharpshooters. Effective artillery support for the raid was supplied by the Texas artillery under the control of Captain Almeron Dickinson and Captain William Carey. Another message was sent out by Travis, this time carried by Captain Juan Seguin, whose San Antonio company of Tejanos formed part of the garrison. In this message, Travis wrote that "It will be impossible for us to keep them out much longer. If they overpower us, we fall a sacrifice at the shrine of our country, and we hope posterity will do our memory justice. Give me help, oh my Country!"

Fannin was at last stirred to action of a sort. On February 26, he left La Bahia for the Alamo, though he halted for a day when a wagon broke down only a few hundred yards along the road. Then on February 27, Fannin retired to La Bahia once more. Some help was forthcoming, however, for at Gonzales the 25 men of Lieutenant George Kimball's Gonzales Ranging Company of Mounted Volunteers decided to assist the garrison of the Alamo. In the early morning of February 29, they slipped through the Mexican lines to reach the Alamo.

It was too late for further assistance to reach the Alamo, but Travis' patriotic pleas finally spurred the Texas convention into action. Reconvened at Washington-on-the-Brazos, the convention declared Texas an independent nation on March 2. Fannin again decided to move in support of the Alamo, with the intention of joining forces with the volunteers that Seguin was rallying for a relief attempt. Yet again, however, Fannin changed his mind.

The Fall of the Alamo

The Alamo had been under fairly constant artillery bombardment that had knocked down large parts of the walls. On March 5, Santa Anna decided that the time was ripe for an assault: some of his artillery had pushed to within 250 yards of the Alamo, and he had been reinforced with another brigade to give him an effective strength of more than 2,000 men. The assault was committed on March 6, and the fort was attacked by four columns of Mexicans starting at 5a.m. By 6:30a.m., it was all over, and the defenders of the Alamo were all dead with the exception of a few women and children, and one Tejano who persuaded the Mexicans he had been a prisoner. Mexican losses were about 600.

Houston arrived in Gonzales on March 11 and found 374 men gathered under Neill and Burleson for the relief of the Alamo. News of the Alamo's fall reached the Texans at Gonzales, and Houston decided to fall back in the face of Sesma's

The Alamo
For further references
see pages
254, 255, 258, 259, 261.

REVOLUTIONARY AND EARLY AMERICAN WARS

The death of Davy Crockett during the final Mexican assault on the Alamo.

advance on the town with 700 men. This retreat to the east was attacked by Houston's political opponents as the "Runaway Scrape." It was also unpopular with part of the Gonzales force, but was in fact very sensible as many of the men lacked weapons, and there were no supplies. The Texas government abandoned Washington-on-the-Brazos at the same time, finally establishing itself at Harrisburg under the newly elected provisional president, David Burnet.

The main Texas force was at La Bahia under Fannin. It was comparatively well trained and adequately equipped. The infantry units were the Georgia and Lafayette battalions, both created out of independent companies, and there was a small detachment of artillery. Fannin now proceeded to waste his force. A company under Captain King was sent to Refugio to evacuate its civilians, but was intercepted by Urrea's detachment and overrun. King and a few other survivors were tied to trees and shot. The Georgia battalion was then sent under Major Ward to find King's company and was also overrun. Reduced to a strength of 300 infantrymen and 25 cavalry, Fannin destroyed the fortifications of La Bahia, spiked the guns he could not move, and marched to join Houston.

The "Goliad Massacre"

Fannin's progress was slow, for his force was weighed down with baggage. Even though a move of only two more miles would have brought the force to the Rio Coleto and its timbered banks, Fannin camped in open countryside and was attacked by a superior Mexican force. Fannin formed his men into a hollow square with cannon in the corners and repulsed the first Mexican cavalry charge. Then, the Texans' rifles took a heavy toll of the Mexicans until the fall of night brought hostilities to a temporary end. On the following day, March 20, the Mexicans received reinforcement, including two cannon. Fannin's force was out of artillery ammunition, and the commander offered his men the opportunity to surrender or fight their way out. The Alabama Red Rovers wanted to fight, but because of their 70 wounded and the Mexicans' promise of fair treatment, the majority chose to surrender. Fannin's force returned to La Bahia under Mexican escort, where they found a number of other prisoners. On March 27, the majority of the Texans were marched out of La Bahia. Those who remained were mainly colonists from Refugio and San Patricio, medical staff, and a number of volunteers who had been captured while unarmed. The Mexicans said that the men being marched out were to be repatriated to the United States, but then opened fire. In this "Goliad Massacre," 342 of the prisoners were killed, and only about 30 escaped. The legal reason for the massacre was a Mexican law of 1835 which decreed the death penalty for all foreigners captured under arms in Texas.

This massacre left only Houston and his force to oppose Santa Anna's total control of Texas. Houston continued to fall back, but after crossing the Rio Brazos, halted and started to turn his force into a more disciplined army, with the 1st Regiment commanded by Burleson and the new 2nd Regiment by Sidney Sherman. Over the next two weeks, two cannon and some reinforcements arrived, giving Houston a strength of about 800 men including a mounted scouting troop under Captain H. Karnes. There was resentment at Houston's inaction, and nearly a mutiny when the threat of summary execution was used to prevent the departure of a small force under Mirabeau Buonaparte Lamar in search of the Mexicans.

Santa Anna's Decisive Mistake

Houston was completely right, for Santa Anna finally committed the error for which the Texan commander was waiting. With his lines of communication completely overextended, Santa Anna sent General Gaona's division north from San Antonio, and General Urrea's division south from La Bahia toward Matagorda and Brazoria. He himself led 750 men of Sesma's division toward Fort Bend, where Sesma was to join him with the rest of the division. Santa Anna's main intention was

Santa Anna surrenders to Houston after the Battle of San Jacinto, and so brings the fighting in the Texas Revolution to an end.

to capture the members of the Texas government.

The Texas government avoided Santa Anna, who turned aside to find and destroy Houston. Santa Anna ordered the balance of his force at Fort Bend to meet him without delay, but in forced marches that covered 60 miles in just over two days, Houston and his Texas army approached Santa Anna before he had been reinforced. On April 20, Houston used his tactical advantage to cross Buffalo Bayou into a good defensive position offered by woods along the Rio San Jacinto. Cos arrived on April 21, bringing Santa Anna's strength to about 1,300 infantry, a few cavalry, and a single gun. Santa Anna located his force behind a barrier of supplies and pack saddles on the flat ground in front of the Texans and waited for the attack. In the Texas ranks, there was the inevitable demand that Houston should order an attack. Houston said that the men should eat their midday meal first and sent a small party to destroy the bridge by which more reinforcements might reach Santa Anna.

The Texans then deployed, with the cavalry on the right flank, hidden from the Mexicans by the woods, and the 1st and 2nd Regiments on the left and right wings, with the Texans' two pieces of artillery between them. These guns, nicknamed "The Two Sisters," were gifts from the citizens of Cincinnati. The Mexicans clearly did not expect a battle to start so late in the day, and while Santa Anna slept in his tent, most of the Mexican force took its customary siesta in the field.

The Battle of San Jacinto

Houston started his advance at 4:30 p.m. on April 21, and the Battle of San Jacinto was a complete rout of the Mexicans. The Texans got within 200 yards of the Mexican position without being noticed, and within 60 yards before the Mexicans had manned their positions and begun to fire. Santa Anna's flanks crumbled, allowing Lamar's cavalry to sweep around onto the Mexicans' left and Sherman's infantry to start passing around their right. The battle was over in just 18 minutes. Of the 783 Texans, two had been killed and 23 wounded, while the Mexicans had lost 600 dead and 730 taken prisoner. Santa Anna was captured on the following day as he tried to escape, but was not executed as Houston realized that the Mexican dictator was essential to any peace negotiations. Santa Anna recognized the independence of the Republic of Texas, although this recognition was later repudiated by the Mexican government. Houston was elected president, and on July 4 the United States recognized Texas. This move stirred considerable resentment in Mexico and contributed to sporadic border skirmishing between Texas and Mexico over the next ten years.

Glossary

Adjutant General The professional head of the army department responsible for matters of personnel.
Ammunition Propelent (gunpowder) and projectiles for artillery and small arms.
Arsenal A depot for the storage of military equipment (especially weapons and other munitions) for distribution in times of crisis or war.
Artillery An overall term for a tube weapon too large for operation by a single man. It is designed to fire solid shot or explosive-filled shells.
Battalion The basic organizational and tactical grouping, mainly of infantry, commanded by a lieutenant colonel and made up of several companies.
Battery The basic organizational and tactical grouping of artillery equivalent to an infantry company.
Bayonet Sword-like blade attached to the muzzle of a musket or rifle for use in close-quarter combat.
Blockade The closing up of a country or region to prevent entry or departure of people and goods.
Blockhouse A small fort, generally built of logs or other locally available materials, for local security along lines of communication.
Brig A two-masted vessel with square sails on each mast.
Brigade The organizational and tactical grouping of two or more regiments, generally commanded by a brigadier general.
Brigantine A two-masted vessel with square sails on the foremast and fore- and-aft sails in the mainmast.
Canister An artillery-fired projectile for use against people, and generally made of a quantity of shot (the size of small cannon balls or large musket balls) in a thin metal container. The "canister" bursts open when it leaves the muzzle of the gun, allowing the shot to spread out into a large but even pattern.
Carriage The mobile or fixed support for piece of artillery, usually including the elevating and traversing mechanisms.
Cavalry The branch of any army intended to move and fight on horseback.
Chain of command Sequence of commanding officers from highest to lowest, through which command is exercised.
Commissary General Commanding officer responsible for food.
Company An organizational and tactical grouping, usually of infantry, commanded by a captain, and grouped to create a battalion.
Corvette A single-deck warship smaller than a frigate and generally used for scouting or, more frequently, raiding merchant shipping.
Court martial Court for the trial of people subject to military law.
Demobilization The orderly disbandment of an army or other armed force at the end of hostilities.
Division Tactical grouping of two or more brigades, often provided with support elements so that it can exist and fight by itself.
Dragoon A cavalryman trained and equipped to fight as an infantryman if needed.
Earthwork Defensive geographical feature created by excavating and mounding dirt.
Enlistment Length of time for which a soldier agrees to serve in the army.
Establishment Any authorized strength of men, weapons, and equipment, seldom matched by actual numbers.
Fighting top A platform built at the top of a mast to support the shrouds stabilizing higher masts. In action, they were manned by marines and sailors with small arms, grenades, and on occasion light swivel guns to fire down onto an enemy ship's decks.

Glossary

Firepower Overall term for a unit's total weapon strength.
Flank The extreme left or right of a body of troops in a military position.
Flotilla Fleet of boats or small ships.
Frigate A single-deck ship of between 28 and 48 guns. It lacks the firepower and protection to take part in a fleet action, but has the speed and maneuverability to scout for line-of-battle ships and harass enemy shipping.
Front Lateral length of a body of soldiers between their two flanks.
Galley A small warship relying on oars instead of sails as its main method of propulsion.
Garrison The unit or units attached to a base or other area for defense and the maintenance of its facilities.
Guerrilla Any man involved in irregular warfare waged by small parties operating independently, usually to harass the enemy's lines of communication, etc.
Howitzer A piece of artillery designed to fire at an angle of elevation higher than 45°. It lobs its shells high over any obstacle for a plunging descent on the target.
Infantry The branch of any army intended to move and fight on foot.
Inspector General The professional head of the army department responsible for training.
Light infantry Infantry equipped more lightly than infantry of the line, and thus able to march more quickly and to operate as skirmishers.
Line(s) of communication The main route(s) over which an army in the field is supplied, reinforced, and provided with orders from a base area.
Magazine A storage area for gunpowder and/or other munitions.
Militia Citizen force with a commitment to annual training and, under specific conditions of geography and time, active service.
Minuteman Able-bodied person prepared to turn out at a minute's notice in times of emergency.
Musket A personal weapon (usually of the infantry) with a comparatively short but smooth-bored barrel that does not impart any spin to its bullet. It offers only modest accuracy and range, but gives a fairly rapid rate of fire.
Operational The adjective used to describe the level of military activity between the tactical and the strategic, and therefore concerned mainly with the coordination of battles to produce a campaign.
Ordnance The collective noun for artillery and its ammunition.
Parallel A trench dug parallel to a defensive feature to provide cover for assaulting soldiers. Parallels were gradually pushed closer to the objective by digging zigzag trenches in the direction of the objective and then digging lateral trenches to make a new parallel at the forward end of the zigzag "sap."
Privateer Civilian ship with a license from its national authorities which was used for raiding merchant shipping.
Quartermaster General The professional head of the army department responsible for supplies (such as food and armament) and accommodation.
Rampart A broad-topped mound of earth, usually with a stone parapet, for defensive purposes.
Rearguard Rearmost element of a fighting force, designed to protect the rear during an advance, and to check the enemy during a retreat.
Reconnaissance Mission by a small group of soldiers to obtain information about the enemy's position, strength, and movements.
Redoubt Outwork of a defensive system, usually lacking flanking defenses.

Glossary

Regiment The basic organizational and tactical grouping commanded by a colonel and made up of two battalions.
Regular soldier Full-time soldier as opposed to part-time militiaman.
Rifle A personal weapon (usually of the infantry) with a comparatively long barrel containing spiral internal grooves designed to spin the bullet. It provides high accuracy and long range, but only a low rate of fire.
Schooner A vessel with two or more masts each rigged with fire-and-aft sails.
Sharpshooter An individual soldier who is accurate enough (usually) with a rifle to be posted where marksmanship is needed.
Ship of the line Warship with more than 60 guns, designed to fight in fleet actions.
Siege Scientifically planned and executed capture of an enemy position by cutting it off and then gradually closing in before delivering the final assault.
Skirmisher A lightly equipped foot soldier deployed forward of the main body of troops to reconnoiter and harass the enemy's advance.
Sloop A small single-masted vessel rigged with fore-and-aft sails.
Small arms General term for weapons operated by one person.
Spiking The act of rendering a piece of artillery useless, generally by hammering a spoke into its touchhole.
Strategic The adjective used to describe the level of military activity above the operational, and therefore concerned mainly with coordination of campaigns to produce a war-winning situation.
Strategy Art of fighting a war or campaign.
Strike a flag To lower a naval flag in surrender.
Tactical The adjective used to describe the level of military activity below the operational, and therefore concerned mainly with winning individual battles.
Tactics Art of fighting a battle.
Topography The art of describing and representing on a map natural and artificial features of a geographical region.
Trail The leg connecting a gun carriage to its towing vehicle of animal. It is used to stabilize the weapon when it is deployed for action.
Volley Hail of fire delivered when many small arms are discharged at the same moment.

Bibliography

Balderston, Marion and David Syrett (ed.). *The Lost War: Letters from British Officers During the American Revolution.*
(Horizon Press, New York, 1975).
First-hand views from the other side.

Baldwin, Leland D. *Whiskey Rebels, the Story of a Frontier Uprising.*
(University of Pittsburgh Press, Pittsburgh, PA, 1939).
The Whiskey Rebellion.

Bemrose, John. *Reminisces of the Second Seminole War.*
(University of Florida, Gainesville, FL, 1966).
Reprint of eyewitness account.

Boatner, Mark M., III *Encyclopedia of the American Revolution.*
(David McKay Co., New York, 1974).
Outstanding alphabetical coverage of all aspects of the war.

Buker, George E. *Swamp Sailors: Riverine Warfare in the Everglades 1835-1842.*
(University of Florida, Gainesville, FL, 1975).
Seminole wars.

Busch, Noel F. *Winter Quarters.*
(Mentor, New York, 1974). Winter at Valley Forge.

Carrington, Henry B. *Battles of the American Revolution.*
(A. S. Barnes & Co., New York, 1877).

Coggins, Jack. *Ships and Seamen of the American Revolution.*
(Stackpole Books, Harrisburg, PA, 1969).
Good details on the construction and handling of ships in the age of sail.

Cuneo, John R. *The Battles of Saratoga.*
(Macmillan, New York, 1967).
The decisive battle, part of a battle series aimed at younger readers.

Davis, Burke. *The Campaign That Won America.*
(Dial Press, New York, 1970).
A more sophisticated account of the Saratoga campaign.

Davis, Burke. *The Cowpens-Guildford Courthouse Campaign.*
(J. B. Lippincott Co., New York, 1962).
Good popular history of the duel of wits between Cronwallis and Greene.

de la Pena, Jose Enrique. *With Santa Anna in Texas.*
(Texas A & M University Press, College Station, TX, 1975).
Dairy of the period.

Downey, Fairfax. *Indian Wars of the U.S. Army 1776-1865.*
(Doubleday & Co, Garden City, NY, 1963).

Espositio, Vincent J. (ed.). *The West Point Atlas of American Wars 1689-1900.*
(Frederick A. Praeger, New York, 1959).
A fine map book coordinated with easy-to-understand text.

Fleming, Thomas J. *Beat the Last Drum: The Siege of Yorktown 1781.*
(St. Martin's Press, New York, 1963).
The origins of the American way of war.

Gifford, John C., (ed.). *Billy Bowlegs and the Seminole War.*
(Dewars Limited Editions, Coconut Grove, FL, 1925).
Reprint of contemporary account.

Hassler, Warren W., Jr. *With Shield and Sword.* (Iowa State University Press, Ames, Iowa, 1982).
General U.S. military history including Seminole and Blackhawk wars.

Holland, James W. *Andrew Jackson and the Creek War: Victory at the Horseshoe.*
(University of Alabama Press, 1968).

Jacobs, James R. *The Beginning of the U.S. Army 1783-1812.*
(Kennikut Press, Port Washington, NY, 1947).

Ketchum, Richard M. (ed.). *The American Heritage Book of the Revolution.*
(American Heritage Publishing Co., New York, 1971).
A lavishly illustrated, fine popular history.

Bibliography

Ketchum, Richard M. *The Winter Soldiers.*
(Doubleday & Co., Garden City, NY, 1973).
Washington's early campaigns showing him to be truly the "indispensible man."

Lancaster, Bruce, *From Lexington to Liberty.*
(Doubleday & Co., Garden City, NY, 1955).

Lord, Walter. *A Time to Stand.*
(Harper & Row, New York, 1978).
An exciting popular history of the siege of the Alama.

Lossing, Benton J. *Pictorial Field-Book of the Revolution.*
(Harper & Brothers, New York, 1852).
Full of good terrain sketches and human interest stories by someone who visited the sites while they remained nearly unchanged from the war days.

Lumpkin, Henry. *From Savannah to Yorktown.*
(Paragon House, New York, 1981).
The war in the south.

Martyn, Charles. *The Life of Artemas Ward, the First Commander-in-Chief of the American Revolution.*
(New York, 1921).

Matthews, William and Dixon Wecter. *Our Soldiers Speak, 1775-1918.*
(Little Brown & Co., Boston, 1943).
First-hand accounts.

Miller, Nathan. *Sea of Glory.*
(David McKey Co., New York, 1974).
The Continental Navy.

Potter, Woodburne. *The War in Florida.*
(University Microfilms, Ann Arbor, MI, 1966).
Eyewitness account of the Seminole Wars.

Rankin, Hugh F. *Francis Marion: The Swamp Fox.*
(Thomas Y. Crowell Co., New York, 1873).
The war's most famous guerrilla leader.

Roberts, Kenneth. *The Battle of Cowpens.*
(Doubleday Co., Garden City, NY, 1958).
Morgan's masterpiece in easy-to-read detail.

Scheer, George F. and Hugh F. Rankin. *Rebels & Redcoats.*
(World Publishing Co., New York, 1957).

Smith, William. *Expedition Against the Ohio Indians.*
(University Microfilms, Ann Arbor, MI, 1966).
Reprint of eyewitness account.

Starkey, Marion L. *A Little Rebellion.* (Alfred A. Knopf, New York, 1955).
Shays' Rebellion.

Sugden, John. *Tecumseh's Last Stand.*
(University of Oklahoma, Norman, OK, 1985).

Tinkle, Lon. *13 Days of Glory: the Siege of the Alamo.*
(McGraw Hill, New York, 1958).

Tucker, Glenn. *Tecumseh, Vision of Glory.*
(Bobbs-Merrill Co., New York, 1956).

Utley, Robert M. and Wilcomb E. Washburn. *The American Heritage History of the Indian Wars.*
(American Heritage Publishing Co., New York, 1977).

Wheeler, Richard. *Voices of 1776.*
(Thomas Y. Crowell Co., New York, 1972).
Eyewitness accounts of the American Revolution.

Index

Page numbers in *italics* refer to illustration.

Act of Union 174
Adams, John 174, 191, 221, 223
Adams-Oris Treaty 214
Adjutant 202
Alabama Red Rovers 262
Alabama River 196
Alabama 196, 237, 243
Alamance Creek 13
Alamo 254 (map), 255 (map), 260-261
Alamo, siege of 255 (map), *259*
Alarm 222
Alarm Companies 30
Albany 72, 73, 79, 80 (map), 146 (map), 185
Alert 222
Alexander, William 57
Alfred 37, 182-185, 221
Allen, Ethan, 20, *23,* 41
Alliance 190-1, *222, 223*
Alliance, U.S.S. 96, 134
Amelia Island 197 (map)
American frontier life 212
amphibious assault 255
Anahuac 258
Andre, John 104, 107
Andrew Doria 187
Annapolis 130, 136
Apalachee Bay 211
Apalachicola River 209-211
Arbuthnot, Marriot 100, 102, 121
Arkansas River 235
Arkinson, Fort 233
Armistead, Walker K. 244
Armstrong, Fort 233
Armstrong, John 202
Army of operations 258
Arnold, Benedict 20, *20,* 40 (map), 41, 44, 74, 78, 79, 80 (map), 81, 104, 106, 120, 121, 138, 185
Arrowstook War 243
Arroyo Hondo 179
Articles of Confederation 50, 146, 149
Ashe 96
Ashley River 100
Assumpink Creek 64
Astoria 178
Athens 197 (map)
Atkinson, Henry 236, 237
Atlanta, H.M.S. 134
Augusta 96, 97 (map), 99, 197
Austin, Sam 252-256

Bad Axe River, Battle of 236-238
Bahamas 187, 206, 220-221
Bainbridge, William 223

Baltimore 62, 123 (map), 130,164 (map)
Barney, William 187
Barrancas, Fort 212
Barry, John 134, *134,* 190, 222-225, 231
Barton, Thomas B 195
Baton Rouge 198 (map)
Baum, Friedrich 76
Beagle 194, 195
Beaufort 101
Bemis Heights 79, 80 (map)
Bemis Heights, Battle of 80
Bend, Fort 262-263
Bennington 74, 80 (map), 109
Bennington, Battle of 76, *78*
Berkeley Sound 195
Bernard, Simon 206
Bey of Algiers 223
Big Cypress Swamp 250
Billingsport Garrison 187
Black Hawk War 235-237
Black Hawk *235,* 236-237, 238
Blodgett's Hotel 201
Blue Licks 134
Board of Admiralty 222
Board of Treasury 153
Board of War 85
Board of War, Abolishment of 107
Bonhomme, Richard 90, 92, *93,* 189
Bonneville, Benjamin L E 235
Boone, Daniel 134, 201
Bordertown 63 (map), 64
Boston *12, 13, 14,* 15, *16,* 17, 18, 19, 22, 23, 25, *28,* 33, 36, 40 (map), 44, *49,* 53, 81, 89, 123 (map), 132, 156, 190, 251
Boston Harbor 225
Boston Massacre *12,* 13
Boston Naval Shipyard 225
Boston, Siege of 19, 24, 38, *45*
Boston Tea Party 14, 15
Bowie, James 256, 259-260
Bowleg's Town 212
Bowlegs, Chief Billy 211, 212
Bradford, William 187
Brandywine 18 (map), 53, 71
Brandywine Creek 70
Brandywine, Battle of the 70
Brant, Joseph 73
Breakwater 195
Breed's Hill *25,* 21, 22 (map)
Brest 188
Breymann's Redoubt 81
Briar Creek, Battle of 96
British Army *21*
Brooke, Fort 239
Brooklyn Heights 18 (map), 56, 57, 61 (map)
Brooklyn Navy Yard 226
Brown, Jacob 202, 219, 232
Browne, Montfort 184
Bryan's Station 132
Buchanan, Franklin 231

Buford, Abraham 101
Bunker Hill 18 (map), 23, 28 (map), 29, 31, 100
Bunker Hill, Battle of 23, 25, *25,* 26-27, 28 (map), 29
Burgoyne, Sir John 22, 42, 43, 44, 67, 70, 72, *73,* 74, 76, 78, 79, *79,* 80 (map), 81, *82-83,* 85, 109, 119
Burnet, David 261
Burrows, William Ward 191
Bushnell, David 60
Butler, John 95
Butler, Walter 95
Byron, John 99

Cabot 184
Cadwalader, James 64
Cadwalader, John 190
Calhoun, John C. 206, 210-211, 214-215, 232, 233, 235
California 248
Cambridge Common 34, *34*
Camden 97 (map), 104, 108, 110, 117
Camden, Battle of *102,* 104
Camp Comanche 248
Campbell, Archibald 96, 97 (map)
Campbell, Richard 108
Canadian Militiamen 243
Cannon, English *112*
Cape Fear River 116, 117
Cape Henlopen 182
Cape Henry 129
Carey, William 260
Carleton, Sir Guy, 41, 134
Caroline Incident 243
Carmick, Daniel 192
Carronade *219, 257*
Cass, Lewis 217, 235, 237, 239
Catawba River 108, 110
Catherine the Great 188
Catlin, George 239
Charleston 53, 55, 56, 96, 97 (map), 99, 101, 104, 107, 108, 110, 117, 118, 120, 124, 131, 132, 136, 164 (map)
Charleston Harbor 55
Charleston, Loss of 100
Charleston, Siege of *102*
Charlestown, 17, 23, 25, *28*
Charleville Musket 205
Charlotte 108, 109, 110
Chattahoochee River 209
Cheraw Hill 110, 116
Cherokee Indians 243-244, 247, 258
Cherub 194
Chesapeake Bay 18 (map), 70, 120, 124, 127, 128, 129, 130, 187, 220, 221
Chesapeake 225, 226
Chew House, The *71,* 72 (map)
Chickamauga Indians 99
Chippewa, Battle of 234

Cincinnati 146 (map), 156, 158, 162, 164 (map), 174
Claiborne, Fort 197 (map)
Clark, George Rogers 96, 188, 191
Clark, Rawson 242
Clark, William 176, 178, 217
Clatsap, Fort 178
Clay, Henry 206
Clermont 228
Cleveland 164 (map)
Clinch, Duncan L 239
Clinton, Sir Henry 22, *23,* 53, 55, 61 (map), 63, 79, 87, 88, 93, 95, 96, 97 (map), 100, 101, 107, 108, 110, 117, 119, 120, 121, 122, 123, 124, 127, 131, 134
Coahuila 253
Collier, Sir George 99
Colombus 221
Colorado 178
Columbia River 178
Committee of Safety 205
Conception Mission 256
Concord 16, 17, 220
Concord, Battle of *19*
Confederates 231
Congress, 145-149, 151-157, 161, 163, 177, 179, 191, 201, 202, 206, 214, 215, 218, 220, 222, 225, 226, 228, 231
Connecticut 19, 148
Connecticut Militia 20
Constellation 223, 225
Constitution 151
Constitution U.S.S. 138, 223, *224,* 226
Continental Army 32-34, 38, 42, 49, 51, 52, 53, 60, 62, 63, 64, 65, 67, 68, 71, 72, 74, 78, 79, 84, 85, 86, 87, 88, 89, 97, 105, 106, 108, *119,* 137, 138, 139, 141, 152, 153, 155, 181, 186, 221
Continental Congress 31, 32, 33, 36, 38, 40, 49, 50, 51, 52, 53, 56, 62, 67, 70, 71, 81, 85, 90, 96, 98, 104, 105, 107, 124, 136, 137, 138, 141, 173, 182, 185, 186, 220, 221, 222
Continental Marines 98, *98, 180,* 182-191
Continental Navy 38, 124, *125,* 182, 184, 220-223
Convention of Saratoga 81
Conway, Thomas 85
Cooch's Bridge 70
Cooper River 100
Coosa River 197
Cornwallis, Lord 61 (map), 62, 63, 65, 66, 71, 97 (map), 101, 104, 108, *109,* 110, 116, 117, 120, 122, 123 (map), 124, 127, 128, 130, 131, *132,* 186, 187
Corps of Artificers 247

269

Cos, Martin Perfecto de 253-255, 257
Cowann's Creek 58
Cowpens 18 (map), 53, 97 (map)
Cowpens, Battle of 110, *111*, 114, 116, 117 (map)
Crawford, William H. 202, 206
Creek Indians 155, 179, 197, 206, 212, 214, 237, 243, 247
Creek Wars 179, 199, 208, 253
Crockett, David 258, 261
Crown Point 20, 40 (map), 43, 44, 85
Cumberland, Fort 143
Cumberland River 164
Cyane 225

D'Estaing, Jean Baptiste le Conte 89, 97 (map), 99, 100
Dade, Francis L. 239
Dale, Richard 225
Dallas, Alexander 202
Dan River 116
Danbury 67
Dawes, John 16
De Barras, Louis le Comte 127, 128, 129
De Grasse, Francois-Joseph le Conte 127, 128, 130, 131
De Kalb, Johann 68, 101, *102*, 104
De la Place, Captain 23
De Lafayette, Marquis 68, *68*, 70, 88, 92, 121, *122*, 123 (map), 127-128, 130
De Rochambeau 107, *107*, 108, 123 (map), 124, 127, 132
De Termay 107
Deane, Silas 221
Decatur, *193*, 223, 230
Declaration of Independence 12, *16*, 49, 50, *50*, *52*
Defiance, Fort 159 (map), 260
Delaware 223
Delaware Capes, First, Battle of 121
Delaware Capes, Second, Battle of 127, 128, 129, 130
Delaware Indians 158
Delaware River, 61-65, 70, 139, 186, 187, 221
Demologos 226
Dennett, Mr. & Mrs. William 226
Department of the Navy 222, 223
Department of War 152, 153, 202, 206, 232, 244, 246
Deposit, Fort 159 (map)
Depot, Chart & Instruments 228
Destouches, Sochet 121
Detroit 146 (map), 147, 175

Dickinson, Almeron 260
Division of the North 202, *219*
Division of the South 202, 211, 219
Dorchester Heights 23, 28 (map), 44
Drake, H.M.S. 90
du Lac, Fort 178
Du Portail, Louis 68
Duncan, Silas 195

Eagle, H.M.S. 60
Eastern and Western Depts 203, 219
Edward 223
Elkton 123 (map)
Elwood, Thomas 191
Emachitochustern 241
Engineers, Corps of 202, 206, 211
Enterprise 98, 181
Erie 146 (map)
Erie Canal 235
Erie Lake 147
Esopus War 152
Essex 193
Eustis, William 164
Eutaw Springs 117, 118
Eutaw Springs, Battle of *118*
Everglades 240
Ewing, James 64

Fajardo 194
Falkland Islands 185
Fallen Timbers, Battle of 159-163
Fannin, James 258-261, 262
Ferguson, Patrick 108
Finch, William B. 228
Firearms, Early American 204-205
First Continental Congress 15, *16*, 22
First Seminole War 206, 210, 212, 214, 240
Fishing Creek 105
Fitzpatrick, John 184
Five Pounder Gun, English *113*
Flamborough Head 189
Flatbush 61 (map)
Flint River 209
Florida 87, 237, 243, 247, 195, 206-210, 214, 219, 232
Foot, 82nd Regiment of 190
Fort
  Detroit 95, 96
  Edward 73, 80 (map)
  Lee 59, 61, 61 (map)
  Mercer 71
  Mifflin 71
  Montgomery 79
  Moultrie 100
  Niagara 95, 96
  Ninety-Six 101, 117
  Oswego 73, 76, 78, 80 (map)
  St. John's 40, 40 (map), 41
  Stanwix 73, 76, 78, 80

  (map)
  Ticonderoga 22, 40, 40 (map), 73, 80 (map)
  Washington 60, 61, 61 (map)
Fort Jackson, Treaty of 199, 208
Founding Fathers 139
Fowltown 197
Fox Indians 236-137
France 174-175, 179, 188-190, 201-202, 222
France, Quasi War with 175, 191, 192
Franco-American Alliance 85
Franco-American Army 123 (map), 127, 130
Fraser 79, 80 (map)
Fraunce's Tavern 136, 137
Frederick the Great 65, 87
Freeman's Farm, Battle of 46, 80 (map)
Fremont Expedition 248
Fremont, John C. 247
French and Indian War 12, 31, 34, 36, 73, 140
French Revolution 174
Fulton 226
Fulton, Robert 226, 231

Gadsen, Christopher 221
Gadsen, Fort 211, 212
Gadsen, James 211
Gage, Sir Thomas 15, 16, 22
Gaines, Edmund 219, 236, 239-240, 243, 254 (map), 256
Gamble, John M. 193, 194
Gaspee 125
Gates, Horatio 34, *36*, 73, 79, 80 (map), 85, 86, 104, 105
Gattenawa, Chief 194
General Recruiting Service 232
General Staff 202, 206
George, Robert 188
Georgetown 101
Georgia 97, 117, 118, 155, 197 (map), 206-210, 214, 237, 239, 240, 244
Georgia, invasion of 96
Georgia Militiamen 210-211, 222, 243
German Mercenaries 46
Germantown 53, 72 (map)
Germantown, Battle of 71, 72 (map)
Ghent, Treaty of 199, 208
Gibson, Fort 235
Girty, Simon 132
Glasgow H.M.S. 184, 185
Gloucester Point 123, 131
Glover, John 57
Golden Hill, Battle of 13
Goliad Massacre 261, 262
Gonzales 254 (map), 255, 260
Governor's Island 56
Graham, George 206
Grampus 195
Grand Union Flag *27*, 37, 221

Graves, Thomas 128, 129, 130, 131
Great Britain 154-155, 172, 174, 175
Great Lakes 237
Great Miami River 156
Green Mountain Boys 20, 31, 76, 78
Greene, Nathaniel 56, *57*, 61, 64, 71, 72 (map), 97 (map), 105, 107, 109, 110, 116, 117, 118, 120, 132, 138, 139
Greenville 139 (map), 162
Greenville, Treaty of 162, 163
Greenwich 193, 194
Grenada 99
Grenada, Battle of 100
Gribeauval, J. B. de 233
Gulf of Mexico 209
Guilford Court House 18 (map), 53, 97 (map), 116, 117
Guilford Court House, Battle of 116, 120
Gun, British 6-pounder 208
Gun, 6-pounder ship's 218
Guns, swivel 233

Haiti 127
Halberds 33
Halifax 45, 48, 53, 56
Hall, Frances and Almina 243
Hamilton 79, 80 (map)
Hamilton Committee 141, 145, 146
Hamilton, Alexander 141, 145, 153, 154
Hampton Roads 120, 128
Hancock, John 182
Hangers *47*
Hannah 38
Hannah 220, 221
Harlem Heights 59
Harlem Heights, Battle of 59, 61 (map)
Harmar's Defeat 159
Harmar, Fort 152
Harmar, Joseph 138, 152, 156-157, 162
Harper's Ferry 154
Harper's Magazine *25*
Harriet 195
Harrisburg 254 (map), 261
Harrison, William 164, 166-*167*, 172
Hartt's Shipyard 225
Hassen, Harry 186
Hawk 221
Hawkin's, Fort 210, 211, 241
Head of Elk 130
Heath, William 61, *124*, 127
Heights of Abraham 41
Heinrich Brothers 204
Henderson, Archibald 195
Herkimer, Nicholas 76, 78
Hesse-Kassel 48
Hessian Garrisons 63, 64, 76
Hessians 56, 65, 70, 71, 72
Hillsboro 101, 104

Hispaniola 192
Hobkirk's Hill, Battle of 17
Hog Island 187
Holmes, Oliver Wendell 225
Hopkins, Esek *38,* 40, 182, 184, *220,* 221
Horseshoe Bend, Battle of 197-199, 206
Hoskins, Gayle 205
House Naval Committee 191
Houston, Sam 198, 252, 254-345
Howe, Robert 96
Howe, Sir Richard 48, 89
Howe, Sir William 22, *22,* 25, 28 (map), 44, 45, 48, 53, 55, 56, 57, 58, 59, 61, 62, 63, 66, 67, 68, 70, 71, 62, 73, 76, 85, 86, 119
Hubbardton, Battle of 73
Hudson River 18 (map), 20, 40 (map), 53, 56, *57,* 59, 60, 61 (map), 63, 66, 68, 70, 72, 79, 80 (map), 93
Hull, Isaac 192, 225, 227
Humphreys, Joshua 141
Huron, Lake 146 (map), 147
Hutchins, Anthony 188

Illinois 236
Illinois Militia 237
Illinois Regiment 191
Illinois Territory 188
Indian & Gulf Campaigns 197 (map)
Indian Territory 164
Indian War *159*
Indiana 159
Inspector General 202
Intolerable Acts 15, 16
Iowa 233
Iroquois 73, 76, 78, 95, 149

Jackson, Andrew 195-199, 202, 210-214, 219, 239, 240, 252
Jackson, Fort 197 (map)
Jacob, John 179
James River 121, 122
Jameson, G 258
Jamestown Ford 123
Java 225
Jay's Treaty 174
Jefferson Barracks 235-236
Jefferson, Fort 159 (map)
Jefferson, Thomas 175-178, 191, 199, 202
Jesup, Fort 235
Jesup, Thomas S 243, 244, 247
John Adams 194
John's Island 100
Johnson, Frank 258
Johnson, John 73
Jones, John Paul *37,* 92, *93,* 95, 188-189, 221, 222

Kansas 233
Kearny, Stephen W. 248
Kentucky 95

Kentucky Militia 157
Kentucky pistol *153*
Kentucky Rifles 205
Kettle Creek 99
King, Fort 239
King George III 15
King's Mountain 108, 109, 120, 140
King's Mountain, Battle of 108, 114
Knox's Brigade of Artillery 106
Knox, Henry 40, 53, 108, 138, 152, 153, 156-157, 161
Knoxville 164 (map)
Kosciuszko, Thaddeus 68, 79

L'Insurgente 223
La Bahia 254 (map), 258, 261-262
La Croyable 233
Lake Champlain 20, 40 (map), 43, 44, 53, 56, 66, 70, 72, 73, 80 (map), 147, 185
Lake Champlain, Battle of 185
Lake George 20, 40 (map), 72, 73, 80 (map)
Lake Okechobee, Battle of 244
Lake Ontario 73, 80 (map)
Lancaster 71
Langdon, John 221
Leary, Dennis 187
Leavenworth, Fort 235
Lee, Charles 34, 53, 55, 61, 62, *62,* 63, 86, 89, *89,* 107, 108
Lee, Ezra 60
Lee, Henry *Lighthouse* Harry 93, *95,* 120
Lee, Henry 154
Legion 144
Leman, Peter 204
Leopard H.M.S. 226
Leslie, Alexander 110
Levant 225
Lewis & Clark Expedition 177-179
Lewis, J. O. 217, 235
Lewis, Merriwether 176-179
Lexington 16, 53, 220
Lexington 195, 222, 223
Lexington, Battle of *18*
Lexington, capture of 222
Lexington Green 17
Liberty Tree 38
Licking Creek 191
Light Artillery Regiment 169
Light Infantry, Corps of *54*
Lincoln, Benjamin 74, 96, 97 (map), 99, *99,* 100, 145, 150
Lindreux, Robert 247
Little Miami River 156
Little Turtle 158, 162, 163
Long Island 53, 56, 57, 59, 61 (map), 69, 123 (map)
Long Island, Battle of 57, *58*
Long Warrior, The 247
Long, Maj. S *214*
Losantiville 156

Louisiana 155, 175, 179, 197, 239, 244
Louisiana Militiamen 243
Louisiana Purchase 176-178 (map)
Louisiana Territory
Louisville 164
Lovell, Joseph 232, 233
Lovell, Solomon 190
Lynchburg 254 (map), 255 (map)

Machias Bay 22
Mackenzie, Fort *246*
Madison, James 199, 201, 202, 206
Magaw, Robert 24
Maine 41, 190, 220, 243
Malcolm, John *13*
Manchester 76
Manhattan Island 45, 56, 59, 61 (map)
Marblehead Regiment 57
Margaretta 22, 220
Marietta 156
Marine Band, creation of 191
Marion, Francis 101, 117
Marquesas Islands 193
Maryland 33, 205
Massachusetts 15, 16, *17,* 146, 148-151, 190, 204-205
Massachusetts Militia 30, 38
Matamaros Expedition 261
Maumee Indians 156-158, 161, 163
Maumee River 206
Maumee War 156, 166
Maury, Fontain 228
Mawhood, Charles 187
Maynard, George W. 134
McAgee, Robert 173
McCail, George 250
McConkey's Ferry 63
McCrea, Jane 74
McIntosh, Fort 149
McKenzie, Alexander S. 231
McLean, Francis 190
Meigs, Fort *206*
Mercer, Brigadier General 66
Mellish 222
Mexico 178
Miami, Fort 147
Michigan 159 (map)
Michilimackinac Lake 147
Middlebrook 68
Midnight Riders 16, *17,* 18
Minutemen 16, 17, *18, 30*
Mississippi *164,* 175, 197 (map)
Mississippi River 12, 14, 96
Missouri River *164,* 178
Mobile 196, 210, 211
Mohawk River 73, 76, 80 (map), 149
Monmouth 53
Monmouth Court House 89
Battle of 88, *88,* 92
Monroe, James *199,* 201
Montgomery, Richard 34, 40

(map), 41, *41,* 42
Montreal 40 (map), 41, 43, 80 (map)
Moores Creek Bridge, Battle of 53
Morgan's Rifle Corps *75,* 79, 80
Morgan, Daniel 24, 40, 74, *74,* 80 (map), 97 (map), 110, 116
Morgan, Nathaniel 138
Morris, Robert 107
Morristown 62, 65, 67, 88, 105, 107
Mortar, American *113*
Moultrie, William 55, *55,* 97
Musket, French Charleville *103*
Muzzleloaders *160*

Napoleon 176, 179, 201
Napoleonic War 226
Nashville 210
Natchez 196
Natchitoches 178
Negro, Fort 209
Netherlands, The 90
New Brunswick 63, 65
New England 17, 67, 74, 80, 147, 155
New England Army 22
New Hampshire 19, 38, 146, 148
New Hampshire Grants 32
New Jersey 51, 61 (map), 62, 63 (map), 65, 67, 71, 148
New Orleans 175, 176, 210
New Providence 40
New York 18 (map), 20, 32, 43, 44, 45, 46, 48, 53, 55, 57, 58, 59, 61, 61 (map), 63, 66, 67, 71, 79, 80 (map), 85, 87, 89, 92, 93, 95, 97 (map), 100, 101, 109, 120, 123 (map), 124, 127, 128, 130, 131, 132, 134, 136, 137, 138, 140, 146, *147,* 149, 185, 187, 228
New York Campaign 61, 80
New York, Invasion of 56, 72
New York Regiment *103*
Newburgh 132, 141
Newport 63, 65, 89, 100, 107, 121, 123 (map), 127
Newtown, Battle of 95
Nicholls, Lt. Col. E. 208
Norfolk 226
Nook's Hill 44
North Carolina 18 (map), 97 (map), 99, 108, 110, 116
Northern Army 40, 52, 63, 67, 70, 73
Nova Scotia 45

O'Brien, Jeremiah 22
Ohio *148,* 156, 158
Ohio Company 155, *158, 161, 162,* 175
Ohio River 14, 132, 152, 156

271

Oneida, Lake 73, 76, 80 (map)
Oriskany, Battle of 78, 80 (map)
Oswegatchie 147
Oswego 146
Oswego River 76
Ottawa 148

Parker, John 16
Parker, Sir Peter 53, 55
Paulus Hook 93
Pausch, George 46
Pee Dee River 101
Pelham, Henry 12
Pennsylvania 14, 18 (map), 33, 61, 62, 63 (map), 95, 120, 123, 148, 149, 154, 157
Pennsylvania State Regiment 84
Pensacola 212
Perth Amboy 63, 65
Petersburg 124, 123 (map)
Philadelphia 15, *16*, 18 (map), 62, 66, 67, 68, 70, 71, 72, 85, 86, 123 (map), 153
Phillips, William 121, 122
Pickens, Andrew 101, 117
Pickering, Timothy 107, 108
Pike, Capt. Z. M. 178
Pistols, flintlock *126*
Pitcairn, John 17
Pitcher, Molly *88*
Pittsburgh 161
Planter 226
Point aux Trembles 40 (map), 41
Pompton 107
Port Royal 97
Portsmouth 99, 121, 122, 123
Portsmouth, NH 226
Powder Tester *105*
Prescott, Dr. Samuel 16
Prescott, William 23, 25
Prevost Augustine 96, 97, 99, 100
Princeton 53, 63, 65, 67
Princeton, Battle of 65, *66*
Providence 132
Provincial Congress 16, 19
Pulaski, Casimir 68
Putnam, Israel *56,* 59, 70, 74

Quasi-War with France 175
Quebec 12, 14, 18 (map), 20, 33, 40, 41, 42, 44, 46, 53, 66, 132, 138
Quebec Act 14
Quebec, Invasion of 40 (map)

Rall, Johann 64
Ramage, V *156*
Raritan River 65, 66
Rawdon, Frances 117
Regiment of Artillery Artificers 106
Regulators 13
Revere, Paul *12,* 16, *17*
Revolutionary War 138-141, 145, 147, 149, 154, 161, 215
Rhode Island 19, 40, 66, 85, 132
Richelieu River 40 (map), 41, 72
Richmond 18 (map), 121, 122, 123 (map)
Rocky Mountains 175, 178
Royal Navy 226

Sabine River 179
Sandy Hook 89
Santa Fe 178
Santee River 104
Saratoga 53, 72, 73, 76, 79, 80 (map), 81, *82-83,* 85, 101, 140
Saratoga, First, Battle of 79, 80 (map), 93
Saratoga, Second, Battle of 80 (map), 81
Savannah 53, 96, 99, 100, 101, 102, 118, 136
Schuyler Philip 40, 41, 73, 74, 78, 79
Scott, Brig. Gen. W. 201, 232
Second Continental Congress 22
Secretary of War 107
Seminole Indians 206-214, *239-250*
Serapis, H.M.S. 93, *94,* 95
Seven Years' War 12
Shawnee Indians 158-159 (map), 163-166, 172-179
Shays' Rebellion 149-151
Shelby, Isaac 108
Sioux Indians *210*
Skenesborough 73
South Carolina 18 (map), 97 (map), 101, 108, 110, 117, 118, 155
South Carolina Militia 53-55, 97
Southern Army 52, 96, 101, 104, 105, 109, 110, 116
Spain 175, 214
Spear *39*
Spirit of '76, The *133*
Split Rock 44
Springfield 149, 151, 152, 154
St. Clair, Arthur 73
St. Clair, Lake 147
St. Clair, Maj. Gen. A. *156,* 157, 166
St. Lawrence River 12, 40 (map), 41, 44, 73, 80 (map), 147
St. Leger, Barry 73, 76, 80 (map)
St. Louis 176
St. Marks 211-212
Stamp Act 13, *14*
Stark, John 74
Stars and Stripes 67, *70*
Staten Island 56, 61 (map), 89
Stephenson, Fort 206
Stewart, Alexander 118
Stewart, John 201

Stillwater 73, 78, 79
Stirling, William 58
Stock, John 76
Stone Ferry 99
Stony Point 93, *94*
Stony Point, Battle of 94
Strother, Fort 197
Sugar Act 13
Sullivan's Island 55
Sullivan's Island, Battle of 55
Sullivan, John 42, 43, *44,* 56, 57, 64, 70, 71, 72 (map), 89, 95, 96
Sumter's Guerrilla Force 104
Sumter, Thomas 101, 117
Swords *48*
Swords, American *35*

Talladega 197
Tallapoosa River 197
Tarleton, Air Banastre 101, 104, 110, *111,* 116, 117, 118
Tecumseh 163, *164,* 179
Tennessee 99
Tenskwatawac *164*
Texas, 175, 178
Thomas, John 43
Ticonderoga 20, 43, 53, 73, 85
Tippecanoe, Battle of 166-171
Toledo 162
Treasury 153
Treaty of Paris 12, 96, 131, 136, 147, 148
Trenton 18 (map), 53, 63 (map), 64, 65, 123 (map)
Trenton, Battle of 63, 64, 65
Trespassy, H.M.S. 134
Trois Rivieres 43
Tryon County Militia 76
Tun Tavern 98
Turtle 60
Twenty-Sixth Regiment of Foot 23

U.S. Army *169, 200,* 207, 213
U.S. Marine Corps 98, 157, *180-195*
U.S. National Guard 154
U.S. Navy 38, 151, 220-225, 226-231
United Kingdom 172, 179, 201, 214
Unity 38

Valcour Island, Battle of 44
Valley Forge 72, 85, 86, 87, 105, 108
Vermont 73, 76
Vermont Militia 20
Verplanck's Point 73
Vincennes, Capture of 96
Vincennes, Fort 160
Virginia 14, 18 (map), 33, 53, 96, 97 (map), 99, 109, 117, 119, 121, 122, 123, 127, 132, *152,* 154
Virginia Riflemen 25
Virginian Coastal Operations 121
Virginian Militiamen 130
Von Breymann, Heidrich 76
Von Knyphausen 100
Von Riedesel 79, 80 (map)
Von Steuben, Friedrich Wilhelm 68, *86, 88,* 121, 122

Wabash River 157, 157, 159 (map), *161*
War of 1812 201, 206
Ward, Artemas 19, 22, 25
Warner, Seth 32, 73
Warren, Joseph *29*
Washington, Fort 146, 156, 157, 162-164, 174-175
Washington, George *31,* 33, *34,* 36, 37, 38, 44, *45,* 48, 50-53, *54,* 56, 57, *58,* 59, *59,* 61, 61 (map), 62, *62,* 63, 64, *64,* 65-68, 70, *70,* 71, 72, 73, 75, 86, *86,* 87, 88, *88,* 89, 92, 93, 100, 101, 104, 105, 107, 109, 121, 122, 123 (map), 127, *127,* 130, 131, *131, 132,* 136, *137,* 137, 139, 145-147, 152, 154, 156, 158, 161, 174, 181, 186, 187, 221, 223, 232
Washington's Cruisers *35,* 38
Washington's Headquarters 67
Washington, William 110, *111*
Waterloo, Battle of 179
Waxhaw Creek, Battle of 101
Wayne, Anthony 71, 88, *92, 93, 121,* 122, 123
Wayne, Maj. Gen. A. 161-162
Wayne's Light Infantry *94*
Weapon procurement 153
West Indies 87, 89, 90, 96, 99, 100, 124, 127, 131, 136
West Point 93, 94, 107, 123, 141, 147, 151, 152, 175, 206
Western Army *143*
Whipple, Abraham 125
Whiskey Rebellion 95, 154
White Plains 89
White Plains, Battle of 59, 61 (map)
Wilkinson, Brig. Ben. J. 176
Willard, A.M. 132
Williamsburg 130
Wilmington 97 (map), 117, 120, 122, 131, 136
Winnsborough 97, 109
Wolfe, James 41

York 71
York River 130, 131
Yorktown 18 (map), 53, 123 (map), 127, 128, 130, 131, *131,* 132
Young, Thomas 114